Seventy-Two Servants of the Word

RETRIEVING THE SEPTUAGINT AS SCRIPTURE

MIKKEL SØTBÆK

The Seventy-Two Servants of the Word of God: Retrieving the Septuagint as Scripture
Copyright © 2025 by Mikkel Søtbæk
Published by The Weidner Institute
A Division of Just & Sinner

All rights reserved. No part of this publication may be reproduced, stored or transmitted in any form or by any means, electronic, mechanical, photocopying, recording, scanning, or otherwise without written permission from the publisher. It is illegal to copy this book, post it to a website, or distribute it by any other means without permission.

All translations of the Septuagint's Koine Greek into English are the author's own.

Just & Sinner, Ithaca, NY 14850
JustandSinner.org

ISBN: 978-1-952295-69-0 (Paperback)

TABLE OF CONTENTS

List of Tables and Figures 5

Introduction 7

Part I: Historical Foundation 12

From King Josiah to Ezra 13

    The Hebraic Change of Writing 18

    Alexander the Great and Hellenization Up Until Christ 22

    Conclusion 29

The Translation of the Seventy-Two *The Lighthouse of Hellenism* 31

    The Birth of the Septuagint and the Letter of Aristeas 33

    The Jewish Reception of the Septuagint 40

    Conclusion 47

Part II: Vetus Testamentum in Novo Receptum: The Old Testament Received by the New 50

Textual Findings and Transmission: *Septuagint Finds in Roman Judaea* 51

    Textual Plurality at the Time of Christ 52

    The Septuagint and Qumran 55

    Conclusion 58

The Old Testament *As it is Written*:
Intermission: A Conceptual Framework 60

    The Use of the Septuagint by Christ 63

    The Use of the Septuagint by the Apostles 72

    Conclusion 80

Part III: The Reception of the Septuagint by the Church 82

The Early Ecclesial and Conciliar Reception of the Septuagint ... 83

    The Early Reception 83

    The Local Synods and the Ecumenical Council 84

    Lex Credendi Lex Orandi 86

The Patristic Reception of the Septuagint: A Digression on the Extent of the Canon 88

A Presentation of the Patristic Reception of the Septuagint 89

Conclusion 115

An Outline of the Early Modern Reception of the Septuagint 117

The Septuagint and Text Criticism Among the Protestants 120

Cross-Confessional Protestant Appraisal of the Septuagint 123

Tridentine Catholicism's Relation to the Septuagint 125

Conclusion 130

Part IV: The Septuagint in the Third Millennium Church 132

A Sketch of the Septuagint's Textual Transmission 133

    The Ancient Copyists 133

    The Common Septuagint 135

    Recensions and Textual Variants 141

    The Kaige 146

    Theodotian and Daniel 147

    From the Medievals to the Moderns 149

    Septuagint Translations 151

    Conclusion 152

Last Remarks 154

    Between the Masoretes and the Seventy-Two 154

    The Insufficiency of the Masoretic Text... 159

    The Lost Messianic Tendency of the Masoretic Text 164

Final Conclusion 178

    The Seventy-Two Servants of the Word of God 178

    The Departure 179

Appendix: Timeline 181

Bibliography 183

LIST OF TABLES AND FIGURES

Figure		Page
1	The two pictures illustrate the same text rendered in the two scripts	20
2	The Khirbet Qeiyafa Ostracon	21
3	Map of Roman Palestine at the time of Christ	25
4	Here a photo of the newly found Septuagint fragment of the Book of Zachariah is seen	51
5	Comparison Chart over Textual Overlap	75
6	Geneological Chart of Translations of the Septuagint	84
7	Chiastic structure of Psalm 22:12-21	172

Table		Page
1	Comparison of Mark 7:6–7 with Isaiah 29:13	65
2	Comparison of Luke 4:18–19 with Isaiah 61:1–2	66
3	Comparison of Matthew 13:14–15 with Isaiah 6:9–10	69
4	Comparison of Matthew 21:16 with Psalm 8:3	70
5	Comparison of Matthew 1:23 with Isaiah 7:14	74
6	Comparison of Galatians 3:16 with Genesis 22:18	78
7	Comparison of Nicene Creed, First Article with Genesis 1:1	87
8	God-Fearers and Gentile Inclusion in Luke-Acts	166
9	Deuteronomy 32:43 in the Septuagint, Dead Sea Scrolls, and Masoretic Text	172
10	Amos 4:13 in the Septuagint and the Masoretic Text	173
11	Acts 15:15-18 compared to Amos 9:11-12 in the Septuagint and Masoretic Text	174
12	Luke 3:6 vs. Isaiah 40:5 in the Septuagint and Masoretic Text	175
13	Romans 15:12 vs. Isaiah 11:10 in the Septuagint and Masoretic Text	175
14	Zephaniah 3:8 in the LXX and MT	176

SEVENTY-TWO SERVANTS OF THE WORD

INTRODUCTION

In the Gospel of Mark 7:6–7, Jesus cites the Old Testament in his rebuttal of the Pharisees. Although this citation does not appear to be a very noticeable passage by itself, it suddenly becomes quite intriguing if one looks up the reference. This is because the passage Jesus cites is wholly unlike the text, which can be read in the Book of Isaiah when one turns the pages of his Bible back to the Old Testament. This example is far from unique, because often the texts referenced in the New Testament will differ from their apparent original text as it is found in the Old Testament. The discrepancies are stylistic and a matter of wording, but they have theological significance as well.

This insight is not a new one, and many explanations have been proposed to explain the differences between the Old and New Testament texts. These include loose citations from memory, theological and rhetorical rewriting of the passages, reapplication of the material to the present exegetical need of the author, a different conceptual approach to citations, and the use of canonical literature, etc. Even though each of these proposals have their own strengths and weaknesses, two insights make them rather superfluous, at least in the vast majority of cases.

Even if such theories contain valid insights, which they certainly do occasionally, these explanations seem to ignore two central problems. The first problem is the alleged correspondence between the quote and the quoted text given in the sources themselves. Mark 7:6 presents the citation as ὡς γέγραπται, that is, *as it is written*. This would seem to exclude the option of a loose handling of the original text. Secondly, the aforementioned theories do not seem to consider the possibility that what readers today denote as *the* Old Testament differs from the actual Old Testament text which the New Testament's authors used.

This second insight draws its inspiration from one of the pivotal debates of the ancient church, the origin of which is to be found in Hellenistic Judaism during the centuries leading up to Christ's birth. From ancient times, controversy surrounded the very identity of the Old Testament text which the authors of the New Testament relied on. The church father Jerome pointed out, with reference to, among others, Matthew 2:15, that the apostles must have used the ancient Hebrew Text in the form which had been passed on in the Jewish Synagogue—the so-called Masoretic Text. This view was unique to Jerome in his day and age, as the church used the

Septuagint or translations thereof. The Septuagint was a Greek translation of the Hebrew Text of the Old Testament from the third century B.C., and it was called Septuagint because it had been translated by seventy-two Jewish translators.

This book will journey with Scripture and its intriguing history to examine the beginning and origin of the Septuagint, how it spread throughout the Mediterranean Basin, how it was received by early Judaism, the authors of the New Testament, and the church. It will also tell the surprising story of how Jerome's peculiar view, which in his own time was both unpopular, novel, and rebuked by major theologians, would grow in time to become the all-dominant position in the Western church. By shedding light on these and related questions, this book hopes to shed light on where and how one might most accurately find the Old Testament *as it is written*.

This book is divided into four parts in order to prove a coherent, chronological story, with each part building on the parts that came before it. The research and analyses have been made in dialogue with early and contemporary scholarship but are primarily focused on the first-hand sources, of which the Old and New Testaments' texts have the primary importance. The first-hand sources do not stand alone, but rather the book will engage with the foremost experts on the Old Testament, Biblical Hebrew, textual criticism, and the Septuagint, and from many more learned authors. It is the assertion of this book that the Septuagint should serve as the textual basis for the Old Testament of the Christian church. This is a controversial thesis, and it will be explained and defended in the following chapters.

This book is not written to cause scandal or to draw controversial headlines. There is nothing new in this work; the thesis is old, and the texts being discussed have been held in the hands of Christians in millennia and studied with diligence and devotion. No flashy, new hidden evidence has been unearthed, excepting the Dead Sea Scrolls, and no new "apocryphal" gospels have moved the needle in this discussion. This work is at best a helpful, distilled summary of the great many voices in defense of the case for the Septuagint, voices which have been put into interaction with the opposing side. This book has also been kept rather short, not in order to exclude information or related discussions of importance, but out of a desire to make this thesis and its defense available in an accessible format and of a length that can fit most peoples' busy schedules and overpacked

INTRODUCTION

reading lists. For those with further interest in the subject, the bibliography can be consulted.

Nor should this book be viewed as an attack on using the Hebrew Masoretic Text. Though this text has certain profound shortcomings, the high degree of overlap between the text of the Septuagint and the Masoretic should not be de-emphasized. It must be said that, though this work will deal primarily with the differences and the strengths and advantages of the Septuagint, in the vast majority of the cases, both texts agree with each other. Neither should it be ignored that the Masoretic Text has served as the textual basis for countless Christians throughout millennia. This is not an attempt to belittle or smear these blessings. These facts are important and deserve to be mentioned here for emphasis. Yet, the differences toward which this book will especially look are crucial, and they form one of the main reasons why it is necessary to present a *positive* case for the Septuagint.

One can justly ask whether such a radical change as the book proposes is desirable, let alone possible. But it must be said that much of the history of Scripture consists in Christians struggling toward ever greater fidelity to the inspired writings and their authentic wording. Ancient copyists carefully transcribed untold numbers of manuscripts, many even noting variants in the margins in a desire to remain faithful to the text. Likewise, Jerome's push toward the abandonment of the Septuagint was guided, not by detestation of the Septuagint, but by an honest wish to come into closer conformity with the original text of the Biblical authors.

This journey toward ever closer fidelity to the text forms the backdrop that the present work wishes to place itself in. A journey seen in the Reformation Era's abandonment of Jerome's Vulgate, also shared by the Roman Catholic Church since Pope John Paul II's Nova Vulgata, and in the publication of new critical editions of the Greek New Testament. As will be argued at length, it is through the lens and presentation of the New Testament itself that the Septuagint is proposed as containing the authentic and genuine inspired text of the Old Testament, a text which the Masoretic Text in comparison fails to convey as adequately.

The question's importance demands that it be given a thorough treatment, and toward that end this monograph has been written to as inclusive an audience as possible in the hope that this might also serve to the edification of the church. It is my hope that this book will be read not only by pastors, clergy, and academics, but especially also by laymen and laywomen, and by all those with an interest in the topic of Scripture.

Therefore, this work is not only intended toward one denomination or faith tradition, but toward all Christians of good faith with a love of Scripture and an interest in drawing ever closer to the Word of God. In the interest of clarity, I will add that I am myself a Confessional Lutheran with a high view of Scripture, yet I can confidently say that this book can be equally read and enjoyed regardless of confessional background. This is not a discussion of one denomination against another, but it is a conversation for the whole body of Christ.

May your reading be edifying! —*Michael*

PART I: HISTORICAL FOUNDATION

PART I
HISTORICAL FOUNDATION

FROM KING JOSIAH TO EZRA

hough this era of Israelite history is rich enough to justify its own monographs, this book will only draw a sketch in so far as it touches on the areas of interest for this present work. Yet before this book can delve into this period, a few historical considerations must be made. The goal of this part of the book is first and foremost to present a historical survey of the history of Scripture as presented in the Old Testament itself. It is beyond the scope of this work to offer a defense for the historical truthfulness of the presentation given in the Old Testament. This will be taken for granted in the following chapters. Though such an approach is open to criticism, it must be added that even if one were to reject the historical reliability of the Old Testament, then such an approach would still be useful in that it would shed light on the Jewish reception and use of material being presented in the historical books of the Old Testament. Whether historical or not, then, the presentation given is an expression of the early Jewish understanding of their own history and their dealings with inspired Scripture. Looking at these considerations more broadly, it must also be noted how this information is crucial because it was formative for the early Christian understanding of the story of Scripture and God's dealings with it and his people. Therefore, whether one is inclined toward *Biblical maximalism* and grants the historicity of the events—e.g. K. A. Kitchen, *et al.*—or takes a more skeptical view as the biblical minimalists do—T. L. Thompson, Niels P. Lemche et al.—then the following will provide fruitful reading, either as the actual history of the written Word of God itself during Old Testament times, or as the Jewish understanding and representation of these events, which would in time become formative for the Christian understanding.

The way that the story of Israel is portrayed in the Old Testament, both in the protocanonical and the deuterocanonical books, especially 1 and 2 Maccabees, often leaves the story of Scripture itself unspoken. When touched upon, it plays somewhat of a secondary role in the narrative. Take for example the portrayal of King Josiah's renovation of the Temple in Jerusalem in 2 Kings 22. The High Priest Hilkiah rediscovers the Book of the Law (סֵפֶר הַתּוֹרָה), or more literally the Torah scroll, in the Temple. When the scroll is read before the king, he tore his clothing asunder and exclaims in verse 12, "Go, inquire of the Lord for me, for the people and for all Judah, concerning the words of this book that has been found; for great is the wrath of the Lord that is aroused against us, because our fathers have not obeyed the words of this book, to do according to all that is written concerning us." The narrative seems to presuppose that the content of the scroll is new and unknown to the King. He already knew of the disobedience of the forefathers; therefore, his astonishment and strong reaction came from his prior unawareness of the existence of the Scriptures. This is significant because it seems to show that the Law, whether we understand that broadly as the Five Books of Moses or more narrowly as the Mosaic Law alone, had somewhat of a precarious existence in ancient Israel.

Such a view also finds support in the following chapter, 2 Kings 23:21, where King Josiah commands the people to "Keep the Passover to the Lord your God, as it is written in this Book of the Covenant" (סֵפֶר הַבְּרִית הַזֶּה). The following verse also strongly indicates that the Law had indeed been absent for a longer period: "Such a Passover surely had never been held since the days of the judges who judged Israel, nor in all the days of the kings of Israel and the kings of Judah." Even though the Word of God never wholly disappeared from Israel, insofar as the prophets spoke both in the absence and in the presence of the written word, multiple texts seem to take for granted the absence of God's written word during longer periods of time.

The motif of the Law not always being available in Israel will also be important later. In concurrence with the decline and fall of Israel, especially after the fracture of the United Kingdom under King David and Solomon, the decline of Hebrew also followed. The Babylonian Exile further diminished the extent of spoken Hebrew. The Old Testament itself bears witness to this development, as shown in 2 Kings 17–18. These chapters describe the fall of the Northern Kingdom around 721 B.C. The Assyrian Empire deported and scattered 10 out of the 12 Israelite tribes and colonized the depopulated former Israelite territories with Assyrian settlers (2 Kings 17:23–24). Even though a few Israelites remained, as 2 Chronicles 30:1 points out, for all intents and purposes the Northern Kingdom had essentially ceased to exist as a political and cultural entity—a change that the Assyrian colonization cemented. The language also switched from Hebrew to Aramaic; the latter being the lingua franca of the Western Assyrian Empire. Even though the Southern Kingdom would survive until the fall of Jerusalem in 586 B.C., yet also Aramaic began its encroachment and expanded its influence in the Judean heartland long before the successful Babylonian conquest centuries later.

PART I: HISTORICAL FOUNDATION

At the dawn of the Assyrian siege of Jerusalem in 701 B.C., a fascinating interaction is provided in 2 Kings 18:17–27. Here the Assyrian representatives negotiate with the Judean court at the city walls of Jerusalem. The chief negotiator of the Judean Kingdom, the supervisor of the royal house Eliakim, the royal scribe Shebna, and the royal secretary Joah, are addressed by the Assyrian emissaries in Judean (Hebrew) yet their response is quite telling. They reply in verse 26, "please speak to your servants in Aramaic for we understand it." Even though the point of the comment is that the royal court wished that the dialogue would be kept in Aramaic out of a fear that the native Jerusalemites might understand the threats of the Assyrians, the comment reveals that already in the eighth century B.C., Aramaic had made its inroads into the Kingdom of Judah, and the use of it had become common. It would have been especially common among the higher classes, to which royal scribes, secretaries and supervisors would be considered.

This development escalated during the Babylonian Exile, which caused the Aramaic language to become the dominant language among the Judeans rather than just being a foreign lingua franca for the learned and higher classes of the kingdom. This development is also seen in the Old Testament books covering this period, such as the Books of Daniel and Ezra, in which longer and shorter passages are written in Aramaic rather than Hebrew. When spoken Hebrew exactly died out as the native langue of the majority of Israelites is highly discussed throughout scholarship. Some scholars, such as Klaus Beyer and Seth Schwartz, put this development around the time after the return from the Babylonian Exile, around 400 and 300 B.C.[1]

Hebrew did not wholly cease to be a native language among Israelites, as it persisted in some pockets of society, especially among the more conservative and religious classes. This development led Hebrew to become an increasingly sacred language, more unfamiliar and less a vernacular of the common populace. Indeed, a majority of Jews were unable to understand Hebrew at the time of the birth of Christ[2]. But it must also be added that spoken Hebrew never disappeared completely, but it was kept in use in parts of the population and written Hebrew also was kept in use for

---

[1] Steven E. Fassberg, "Which Semitic Language Did Jesus and Other Contemporary Jews Speak?," *The Catholic Biblical Quarterly* 74, no. 2 (April 2012): 263–80, https://doi.org/10.2307/43727847, 274.

[2] G. Scott Gleaves and Rodney Eugene Cloud, *Did Jesus Speak Greek? : The Emerging Evidence of Greek Dominance in First-Century Palestine* (Eugene: Pickwick Publications, 2015), chapter 1.

the composition of new literary works. The findings at the caves around Qumran, the commonly named Dead Sea Scrolls, provide many such examples, and they will be discussed more thoroughly later in this work. Later in the second century A.D., written Hebrew was used again, for example around the time of the Bar Kokhba revolt circa A.D. 132. Many letters from this time include contemporary compositions in Hebrew. These letters are also intriguing because some of them show linguistic signs of organic development, which points toward the fact that Hebrew had not yet become a dead literary language in the first half of the second century A.D.[3]

Some scholars have put forth evidence of such organic development to suggest that Hebrew might even have been a commonly spoken language at this period[4], but this conclusion should be viewed as conjecture. A collection of letters from the Bar Kokhba Revolt have been found in a cave near the Dead Sea, and they provide a good window into the linguistic reality of the time. A majority of the letters, 15 having been found in total, were composed in Hebrew and Aramaic. Some scholars argue that these languages must have been dominant at the time[5]. This finding, coupled with the organic developments shown by some Hebrew writings, as mentioned above, have led some scholars to conclude that Hebrew was indeed still a living and common language during this time period.

Contrary to such conclusions, it should be considered that, even though a language shows signs of undergoing natural and organic changes, one cannot necessarily conclude that it is a living language with native born speakers. Consider Latin in Medieval Europe, the development of which also showed signs of change though it never was a native language anywhere in Medieval Europe, even if widely spoken in certain societal classes. Words evolved and changed their semantic range, syntactical and morphological changes occurred, pronunciation developed certain regional flavors, and new words were coined even when it only was a second language for its speakers.

The Bar Kokhba Letters are also interesting because they also point toward the limited knowledge of Hebrew. Some of the letters are actually

---

[3] Armin Lange, Emanuel Tov, and Matthias Weigold, *The Dead Sea Scrolls in Context: Integrating the Dead Sea Scrolls in the Study of Ancient Texts, Languages, and Cultures*, 2 Vols (BRILL, 2011), 131.

[4] Lange, et al. *The Dead Sea Scrolls in Context*, 137.

[5] Letizia Rivera, "Multilingualism and Rebellion in 2nd-Century Judaea," ed. Pedro Jesús Molina Muñoz, *Researchers in Progress II: Languages in Contact: Languages with History*, 2017, 117.

PART I: HISTORICAL FOUNDATION

written in Koine Greek, of which especially the letter *P. Tadin 2 52* draws attention. It states in the latter that "this is written in Greek, because we couldn't find [a way to write it] in Hebrew".[6] Since these religious conversative nationalist writers had access to scribes, these clues indicate that the knowledge of Hebrew was not nearly as widespread as some have thought. In the absence of any knowledge of Hebrew, Greek had to be used instead. Greek proficiency appears to have been easier to encounter than a working knowledge of Hebrew. Letizia Rivera from the University of Torino has studied the Bar Kokhba Letters in depth and concludes that, "scholars acknowledge that it [Hebrew] was hardly ever spoken anymore".[7]

The extent of the use of the Greek language can also be seen in the finding of a similar collection of letters, which were actually found in the same cave as the Bar Kokhba Letters. This collection though, known as the Babatha Letters, deals mostly with judicial matters; but they are contemporaries of the Bar Kokhba collection. What makes this second collection fascinating is the fact that the vast majority of the letters, 26 out of 36, are written in Koine Greek.[8] This puts the Bar Kokhba finding in perspective and indicates that the extent to which Hebrew was used could have more to do with ideological choices rather than being reflective of the relative extent of the different languages spoken at the time. As a more conservative rebellion seeking to liberate and establish a divinely sanctioned Israelite kingdom, the choice of Hebrew, with its roots in national history and tradition, served to strengthen the religious and cultural ties between Israel's past and Bar Kokhba's program. The Babatha Letters on the other hand, serving mostly practical purposes such as trade, purchases, house titles, and more, had no such pretentious considerations. They used Greek, as it will be argued later, not just because it was the lingua franca of the time and of the area, but also because it was the most widely spoken language, being used and known across the lines of the different cultural and social groups inhabiting Roman Judaea.

The Old Testament itself also bears witness to the post-exile decline of spoken Hebrew. The Book of Nehemiah narrates how the Jews began their rebuilding efforts in Jerusalem after their return to Judah. After the Babylonian Exile, the Aramaic of the Babylonians became ever more

---

[6] Rivera, "Multilingualism and Rebellion in 2nd-Century Judaea ," *Researchers in Progress II*, 118: ἐγράφη δ[ὲ] Ἑληνεϛτὶ διὰ τ[ὸ η]μᾶς μὴ εὑρηκ[έ]ναι Ἑβραεστὶ.
[7] Rivera, "Multilingualism and Rebellion in 2nd-Century Judaea ," *Researchers in Progress II*, 118.
[8] Rivera, "Multilingualism and Rebellion in 2nd-Century Judaea ," *Researchers in Progress II*, 117.

common among the Jews, becoming the native tongue for many including in more conservative, learned classes[9]. In chapter 8 of Nehemiah, Ezra reads the Book of the Law for the whole people after their return from Babylon, and verses 7 and 8 describe how the Levites "explained [מְבִינִים] the law (...) made clear [מְפֹרָשׁ] the meaning, so that which was read could be understood." Especially this latter comment is significant, depending on which word is used to render the term פָּרַשׁ into English. This term appears six times in the Hebrew protocanonical books of the Old Testament, but the context of the passage and the use of the word in the related Book of Ezra, indicates that the word ought to be rendered as *translated*. In Ezra 4:18, it states that the letter which King Artaxerxes had received from Jerusalem "has been read in translation [מְפָרַשׁ] before me" as translated by the New Revised Standard Version. Even though the grammatical form of the word is a bit different here, it is the same word root being used in Nehemiah 8:8. The context, where Aramaic had been making ever deeper inroads for generations into the Hebrew population in Babylon, points toward the fact that the Law must have been translated, so that which was read could be understood, just as the letter from Judea to the Persian king had to be translated. This is also acknowledged by different Bible translations, such as the New American Standard Bible, the Holman Christian Standard Bible, La Biblia de las Americas, etc. The decline of the Hebrew language in post-exilic times is also underscored by Nehemiah 13:23–24. Here it is recounted how the many Jewish men who had married foreign wives, had fathered children half of whom "were unable to speak Judean." The waning knowledge of Hebrew in this period meant that the obscure and incomprehensible Hebrew text had to be translated by the Levites into Aramaic, which was far more widely spoken and understood. The Aramaic term for this process was *targum* (translation or interpretation) and is from where the Aramaic translation of the Law derives its name.[10]

THE HEBRAIC CHANGE OF WRITING

Another great change which took place on account of the exile was that the old Paleo-Hebrew script disappeared and was replaced with an Aramaic script. This change and its importance are often overlooked. Today the Old

---

[9] Mark Leuchter, "The Aramaic Transition and the Redaction of the Pentateuch," *Journal of Biblical Literature* 136, no. 2 (January 1, 2017): 249–68, https://doi.org/10.1353/jbl.2017.0018, 254.

[10] Gleaves and Cloud, *Did Jesus Speak Greek?*, chapter 2.

PART I: HISTORICAL FOUNDATION

Testament in Hebrew is published exclusively in Aramaic Script, as this script simply supplanted the earlier Paleo-Hebrew[11], and is considered to be *the* Hebrew script. The rupture of continuity can best be illustrated by comparing a pre-exilic fragment with a post-exilic rendering. In 1979, a team of archeologists found two small plates of silver at Ketef Hinnom, measuring around 3 x 10 cm and 1 x 4 cm each. They contained the Priestly Blessing as written in Numbers 6:24ff, "The Lord bless you and keep you. The Lord make his face shine upon you, and be gracious to you. The Lord lift up His countenance upon you, and give you peace." This finding has been dated to around the seventh and early sixth centuries B.C.[12]

As can be seen from the comparison between the two inscriptions above, the original Paleo-Hebrew inscription is on the left while the text on the right is in the now common Aramaic script, these two writing systems are not mutually intelligible or readable. The shift away from Hebrew was double then, as it consisted firstly in the steadily increasing movement away from spoken Hebrew to spoken Aramaic and secondly in the transition away from the historic and traditional script of Israel to that of the Assyrian and Babylonian Empire. The current version of the Aramaic Script used to render Hebrew is simply the original Aramaic Script of the time of the Exile[13]. This naturally means that any current Hebraic Old Testament would have been indecipherable to a pre-exilic Israelite and quite unlike that Scroll of the Law which was found by King Josiah, or the material that King Solomon, King David, or Moses had at their disposal. Interestingly, this transition is also mentioned in the Talmud:

> Originally the Torah was given to Israel in Hebrew characters and in the sacred [Hebraic] language; later, in the times of Ezra, the Torah was given in Assyrian script and Aramaic language (Talmud Bavli, Sanhedrin 21b–22a).

---

[11] Talmud Bavli, Sanhedrin 21b–22a.
[12] Gabriel Barkay et al., "The Amulets from Ketef Hinnom: A New Edition and Evaluation," *Bulletin of the American Schools of Oriental Research* 334 (May 2004), https://doi.org/10.2307/4150106, 52.
[13] Barkay, et al., "The Amulets from Ketef Hinnom," *Bulletin of the American Schools of Oriental Research* 334, 52.

- - (כ)הברו - -
- אָנִיהוּ -
- ר יהו(ו)
- - בָעה - -
- שיברב
ו יהוה
(י)שמרכ
יאר יה
(וה) פניו
(אל)יכ וי
שמ לכ ש
לו(מ) - -
- - - - -
- - -
- - כמ - -
- - - - -
- ור - נ -
- - - - -

Figure 1 - The two pictures illustrate the same text rendered in the two scripts

This point is significant because of the equation often drawn between the Old Testament as transmitted by the Rabbis of the synagogue on the one hand and the original Old Testament as mentioned by Scripture itself—such as the Book of the Law—as possessed by David, Solomon, and others on the other hand. But these are not the same and cannot therefore be equated. They differ in regard to both content, as will be shown at length later in this work, and in form. The most widely used current edition of the Hebrew Old Testament by far, the *Biblica Hebraica Stuttgartensia*, would have been strange and unintelligible to any pre-exilic Israelite because of its alien alphabet and its hitherto unknown addition of different vowel signs and accentuations. This insight is far from new and was known by Christian writers both in antiquity and later. The famous Roman Catholic cardinal Robert Bellarmine mentions this in his work *De Verbo Dei*, book II chapter one, when he writes:

PART I: HISTORICAL FOUNDATION

Blessed Jerome in the Galeatic Prologue says that Ezra invented new Hebrew letters and the old ones indeed he left to the Samaritans but the new ones he handed over to the Jews, and they use them even now. For, as the same Jerome testifies on ch.9 of Ezekiel, the last letter of the ancient Hebrew alphabet was similar to the 'T' of the Greeks and carried the shape of a cross, since the end of the law is Christ crucified; but now the last letter of the alphabet seems to have no likeness to the cross. Therefore without doubt we have new letters. But about the new edition of the sacred books made by Ezra, Jerome says nothing, although however that was most especially the place to say it.[14]

One example where these new letters are seen is on the *Khirbet Qeiyafa* ostracon, a pottery fragment with a short Hebrew inscription from 1000 B.C., one of the earliest fragments found. The last line second letter from the right is a Paleo-Hebrew letter *tet*, described by Bellarmine as having the form of a cross as is clearly seen in this example, compared to the ת of the Aramaic and current Hebrew script.

Figure 2 - The Khirbet Qeiyafa Ostracon

These observations are important with regard to the discussion of the use of the Septuagint in so far as they dispel the assumption that this edition of the Old Testament is foreign and novel wholly unlike the *authentic* Hebrew Old Testament we use today, such as the Biblica Hebraica. This assumption does not take seriously the major changes the Hebrew text underwent not only during the exile but especially later at the hands of the Rabbis in the centuries after Christ. It must therefore be stated clearly that one cannot simply equate the pre-exilic Old

---

[14] Robert Bellarmine, *Controversies of the Christian Faith*, trans. Kenneth Baker (Saddle River, New Jersey: Keep The Faith, Inc, 2016), book 2, chap. 1.

Testament with that edition known as Biblica Hebraica as if they were the same. The apparent disappearance of the Scriptures, and their reappearance as shown in 2 Kings 23:2, Nehemiah 8:9, and others, are also relevant because they show that the Old Testament writings were not necessarily kept in an unbroken chain of transmission. Rather, the Word of God existed partly in an oral and prophetic presence, and in other periods a written presence, during longer and shorter periods.

ALEXANDER THE GREAT AND HELLENIZATION UP UNTIL CHRIST

"And it happened, after that Alexander son of Philip, the Macedonian, who came out of the land of Chettiim, had smitten Darius king of the Persians and Medes, that he reigned in his stead, the first over Greece, And made many wars, and won many strong holds, and slew the kings of the earth, And went through to the ends of the earth, and took spoils of many nations, insomuch that the earth was quiet before him; whereupon he was exalted and his heart was lifted up. And he gathered a mighty strong host and ruled over countries, and nations, and kings, who became tributaries unto him."

— 1 Maccabees 1:1–4

"Now such was the height of Hellenism [Ἑλληνισμοῦ], and increase of heathenish manners, through the exceeding profaneness of Jason, that ungodly wretch, and no high priest (...)"

— 2 Maccabees 4:13a

After the final victory of Alexander the Great over the Persian Empire at the Battle of Gaugamela in 331 B.C., around 200 years after the return of the Jews to Jerusalem from the Babylonian Exile, a new epoch of great cultural, linguistic, and demographic change was ushered in. Though his empire would prove itself exceptionally short-lived, its influence would prove very enduring. Although Greek culture and language had exercised some influence in the Near East prior to the advent of Alexander, his immeasurable conquests initiated a flood of Greek influence and Hellenization. In his work on the Greek translation of the Old Testament, *When God Spoke Greek*, Professor Timothy Law underscores that Alexander's influence cannot be overstated:

PART I: HISTORICAL FOUNDATION

There has never been such a widespread adoption of culture in history. If the closest analogy is the spread of Arabic language and Islamic culture in the wake of Mohammed's victories, even this wasn't as widespread or rapid as the Hellenization of the world from Greece to India between the fourth and first centuries BCE.[15]

Numerous colonies and trade stations with Greek settlements were planted throughout the new empire, including the area covering the former Israeli kingdoms. When Alexander's empire collapsed in the wake of its founder's early death, the Greek influence remained and exercised its impulses through different Greek successor kingdoms founded by his generals, the so-called Diadochi. Two of these successor kingdoms are especially relevant in the scope of this book, namely the Seleucid and the Ptolemaic Kingdoms. Around 281 B.C., the Seleucid Kingdom covered, from West to East, most of Anatolia—the old Persian heart lands—all the way to India. Ptolemy and his successors governed Egypt and its surrounding areas. Between these two Hellenic juggernauts, the tiny province of Judah was positioned, which all too often served as both a battlefield and a war goal of the countless conflicts between Alexander's successor kingdoms. It is worth noting that the battle for dominance over Judah did not take place between a Persian or Egyptian power, or a Greek and Oriental kingdom. Rather, the struggle was now only a question of *which* Greek power should dominate the area, and not whether Greek dominance would be exerted or not.

The process by which non-Greeks picked up Greek culture and way of life has been described in many places (including 2 Maccabees) as Hellenization. The Athenian rhetorician Isocrates, who died in 338 B.C., anticipated this development, writing:

> And so far has our city [Athens] distanced the rest of mankind in thought and speech that her pupils have become the teachers of the rest of the world; and she has brought it about that the name "Hellenes" suggests no longer a race but an intelligence, and the title "Hellenes" is applied rather to those who share our culture than to those who share a common blood.[16]

---

[15] Timothy Michael Law, *When God Spoke Greek: The Septuagint and the Making of Western Civilization* (New York: Oxford University Press, 2013), 13.

[16] Goerge Norlin, trans., "Panegyricus," in *Isocrates, Volume I* (Cambridge, Massachusetts: Harvard University Press, 1980), 49–50.

This development, and the cultural conflict between Hellenized Jews and more nativistic-minded Jews which follow in its wake, is described thoroughly in the Books of Maccabees. It must be noted that the battle was not fought over *whether* Greek language and culture would be received but only about the degree to which it would be. The Maccabees, who led multiple rebellions against the control of the Seleucid kings, were themselves highly Hellenized, though they represented the most traditionally-minded and reactionary part of Jewish society at the time. Judas Maccabeus, who died in 160 B.C. and who led the struggle against the Seleucids, sent his representative Eupolemus, on different diplomatic missions.[17] Eupolemus, a Greek name meaning *good fighter*, was the author of a large work about the Judean kings of old, written in Greek.[18] This book was similar to the book of 2 Maccabees, which narrates the successful struggle for independence and is itself composed in Greek rather than Hebrew or Aramaic.[19] Facts like these indicate the growing dominance of Greek, even in times of growing Jewish nationalism and reacquired national self-determination following the success of the Maccabean Revolt. Hellenism became more widespread and became nativized, and though Hebrew was still the liturgical and religious language, and Aramaic the native language of the people at large, Greek continued to gain ground.

In his book *Did Jesus Speak Greek?*, G. Scott Gleaves, professor of Biblical languages and New Testament Studies, describes how Greek became the dominating language around the time of Christ. By surveying the scholarship written on the topic, the archeological evidence, and the comments made by contemporaneous written sources, he finds evidence justifying the conclusion that Greek influence had already begun around the return from the Babylonian Exile, after which its influence grew to an established dominant position from the period between the conquests of Alexander the Great up until A.D. 1. As an example of maybe the earliest Greek influence, professor Gleaves mentions how the book of Daniel chapter 3:3–5, 7, 8 and 15 describes multiple musical instruments, all of which have common Aramaic names. Yet in spite of this, the passage, which is written in Aramaic, uses Greek loan words for the items even though already existing Aramaic terms could have been used[20]. This is significant because

---

[17] 1 Macc. 8:17; 2 Macc. 4:11.
[18] Gleaves and Cloud, *Did Jesus Speak Greek?*, chap. 2.
[19] Gleaves and Cloud, *Did Jesus Speak Greek?*, chap. 2.
[20] Gleaves and Cloud, *Did Jesus Speak Greek?*, chap. 2.

PART I: HISTORICAL FOUNDATION

it indicates a particularly early example of Greek influence. Indeed, the text mentions קִיתָרֹס (qitharos) from the Greek word κίθαρις (citar), and פְּסַנְטֵרִין (pesanterin), from the Greek word ψαλτήριον, which is a stringed instrument, akin to a harp, and other instruments as well.

But it was the campaigns of Alexander the Great which were to cause the greatest transformations for Hellenization. Following in the steps of the advancing army, a string of Greek colonies were founded, which would in due time became centers of Hellenism. The process of colonization was continued by the Diadochi, and around the time of Christ large parts of the area of the historic Israeli kingdom were heavily colonized and Hellenized. Though Greeks, who lived in many towns and cities, never constituted a majority of the population, except possibly in a few colonies such as Pella, Dion and Philo-teria, yet their influence far excee-ded their numerical size, and their culture and lang-uage quickly be-came dominant. In the New Testament, the area known as the *Decapolis*, or the *Ten City States*, is often mentioned.

Figure 3 – *Map of Roman Palestine at the time of Christ*

The states were a loose confederacy of small city states that were united by their shared Greek culture and lang-uage.[21] Other already established towns were settled by Greeks and influenced by the Decapolis.

The city of Akko changed its name and became known as Ptolemais, Rabbat-Ammon became known as Phila-delphia, and Beth-Shan as Scytho-polis, which

---

[21] Gleaves and Cloud, *Did Jesus Speak Greek?*, chap. 2.

to-gether with Gerasa and Pella, among others all shown on the map above, were part of the Deca-polis. These towns were heavily Hellenized and had temples to the Greek gods, Greek-style city planning, and road systems. Caesarea Maritima also had a Greek amphitheater of stone construction built by Herod the Great, and a characteristically Greek *agora*—a large, open city squares—along with public baths, and a gymnasium with Greek sports and plays.[22]

The Greek influence in this area was so strong that the inhabitants of the coastal area toward the East, the old Phoenician area, were even called *Hellenes*, which means Greeks.

ἡ δὲ γυνὴ ἦν Ἑλληνίς, Συροφοινίκισσα τῷ γένει καὶ ἠρώτα αὐτὸν ἵνα τὸ δαιμόνιον ἐκβάλῃ ἐκ τῆς θυγατρὸς αὐτῆς. (Gospel of Mark 7:26)

The woman in the passage above is introduced as a Greek, Ἑλληνίς, though she is also explicitly described as being ethnically Syro-Phoenician. This is significant because it simultaneously describes her double identity, that is, her socio-cultural identity as a Greek as well as her ethnic background as a Syro-Phoenician.

Looking at the map above, it also becomes apparent that, though Greek influence was extensive in all of Israel, it was more prevalent in the North than in the South, with Hellenism also being very prominent in Jerusalem. Sepphoris, marked out on the map, lay only six kilometers (3.7 miles) northwest from Jesus' hometown of Nazareth, and it was one of the most Hellenized towns of Galilee, along with Caesarea and Tiberias[23]. Jesus and his father Joseph, being skilled carpenters and craftsmen (τέκτων) – Matthew 13:55 and Mark 6:3—most likely traded and at times worked in Sepphoris[24], especially considering the grand building programs ordered by Antipas in the city. Urban Hellenic culture was therefore formative in Jesus' upbringing and early life. Professor Gleaves cites Richard Batey, professor

---

[22] Josephus, *Antiquities of the Jews* 15.9.6; *The Jewish War* 1.21.8, 1.21.11 ($422).

[23] Gleaves and Cloud, *Did Jesus Speak Greek?*, chap. 2.

[24] Joseph is explicitly denoted as a τέκτων in Matthew 13:55, that is an educated craftsman, and though there is no explicit proof demonstrating that he and Jesus went to Sepphoris, then it is highly probable when considering its central locality and its function as commercial hub. See Eric Meyers, "Jesus and His Galilean Context," in *Sepphoris in Galilee: Crosscurrents of Culture*, ed. Rebecca Martin Nagy et al. (Raleigh, NC: North Carolina Museum of Art; Winona Lake, IN: Eisenbrauns, 1996), 63; Josephus, *Antiquities of the Jews* 14.5.4 (§§90–91), where Sepphoris is described as the regional capital.

PART I: HISTORICAL FOUNDATION

of religion, in his book and states, "Jesus lived in a Galilean culture much more urban and sophisticated than previously believed".[25] The town of Sepphoris also serves as an illustrative model for how Hellenism expressed itself in the time around the birth of Christ. Urban centers such as these were centers of culture and Greek influence; for example, Sepphoris possessed an amphitheater with four thousand seating spots. It must therefore be noted that when Jesus uses explicitly Greek words from a theatrical context, such as ὑποκριτα (hypocrite),[26] as Professor Gleaves also notes, then he might very well be drawing on a familiar cultural context. This influence was not limited to the coastal areas either, and inland cities like Sebaste, Gerasa, and Sepphoris have confirmed the broad influence of Hellenism throughout the country through archeological finds such as amphoras, Greek seals, characteristic Greek architecture, and even common housing.

Much evidence also points toward Greek being the dominant language in the time around the birth of Christ. Josephus mentions in his famous work *Jewish Antiquities*, which was naturally published in Greek, that when Julius Caesar wanted to erect bronze tablets for the publication of senatorial decrees from Rome in the Judean province, these were inscribed in Latin and in Greek.[27] The choice of Latin is not a surprise, as it was the official language of the Roman state and the Roman Senate. But the choice of Greek, and the exclusion of any other language, is interesting, as this presupposes that the language by which the decrees could be communicated to the general public was Greek.

Compared to Aramaic, which was the native language for most of the indigenous inhabitants of the country, Greek was the language of the urban elite, travelers, traders, the colonists, soldiers, Roman visitors, and more. Thus, the use of Aramaic was confined to one specific socio-linguistic group, namely that of most of the indigenous inhabitants, while Greek was the natural medium for communication between the many different social and cultural groups inhabiting the area. Though Greek did not replace Aramaic, there are many strong indications that Greek was used and understood also by the Aramaic-speaking population.

The twelve disciples, who were common Galileans, craftsmen and fishermen (Matthew 4:18–22), and a few more educated men such as tax

---

[25] Gleaves and Cloud, *Did Jesus Speak Greek?*, chap. 2.
[26] Gleaves and Cloud, *Did Jesus Speak Greek?*, chap. 2.
[27] Josephus, *Antiquities of the Jews* 14.10.2.

collectors (Matthew 10:3), yet their names are indicative of thoroughly Hellenized culture. Many of them did not even have Jewish names, but explicitly Greek names, such as Phillip, Andrew, and Peter, who was also called Simon. The name Simon, Σίμων, is itself either directly a Greek name, as witnessed to by early authors such as Aristophanes, or a Hellenized version of the Jewish name Symeon, Συμεών. Phillip, who also came from Bethsaida, as did the brothers Simon and Andrew (John 1:44), are also interesting examples of the degree of assimilation into Hellenic culture. Apart from their Greek names, one can read that they were also fluent in spoken Greek. The Gospel of John 12:20 describes how some Greeks (τινες Ἕλληνες) came to Phillip and spoke with him, an episode that further underscores how widespread the knowledge of Greek was in that time. Also, Peter's conversation with the foreign proselyte Cornelius, in the heavily Hellenized town of Caesarea, was most likely held in Greek (Acts 10:24f). This is because the conversation took place in a Hellenized town, with a foreign soldier stationed there, and his family (verse 44f), as Peter apparently spoke not only to Cornelius but also to his family—the multiple Gentiles that were mentioned.

That the knowledge of Greek was not restricted to urban elites, but also widespread among the commoners, such as Galilean fishermen, is not only supported by written sources but also by archeology. The amount of Greek burial inscriptions found in the region around Galilee and Jerusalem in the time around the first and second century points toward the fact that a majority of the population had a knowledge of Greek.[28] Professor Gleaves Scott cites Professor of New Testament Studies Pieter van der Horst's study of burial inscriptions in the first century:

> [F]or a great part of the Jewish population the daily language was Greek, even in Palestine. This is impressive testimony to the impact of Hellenistic culture on Jews in their mother country, to say nothing of the Diaspora.... In Jerusalem itself about 40 percent of the Jewish inscriptions from the first-century period (before 70 C.E.) are in Greek. We may assume that most Jewish Jerusalemites who saw the inscription in situ were able to read them. In a first-century C.E. tomb near Jericho, a Jewish family nicknamed the Goliaths (because of their extraordinary stature) inscribed more

---

[28] Gleaves and Cloud, *Did Jesus Speak Greek?*, chap. 4.

than half their epitaphs in Greek ... a majority of the Jews in Palestine and the western Diaspora spoke Greek. That is probably one reason why there is so little evidence of influence of the Mishnah outside rabbinic circles.[29]

In other words, Greek was the dominant language, though it was not the only spoken language. It did not supplant Aramaic, but it was the primary language through which communication between the nation's different social and cultural groups was enabled and conducted. Even in more conservative pharisaical circles, Greek exerted its influence. The Pharisee Nikodemus, which is also a Greek name, was a member of the Jewish Sanhedrin. Sanhedrim itself is also a Greek loan word, συνέδριον, which again points toward the universal influence of Greek. Even Paul's pharisaic rabbi Gamaliel (Acts 22:3) was himself a Hellenist. His son, Simeon, recounts how the students of Gamaliel devoted themselves to the study of Greek literature[30]. Therefore, it should not be a surprise that Paul, being a student of Gamaliel, multiple times cites Greek poets such as Meander in 1 Corinthians 15:33 and discusses in Greek philosophy in Athens in Acts 17:16ff, in addition to using Greek rhetoric and stylistic devices.[31] One cannot, therefore, imagine a false antithesis between Hellenized cosmopolitan Jews and more "authentic" and nativistic pharisaical Jews. Rather, Hellenization was widespread and common among all layers of Jewish society in First Century Judea.

CONCLUSION

This journey through the history of the Israelites was undertaken in order to show how the assumption of a one-to-one relationship between the old Israel, the writings of the Hebrew Old Testament, and the current editions of the Old Testament, such as the Biblica Hebraica, copied and formed by their transmission through the hands of the Masoretes, cannot be made. The Israelites underwent changes of language, from Hebrew to Aramaic, where they even lost their original alphabet, or more precisely *abjad*, and received a new, foreign one.

Later, with the conquests of Alexander the Great, Greek language and culture became increasingly more embedded into Jewish culture. The

---

[29] Gleaves and Cloud, *Did Jesus Speak Greek?*, chap. 4.
[30] Gleaves and Cloud, *Did Jesus Speak Greek?*, chap. 4.
[31] Gleaves and Cloud, *Did Jesus Speak Greek?*, chap. 4.

concept of a never changing, authentic Hebrew text used by the Israelites must be rejected as much too simplistic and imprecise. Israel was not a monolithic and monocultural Hebrew-speaking nation, rather Hebrew went from being the native tongue to being a liturgical language, spoken and kept alive by a small elite—the priesthood, scribes and scholars—but regarded as alien and strange by most of society. In the words of professor Gleaves, during the time of Christ "The majority of Jews no longer understood Hebrew",[32] and for many Israelites, Hebrew was as strange and foreign to them as Old Norse Runes might be to many modern Scandinavians, or Sanskrit to modern Indians.

Concurrent with the estrangement of Hebrew, Greek became ever more familiar, changing its role from a foreign language of trade and culture to an intimate and homely language. Israelites increasingly began to use Greek for items as personal and intimate as their first names and their burial inscriptions. The knowledge of it became more common in the area covering the Davidic Israelite Kingdom. These facts, and the role of the written Word of God, which in certain times could be absent and later rediscovered—though never leaving Israel—will become significant in the next chapters, where the birth and the reception of the Septuagint will be examined.

---

[32] Gleaves and Cloud, *Did Jesus Speak Greek?*, chap. 1.

THE TRANSLATION OF THE SEVENTY-TWO
THE LIGHTHOUSE OF HELLENISM

The grandest and most important city that rose up in the aftermath of the conquests of Alexander the Great was Alexandria of Egypt. The conqueror king brought with him an unprecedented colonization effort, planting towns as pearls on a string in the wake of his army. Settled by veterans, native Greeks, merchants, locals, and others, these colonies became centers of Hellenism, or in other words, hubs for Greek culture and language. Though these cities were numerous, spanning from Asia Minor to the Hindu Kush, one city was wholly unrivaled among all of them. In 331 B.C., at the mouth of the Nile where the rich delta met the warm waters of the Mediterranean, the Macedonian king founded Alexandria, a city which had from its beginning a strong Jewish presence. The relationship between Israel and Egypt was far from new. In many regards, Egypt acted as the womb of the people of Israel, wherefrom they were delivered by Moses with much pain and travail during the Exodus. The role of Egypt in redemptive history was paramount, and the close relationship between Israel and Egypt is, as it will be shown, also a crucial element in explaining the origin of the Septuagint.

Just as significant in Israel's history, yet much less well known, is the Egyptian Exile which took place simultaneously with the Babylonian Exile. This exile is mentioned in passing in the Book of Jeremiah, where groups of Judeans chose to flee to Egypt, faced with the prospect of an imminent attack of Babylon on Judah. A later group of Judeans who were on their way to Babylon, consisting of poorer Judeans from the countryside who had been freed, also made their way to Egypt. This group is described in Jeremiah 43:

> So Johanan the son of Kareah, all the captains of the forces, and all the people would not obey the voice of the Lord, to remain in the land of Judah. But Johanan the son of Kareah and all the captains of the forces took all the remnant of Judah who had returned to dwell in the land of Judah, from all nations where they had been driven, men, women, children, the king's daughters, and every person whom Nebuzaradan the captain of the guard had left with Gedaliah the son of Ahikam, the son of Shaphan, and Jeremiah the prophet and Baruch the son of Neriah. So they went to the land of

Egypt, for they did not obey the voice of the Lord. And they went as far as Tahpanhes. (Jeremiah 43:4-6)

Though no exact number is given, the size of the group does not seem to be insignificant. The details about the prophet Jeremiah and his scribe Baruch coming along are also important insofar as the arrival of this group to Egypt signals not only the re-entrance of Israel into Egypt, but also the return of the presence of the Word of God to Egypt. Jeremiah's prophetic ministry would continue in Egypt (Jeremiah 43:8f), not to mention the written Word of God through the efforts of Baruch. Baruch was Jeremiah's scribe and the one who likely wrote down the Book of Jeremiah, according to Jeremiah 36:32. From this perspective, it can reasonably be concluded that parts of the book were written in Egypt, since Jeremiah's prophetic work continued there. This makes the Egyptian Exile quite important as it signifies the beginning of a new epoch wherein the Word of God is revealed and also written down in Egypt. Egypt was the same land wherefrom Scripture itself was birthed originally by the hand of Moses, as he began writing the Pentateuch during the Exodus and in the Wilderness of Egyptian Sinai.

The Jewish settlements during this exile were not trivial. Already in the time of Jeremiah, around the first half of the sixth century B.C., he writes, "The word that came to Jeremiah concerning all the Jews who dwell in the land of Egypt, who dwell at Migdol, at Tahpanhes, at Noph, and in the country of Pathros" (Jeremiah 44:1). Multiple Jewish settlements were scattered throughout Egypt even at this time. Around three hundred years after these events, when Alexander the Great had founded Alexandria, this presence grew as well as he chose to deport a multitude of Jews from Judah and Samaria to his newly founded city.[33] The Jewish historian Josephus, who died around A.D. 100, describes these events in a couple of his works, including in *Against Apion*. Josephus relates how Alexandria from its very founding had a significant Jewish population, who even received the same civil rights as the Greek settlers. The Jews received their own quarter in the city,[34] and made up a significant part of its population.

Culturally and linguistically, the city was thoroughly Greek and served as the seat of power of Ptolemaic Egypt, which was ruled by a dynasty descending from Alexander's general Ptolemy until its last ruler was deposed by the Romans in 30 B.C. Cleopatra, the last ruler of the Ptolemaic

---

[33] Josephus, *Jewish Antiquities* 12.1.8.
[34] Josephus, *Against Apion* 2.4.1.

PART I: HISTORICAL FOUNDATION

dynasty, demonstrated the Greek character of this dynasty and the great influence of Hellenism in Egypt. She was not only a native Greek speaker but was actually the only regent of the dynasty who made any effort to gain even a small proficiency in Demotic, the native language of the indigenous Egyptians.[35] This mixture of Greek and Jewish culture in Alexandria made the ground fertile for one of the greatest cultural projects of Antiquity which would define the religious landscape for centuries. The scene was set for the birth of the Septuagint—the first full translation of the Old Testament into Greek.

THE BIRTH OF THE SEPTUAGINT AND THE LETTER OF ARISTEAS

"Now, as I have already said, they met together daily in their own place, which was pleasantly situated for its calmness and brightness, and carried on their prescribed task. But the outcome was such that in seventy-two days the translation work was completed, as if such a result was achieved by some design [κατὰ πρόθεσιν τινα]."

— The Letter of Aristeas §307

Egypt, with its unique connection to Israel and the history of the Old Testament, would also here play a defining role in this monumental task of ancient literary history. As discussed in the previous chapters, shifting languages and even changing writing systems were not new to the turbulent history of the books of the Old Testament, which had originally been written in Hebrew and Aramaic in Paleo-Hebrew script. Alexandria, being the meeting place of Egyptian, Jewish, and Hellenic culture, became the catalyst for the translation of the Old Testament books into Greek. Even though the Old Testament books were written in different languages and had undergone a change of writing system, and would later undergo substantial changes by the hand of the Masoretes, as will be discussed later, this translation was indeed a manifestation of something new. A translation project as ambitious as this had never been carried out before. Dr. Scott Gleaves writes, "It was truly a remarkable undertaking in that it was the first attempt to translate the Hebrew Scriptures into another language. The translators began in the third century BCE and appear to have taken nearly a century to complete the task".[36]

---

[35] Plutarch, *Vita Antonii*, chap. 27.
[36] Gleaves and Cloud, *Did Jesus Speak Greek?*, chap. 2.

SEVENTY-TWO SERVANTS OF THE WORD

The earliest and most important source describing the birth of the Septuagint is without a doubt the work called the Letter of Aristeas, or the Book of Aristeas. According to the letter itself its author is a certain Aristeas, living in Alexandria, who is writing the letter to his brother Philokrates. Aristeas describes how the Pentateuch was translated into Greek. Demetrios, the leader of the famous library in Alexandria, was tasked by king Ptolemy II, who reigned from 281 to 246 B.C., to collect all the books of the known world and have a copy made of each for the royal library at the king's expense. Demetrios then told the king about the famous law of the Jews, which he wished to have added to his collection at once. As a gesture of good will, the king had a large number of Jewish prisoners released so that they could return to Judaea, and wrote a letter to Eleazer, the high priest in Jerusalem, where he expressed his desire to have a group of skilled translations sent from Judaea to Alexandria, so that they could translate the book of law. One of those dispatched from Alexandria with the letter to the high priest was none other than Aristeas. Eleazer gave his assent and sent six men from each of the 12 tribes who were skilled in Greek and Hebrew along with a Hebrew copy of the Torah. These Seventy-Two translators, whereof the name *Septuagint* arose, Latin for seventy, were presented before the king and began to translate the Pentateuch. They were isolated on a small island near Alexandria, which provided the tranquility necessary for the task. They completed their work in seventy-two days, after which they presented their new Greek translation before the king, the chief librarian Demetrios, and the Jewish populace of Alexandria.

The Letter of Aristeas had a great influence on later writers, both Jewish and early Christian, and it is cited as history by Josephus and many Christian authors. Philo of Alexandria, who shows no direct knowledge of the letter, also passes on the same story[37]. The work frequently appears in many Byzantine Septuagint manuscripts as a form of apology,[38] and the letter was generally seen as historical up until after the Reformation. Today, the work has received much criticism with regard to its value as a source of the history for the Septuagint and its credibility is rejected by many[39]. The points of criticism center around what, by many, are seen as legendary features of the

---

[37] Sidney Jellicoe, *The Septuagint and Modern Study* (Eisenbrauns, 2013), 30.
[38] Fernández Marcos, Natalio, *The Septuagint in Context: Introduction to the Greek Version of the Bible* (BRILL, 2000), 37.
[39] Bruce M. Metzger, *The Bible in Translation: Ancient and English Versions* (Grand Rapids, Michigan: Baker Academic, 2001), 15.

PART I: HISTORICAL FOUNDATION

narrative and the seeming apologetic nature of the work. The apologetic tone is interpreted as indicating that the letter should rather be seen as a pseudepigraphic work of Jewish polemic directed against the surrounding Hellenic society. The use of the Letter of Aristeas is therefore controversial among current Septuagint scholars since, if judged as authentic or at least as possessing a historic kernel of truth, it would by far be the earliest and most important source about the origin of the Septuagint.

This earlier skeptical consensus has been challenged recently and is rejected by many contemporary scholars. Even though Professor Timothy Law calls the letter "a legend written by a Jew, who pretends to be a courtier of Ptolemy to give the story credibility",[40] many other important scholars criticize such an interpretation. Mogens Müller, then professor at the University of Copenhagen, wrote that the legendary features of the story have caused an undue amount of skepticism toward the actual historic content of the letter.[41] Müller adds that much of the information provided by the letter matches what we already know about the era and the recounted events. It is well established that king Ptolemy was a lover of wisdom and learning, who had different texts and law codices translated into Greek, among which were the Laws of the Lagides which was translated around 275 B.C. and was a law code used by his demotic subjects. This took place, among other reasons, so that the royal court could get a better knowledge of the different governed peoples.[42] It is therefore not unlikely that something very similar could have happened with the law of the Jews, a group which made up a significant part of the population of Ptolemaic Egypt, especially in the capital of the kingdom.

Professor Fernández Marcos, one of the leading Septuagint experts, also points to other characteristics which add credibility to the letter's historicity. In his influential monograph *The Septuagint in Context*, he summarizes the scholarly consensus concerning Aristeas' letter and the motives lying behind the translation of the Septuagint. Modern scholarship points toward especially two reasons for the translation: first, the liturgical needs of the large Jewish population of Alexandria, who were almost wholly native Greek speakers, and secondly, an official royal initiative by the

---

[40] Law, *When God Spoke Greek*, 167.
[41] Møgens Müller, *The First Bible of the Church: A Plea for the Septuagint*, Journal for the Study of the Old Testament Supplement Series, vol. 206 (1996; repr., Sheffield Academic Press, 2009), 60.
[42] Fernández Marcos, *The Septuagint in Context*, 63.

Ptolemaic court, which is judged to be the crucial *raison d'etre* on account of the judicial and cultural importance of this work.⁴³ Because most recent publications about the Septuagint point toward the official initiative as the decisive reason for the translation, the case for the historicity of the main claim of Aristeas' letter is strengthened, insofar as the letter underscores the royal initiative as the cause for the undertaking. This also casts doubt on an alternative hypothesis explaining the origin of the Septuagint, most famously put forward by Paul Kahle in the first half of the twentieth century, who argued that multiple more or less official translations were made by private initiative,⁴⁴ a view which is contrasted by Aristeas' claim of one official and uniform translation. That being said, the two different motives, the local liturgical need and the royal initiative, should not necessarily be seen as contradictory, but rather that the former contributed to the latter. Kahle's hypothesis, on the other hand, must be rejected, first and foremost because a single, stable, and apparently official Greek text appeared and was received, as will be discussed in depth later.

Other significant details in the letter which deserve to be mentioned indicate an early dating of the letter, around the third century B.C. The biblical scholar and Septuagint expert Sidney Jellicoe brings up the curious fact that Aristeas describes the priestly breastplate worn by the high priest Eleazer in Jerusalem, but this practice of wearing the breastplate was ended by the Pharisees around 200 B.C.⁴⁵ Jellicoe cites the biblical scholar W. F. Albright, who remarked that the list of names of the seventy-two translators "contains authentic personal names of the third century".⁴⁶ These details would be hard to replicate generations later. The highest view of the historicity of the Septuagint is found in the writings of Dr. Nina Colins, who in her peer-reviewed article "282 BCE: The Date of the Translation of the Pentateuch into Greek under Ptolemy" argues that it is possible to fix the exact year of the translation to 282 B.C. Even though her approach has been criticized by others, such as Wright,⁴⁷ this indicates the historicity of the work and the degree to which it is possible to trace it. Some details in the letter are disputed, such as the exact identity of Demetrios, who seemingly

---

⁴³ Fernández Marcos, *The Septuagint in Context*, 62-63.
⁴⁴ Jellicoe, *The Septuagint and Modern Study*, 59.
⁴⁵ Jellicoe, *The Septuagint and Modern Study*, 49.
⁴⁶ Jellicoe, *The Septuagint and Modern Study*, 49.
⁴⁷ Benjamin G. Wright III, "The Septuagint and Second Temple Judaism," in *T&T Clark Handbook of Septuagint Research*, ed. William A. Ross and W. Edward Glenny (New York: Bloomsbury Publishing Plc, 2021), 282.

PART I: HISTORICAL FOUNDATION

was the chief librarian under Ptolemy I and not Ptolemy II. It must be considered that the historical sources disputing this are somewhat unclear, and some scholars including Collins reject such an argument against the Letter of Aristeas and see no issue here, as there are good reasons to harmonize the historical accounts. One other argument against the letter, namely that 10 out of the 12 tribes had become lost at this point in time must be addressed. While it is true that the 10 tribes as such had been lost then this was not the case universally. Apart from the tribes of Benjamin and Judah surviving in Judah itself, the tribe of Levi, Luke 1:5, and northern tribe of Asher is also mentioned as having survived in the southern Judah, Luke 22:30. It is therefore not inconceivable that members of the other tribes were present as well when the northern most tribe of Asher was. Likewise it must neither be forgotten that a minority of the 10 tribes remained in Israel and later became the Samaritans.

The letter, therefore, ought to be used as an important and early source of the origin of the Septuagint and its reception, even if one rejects certain parts of the letter as exaggerations. The letter describes how a single Greek translation of the Pentateuch arose on account of a royal enterprise. If Aristeas' explanation is accepted, three facts concerning the Septuagint can also be explained easily. First, it can be explained why the Septuagint was so quickly received by the Jews not only in Egypt and in Israel, which will be discussed later, but also those scattered throughout the diaspora. This is explained by the fact that the Septuagint not only enjoyed a royal approval but a religious approval as well. By giving his assent and offering manuscripts for the work, Eleazer the High Priest conferred a form of religious credibility to the Septuagint because it was sanctioned by the highest religious authority in Israel, who also provided the Hebrew text for the translation from the very Temple of Jerusalem itself. This detail in the letter is in part supported by some observations made by the leading expert in Hebraic Old Testament textual criticism, Emmanuel Tov. He notices, as will be elaborated later, how the special Hebrew Vorlage (original document, being translated) of the Septuagint shows signs of an early dating on account of its different wording and its variants compared to the later proto-Masoretic Text.[48] Because the Septuagint reflects a very early text, which was in circulation prior to the later proto-Masoretic Text, it seems likely that the date of translation can be put before this later text became common,

---

[48] Emanuel Tov, *The Text-Critical Use of the Septuagint in Biblical Research* (Winona Lake, Indiana: Eisenbrauns, 2015), 219.

which according to Dr. Tov only happened after the purported date of translation of the Septuagint,[49] as will be detailed later.

Secondly, if the reliability of the letter is assumed, it can easily be explained why a multitude of diverse translations of individual Old Testament books never appeared. This would have to be expected, if the Septuagint was the result of different private enterprises, where multiple translations arose without anyone enjoying special religious or regal sanction. But in reality, we find the opposite to be the case. Almost three hundred years would pass before another Greek translation of the Old Testament received any kind of dissemination, namely that of Aquila. The period prior to Aquila's translation stands in stark contrast to the later age, such as at the time of Origen of Alexandria, who was active in the first half of the third century. In his compilation of the Old Testament, the Hexapla, Origen included not only the original translation of the Septuagint, but also a Greek edition of Symmachus, one of Theodotian, and of course the version by Aquila. Later still, during the reign of the emperor Justinian, a decree was issued declaring that only the translations of the Seventy-Two and of Aquila may be used in the synagogues of the Roman empire[50]. The total absence of any other Greek translations of the Old Testament between Ptolemy II and Aquila, who lived 300 years later, gives a strong indication that there were no other Greek translations in circulation, which supports the claims of religious and royal authority of the semi-official Septuagint translation.

Thirdly, though the Letter of Aristeas explicitly relates how the Pentateuch was translated, it also contains an interesting remark about how the king made known to the chief librarian Demetrios in chapter 28 that the books of the Jews, that is, τῶν Ἰουδαϊκῶν βιβλίων ἀντιγραφῆς, should be translated and copied. This fits with the known chronology of the Septuagint. The Pentateuch, we can imagine, was translated as recounted by Aristeas, and is therefore in all parts the same and exerts a great influence on the tone and style of the translation of the remaining books, all of which imitate the Septuagint's Pentateuch in both style, terminology, and semantics.[51] The following books, the historic books, the prophetic books, and the wisdom literature, were likely translated later with a basis in the

---

[49] Tov, *The Text-Critical Use of the Septuagint in Biblical Research*, 219.
[50] Mikhail G. Seleznev, "The Septuagint in the Eastern Orthodox Tradition," in *T&T Clark Handbook of Septuagint Research*, ed. William A. Ross and W. Edward Glenny (Bloomsbury Publishing, 2021), 40.
[51] Jellicoe, *The Septuagint and Modern Study*, 49.

PART I: HISTORICAL FOUNDATION

official translation work taking place in Alexandria. Henry Thackeray, one of the most prominent Septuagint scholars, comes close to such a view and notes, "We shall find indications of the existence of a second company, analogous to the pioneering body responsible for the Greek Pentateuch. This second instalment was also, it seems, in large measure a semiofficial production".[52]

Thackeray, who was also an expert in Koine Greek, and who among other works translated the works of the Jewish historian Josephus from Greek into English, describes how the great prophets Isaiah, Jeremiah, and Ezekiel, as well as the Twelve Minor Prophets, in all likelihood were translated subsequent to the Pentateuch, with which they share many stylistic features in their translation.[53] Next came what he calls the early prophets, that are the Books of Samuel followed by the category commonly denoted as the Writings—the Book of Psalms, Proverbs, etc. Thus, the traditional threefold division of the Old Testament into the Law, the Prophets, and the Writings was more or less followed. Even though the exact order is somewhat unclear, Thackeray for example counts the Book of Joshua as having been translated very early as an appendix of sorts to the Pentateuch, nevertheless this explanation fits well with the story found in the Letter of Aristeas.

Here, an official translation of the Pentateuch is produced with the support and approval of the high priestly authority of Jerusalem under the auspices of the royal librarian of Alexandria, who also made an explicit request for the translation of the remaining sacred books. Though this latter effort is not described by the letter, this undertaking seems to have taken place as the other books were translated with a basis in the already officially established work of translation in Alexandria. Thus, the authoritative character of the pioneering work of the five Mosaic books was passed on in a derivative sense to translations which took place subsequent to the translation of the Pentateuch and which emulated its tone, style, and vocabulary.

Emmanuel Tov, who is described by the aforementioned Professor Timothy Law as "the greatest modern authority on the Hebrew Textual tradition"[54] also affirms that the Pentateuch of the Septuagint clearly has an

---

[52] Jellicoe, *The Septuagint and Modern Study*, 66.
[53] Jellicoe, *The Septuagint and Modern Study*, 67.
[54] Law, *When God Spoke Greek*, 23.

Egyptian origin[55], though he is uncertain about the origins of the later Old Testament books and personally leans toward a Palestinian origin. He acknowledges that "the Alexandrian background of these books [the remaining Old Testament books] is presupposed by many, if not most scholars",[56] a fact corroborating Aristeas' explanation. Professor Jellicoe also agrees with Professor Olinsky, another Septuagint expert, and notes strong evidence supporting the claim that originally there was only one Greek translation of each individual Old Testament book,[57] which fits well with Aristeas' description of Alexandria as the birthplace of the official translation work of Jewish books into Greek. This process began with the Pentateuch but ended only after the completion of the whole Old Testament.

THE JEWISH RECEPTION OF THE SEPTUAGINT

"The clearest proof of this is that, if Chaldeans have learned Greek, or Greeks Chaldean, and read both versions, the Chaldean and the translation, they regard them with awe and reverence as sisters, or rather one and the same, both in matter and words, and speak of the authors not as translators but as prophets and priests of the mysteries, whose sincerity and singleness of thought has enabled them to go hand in hand with the purest of spirits, the spirit of Moses."

— Philo of Alexandria, *Life of Moses*, §40

If the Letter of Aristeas can be dated early, which seems likely according to the previous arguments, then the letter would provide us with an early window into the very first reception of the Septuagint by the Jews. Regardless of whether the letter truly was written by a certain Aristeas connected to the court or whether it is a pseudonym used by a Jewish citizen of Alexandria who wrote it primarily as an apologetic work seeking to defend the authority of the new translation, in either case it is a valuable source to the earliest reception of the Septuagint.

In the last paragraphs of the letter, the reception of the Septuagint by the Alexandrian Jews is described. Demetrios had summoned the entire Jewish population of the city to whom the translation was then presented and publicly read. The Jews praised the translation and asked their leaders to make copies of it (paragraph 308–9). After the Septuagint had been read

---

[55] Tov, *The Text-Critical Use of the Septuagint in Biblical Research*, 201.
[56] Tov, *The Text-Critical Use of the Septuagint in Biblical Research*, 202.
[57] Jellicoe, *The Septuagint and Modern Study*, 341.

PART I: HISTORICAL FOUNDATION

to them, the Jewish priests stood up along with the elders and the aforementioned leaders, who in unison explained that the translation was "beautiful, holy, and translation with utmost precision" (καλῶς καὶ ὁσίως διηρμήνευται καὶ κατὰ πᾶν ἠκριβωμένως, paragraph 310). The letter then describes how the superb quality of the translation and the reception of it by the people made them put a curse on anyone who, "sought to change anything in it, to add something to it, or to subtract something from it" (paragraph 311).

The reception of the Septuagint shares many similarities with the reception of the Law and its recitation to the people at Mount Sinai, where the Lord also explicitly forbade anyone to "add to the word which I command you, nor take from it" (Deuteronomy 4:2). The motif of the absent Law, which is subsequently rediscovered and received with joy, is also well known, as described earlier in the episode of Josiah's rediscovery of the Law and his commandment to celebrate Passover for the Lord (2 Kings 22ff) and in the case of Ezra's representation of the Law to the lawless Jews returning from Exile (Nehemiah 8:1ff).

The Letter of Aristeas, then, shows how the Septuagint was received as a divine law, *beautiful and holy (καλῶς καὶ ὁσίως)*, and protected by the same inviolability, that is unchangeableness, as the Pentateuch itself in order that nothing may be added and nothing may be subtracted, a point which Professor Müller also emphasizes.[58] It seems likely that the ceremony at the reception of the Septuagint itself also consciously drew on these strong parallels so as to emphasis the authority and quality of the work. The work of translation is also presented as having been implicitly effectuated by divine aid, in that it was finished "according to some purpose" (paragraph 307). This is noted as well by the biblical scholar Stanley E. Porter who says, quoting his colleague Wever, "The translators realized that their product was itself God's word; it was declared canonical, and presumably served as the synagogal Scriptures in Alexandria".[59] This strong focus on the text and its sublime character and divine sanctioning are facts that support an early dating of Aristeas' letter. Such a strong defense of the Septuagint would simply have been unnecessary at a later date since, as discussed above, there were no other competing translations, and because the Septuagint quickly

---

[58] Müller, *The First Bible of the Church*, 50.
[59] Stanley E. Porter, "The Septuagint: A Greek-Text-Oriented Approach," in *T&T Clark Handbook of Septuagint Research*, ed. William A. Ross and W. Edward Genny (Bloomsbury Publishing, 2021), 419.

established itself as the authoritative text. Thus, the Jewish reception of the Septuagint is now to be explored.

Artapanus the Historian, circa third to second century B.C.
Only fragments have survived from this author's hand, and were quoted in the works of Clement of Alexandria and Eusebius of Caesarea. But Artapanus' presentation of Moses in Egypt, such as the Ten Plagues, among others, shows that he is textually dependent on the Septuagint.[60] Sadly, nothing else is known about this author, and the dating of his works are very difficult. It is hard to judge *how* early a witness to the Septuagint he was, but it is accepted that he was a very early witness.

Demetrios the Chronographer, active around the time of King Ptolemy IV, 221–205 B.C.
Demetrios was a Greek-speaking Jewish historian who likely lived in Alexandria. All his works are now lost, with the exception of those parts which have been cited in other works. Eusebius of Caesarea's *Praeparatio Evangelica* cites him, and parts of his works are also found in Clement of Alexandria's writings. His history is written in Greek and chiefly concerns itself with the chronology of the Old Testament, the Flood, and Abraham. The work is especially interesting because it clearly follows the wording and chronology of the Septuagint where it differs from the later Masoretic Text.[61, 62] This is noteworthy, as this Greek-speaking Jew is most likely one of the very earliest witnesses to the Septuagint text whose works are known.

Ezekiel the Tragedian, circa Second Century B.C.
Small fragments of Ezekiel's works have survived in quotation, chiefly by Eusebius of Caesarea and Clement of Alexandria. He also used the Septuagint as the textual basis for his dramatic plays.[63] Little else is known about him.

---

[60] Wright III, "The Septuagint and Second Temple Judaism," *T&T Clark Handbook of Septuagint Research*, 281.
[61] Fernández Marcos, *The Septuagint in Context*, 261.
[62] Wright III, "The Septuagint and Second Temple Judaism," *T&T Clark Handbook of Septuagint Research*, 280.
[63] Wright III, "The Septuagint and Second Temple Judaism," *T&T Clark Handbook of Septuagint Research*, 281.

PART I: HISTORICAL FOUNDATION

Aristobulos, circa 181–124 B.C.

The early dominance of the Septuagint is also seen through Aristobulos, an early Jewish philosopher whose works are now sadly lost, but which are found in long excerpts in the texts of authors such as Eusebius of Caesarea and Clement of Alexandria. Aristobulos lived during the reign of King Ptolemy VI, 181–145 B.C., and he is interesting because he describes first, how small, partial translation of segments of certain books of the Old Testament existed, secondly, how the translation of the whole Pentateuch took place during the reign of Ptolemy II, and thirdly, that this work was arranged by Demetrios of Phalerum.[64] This is significant because the second and third points directly support Aristeas' story of the birth of the Septuagint.

Since Aristobulos' narrative is quite short, and since he does not provide any defense of the Septuagint, his text seems to reflect a later period in which the Septuagint had already become dominant and the use of it could be taken for granted. This is unlike the earlier time periods that Aristeas was purported to be writing in, a time wherein the novel nature of the Septuagint required an apology. Professor Müller also notes "Significantly Aristobulus refers to this event as a matter of course, thus indicating that he relies on an extant tradition".[65] Aristeas' account of the origin of the Septuagint therefore seems to have been known and accepted already at the time of Aristobulos, and thus he provides a window into the dissemination of the story of the Septuagint and into how quickly it was received by the Jews. It should also be interesting to note that when Aristobulos cites from the Old Testament—Exodus 13:9, 3:20, and 9:3 for example—that it is the Septuagint he is citing from.[66] This underlines the authoritative nature the Septuagint had acquired at his time, because Aristobulos here uses the text dogmatically to expound how the anthropologic language of the Pentateuch is to be understood in relationship to theology proper.

Jeshua ben Sirach, circa 132 B.C.

In the prologue to the Book of Sirach, a part of the deuterocanonical books of the Old Testament, many important comments are made. Joshua, the son of Sirach, went to Egypt in 132 B.C. to translate from Hebrew into Greek a

---

[64] Eusebius, *Praeparatio Evangelica* 13.12.
[65] Müller, *The First Bible of the Church*, 59.
[66] Wright III, "The Septuagint and Second Temple Judaism," *T&T Clark Handbook of Septuagint Research*, 280.

book written by his grandfather. The prologue is especially noteworthy because it describes in verse 20 the challenges of translation, that "which was by itself said in Hebrew, and then translated into another language does not have the same strength (ἰσοδυναμεῖ)." Even more interesting, though, is the additional comment in verse 25 that this is not only the case with the Book of Sirach but "not only this (book) but also the very Law and the Prophets and the rest of the Scriptures (τὰ λοιπὰ τῶν βιβλίων)" [ibid.]. This comment is poignant as it plainly assumes that all of the Old Testament was translated and available in Greek, at the latest around 135 B.C., if not earlier, a point which has also been noticed in the scholarship[67, 68] and has been often discussed.[69]

Philo of Alexandria, circa 20 B.C. to A.D. 50

Philo was the most skilled and famous of the Jewish philosophers of the antiquities. He lived and worked in Alexandria and combined Greek philosophy with Old Testament exegesis and theology. Multiple works of his have survived till today, of which his work *The Life of Moses* is especially important for this present work. In it, Philo narrates how the Septuagint came to be, though he does so in such a way that his narration seems independent from the tradition provided by the authors mentioned before. First of all, he mentions in *The Life of Moses* 2:36 how the translation of the Septuagint included "the holy books (τὰς ἱερὰς βιβλίους)," which seems to show that Philo assumed that the Seventy-Two translators had translated the whole Old Testament and not just the Pentateuch, as would also become an almost universal view among the church fathers in the generations following Philo. This view could also be explained by the fact, as Joshua the son of Sirach alluded to, that the whole Old Testament had been available in Greek for quite some time already when Philo was active.

Secondly, Philo also expresses the common view at his time that the Septuagint was a divinely inspired work. As quoted in the beginning of this chapter, Philo saw the Hebrew text of his day and the Septuagint as "sister texts" (*The Life of Moses* 2:40), and he viewed the Seventy-Two translators of the Septuagint "not as translators (ἑρμηνέας) but as prophets and the speakers of divine things (ἱεροφάντας)." These Seventy-Two prophets who wrote the Septuagint were even led by "the purest Spirit, the Spirit of Moses"

---

[67] Gleaves and Cloud, *Did Jesus Speak Greek?*, 33.
[68] Fernández Marcos, *The Septuagint in Context*, 264; Law, *When God Spoke Greek*, 40.
[69] Law, *When God Spoke Greek*, 71.

PART I: HISTORICAL FOUNDATION

(*The Life of Moses* 2:40 and 41). According to Philo then, the Septuagint was wholly equal to the Hebrew text insofar as they were sisters of the same divine father, rather than the Septuagint being a daughter, so to speak, of the Hebrew text. It possessed the same authority since one and the same Spirit, who spoke through the prophets and through Moses, had also spoken through the Seventy-Two.

Unsurprisingly, then, the Septuagint was the Old Testament text used by Philo in his theological and philosophical works.[70] His own native language was also Greek, which can be seen in his work *On the Confusion of Tongues*, a work also written in Greek. In it, he writes that the name Penuel is Hebrew, "but in our own (*language*) it means 'turning oneself away from God'".[71] This also underscores the advance of the Greek language and culture among many Jews, especially of the Diaspora at the time, to whom Greek was not only a comfortable second language but the native tongue of many. One last interesting detail concerning Philo is that he mentions the existence of a yearly celebration of the Septuagint:

> ...even to this very day, there is every year a solemn assembly held and a festival celebrated in the island of Pharos, to which not only the Jews but a great number of persons of other nations sail across, reverencing the place in which the first light of interpretation shone forth, and thanking God for that ancient piece of beneficence which was always young and fresh.
>
> — The Life of Moses 2:41

Thus, Philo is also an interesting witness to how the story of the Septuagint was passed on as a part of the culture and collective remembrance of the city.

Josephus the Historian, A.D. 38–100
Josephus also provides an account of the origin of the Septuagint, though it differs quite a bit from Philo's account. In his work *Jewish Antiquities*, Josephus copies around two-fifths of the Letter of Aristeas.[72] Josephus knew and read both Hebrew and Aramaic, in addition to Greek, and did not

---

[70] Fernández Marcos, *The Septuagint in Context*, 264; Law, *When God Spoke Greek*, 129-130.
[71] Philo, *On the Confusion of Tongues*, trans. F. H. Colson and G. H. Whitaker, Loeb Classical Library, vol. IV (1932; repr., Cambridge, Massachusetts: Harvard University Press, 1985), 10.4159/DLCL.philo_judaeus-confusion_tongues.1932, §129.
[72] Jellicoe, *The Septuagint and Modern Study*, 288.

restrict his use of the Old Testament to the Septuagint, but actively used the Hebrew text as well.[73] In many cases, it is almost impossible to judge with certainty whether he used the Septuagint or the Hebrew text, as he rarely cites verbatim but often paraphrases the biblical quotations.[74]

Rather interestingly though, it has been observed that Josephus either did not use, or did not know, the later Masoretic Text type, or he used the Septuagint. This can be seen, among other places, in his use of the Book of Samuel, which in the Septuagint differs strongly from the Masoretic edition. Josephus follows the peculiarities of the Septuagint rather than the Masoretic Text.[75] Likewise, his use of the books of Esther and 1 Esdras,[76] in the Masoretic Text known as Ezra and Nehemiah, shows the same tendency. He also uses and comments on Artaxerxes' decree to Haman, the prayer of Esther, the entrance of Esther before the king, and Artaxerxes' decree in defense of the Jews— these are five episodes which either differ substantially or are wholly missing from the Masoretic Text, but which are present in the Septuagint.[77]

Josephus' use of the Septuagint, or a Hebrew text of the same text type as the Septuagint, is also seen in the chronology presented by the historian. In *Jewish Antiquities*, Josephus recounts the genealogy of Adam following that of the Septuagint[78], which differs quite a bit compared to the Masoretic text. Josephus himself adds a very crucial comment, he says, "Those antiquities contain the history of five thousand years; and are taken out of our sacred books: but are translated by me into the Greek tongue," and again, "For, as I said, I have translated the Antiquities out of our sacred books. Which I easily could do; since I was a priest by my birth; and have studied that philosophy which is contained in those writings".[79] If this is to be understood at face value, as the natural reading of the comments imply, then Josephus is a chief witness to a Hebrew textual tradition, existing in his time, that supports the Septuagint's readings where they either differ from the Masoretic Text or where they are lacking in the Masoretic Text. This has been noted, among

---

[73] Jellicoe, *The Septuagint and Modern Study*, 288.
[74] Tessa Rajak, "Josephus and the Septuagint," *Oxford University Press EBooks*, February 10, 2021, https://doi.org/10.1093/oxfordhb/9780199665716.013.55, 424-26.
[75] Rajak, "Josephus and the Septuagint," 429.
[76] Rajak, "Josephus and the Septuagint," 429-30.
[77] Rajak, "Josephus and the Septuagint," 429-30.
[78] Josephus, *Antiquities of the Jews* 1.3.4.
[79] Josephus, *Against Apion* 1.1, 1.54.

PART I: HISTORICAL FOUNDATION

others, by Etienne Nodet, a French historian and biblical scholar, who notes that Josephus' Hebrew text "probably came from the Temple library".[80]

If Nodet is correct, then that would furnish strong support to Aristeas' claim that the manuscripts from which the Septuagint was translated really did come from the Temple in Jerusalem through the hands of the High Priest Eleazer, since the variants of the Septuagint are shared by and witnessed to by the text of Josephus. This is a fact that can be explained by the existence of a parent text from the Temple, as Nodet and Aristeas suggest. Whether Josephus uses the Septuagint or a Hebrew text related to it, he nevertheless grants the Septuagint a very high authority. He provides, quite like Philo before him did, the Septuagint with sacredness, writing "that since the interpretation was happily finished, it might continue in that state it now was, and might not be altered",[81] and that any change to it must be reverted back to the original wording.

CONCLUSION

Despite the tumultuous history of the Letter of Aristeas—its historicity once being taken for granted, later almost universally rejected as the stuff of legend, to now having being rehabilitated—it must not be forgotten that, even if one rejects certain parts of the letter as fictitious, either on account of exaggeration, legendary features, or apologetic tone, nevertheless a historical core remains even if one were to doubt some aspects. The letter provides an important historical witness to the origin of the Septuagint, a witness which finds corroborative support in other ancient sources and with modern scholars such as Collins, Etienne, and more. Its content should be treated seriously, on account of both its historical value and its immense influence as seen in its reception by authors throughout subsequent periods.

The Septuagint was, from its very beginning, much more than a translation. Aristeas presents it as beautiful and holy and protected by the same inviolability as the Old Testament itself, made according to a certain design. This high view is even clearer in Philo, who sees the text not as a mere translation but as a sister text, written by prophets being led by the Spirit of Moses and equal to the Hebrew text itself, according to the purpose of God. The quick and impressive dissemination of the work is witnessed to

---

[80] É. Nodet, "Josephus and the Pentateuch," Journal for the Study of Judaism 28, no. 2 (January 1, 1997), https://doi.org/10.1163/157006397X00138, 192-194.

[81] Josephus, Antiquities of the Jews 12.2.

by how it became the dominant text of the Old Testament, used by people as different as Jewish theologians, dramatists, and historians in the third and second century B.C. Though Aristobulos mentions the existence of partial translation of certain passages of the Old Testament, no rival translation would challenge the dominance of the Septuagint until Aquila published another version around A.D. 130, a fact further underscoring the unrivaled position of the translation of the Seventy-Two for centuries.

Josephus' case is particularly interesting in that he, living in Roman-occupied Judaea and using, according to his own comments, a Hebrew text of the Old Testament, still supports the Septuagint's text as authoritative. Josephus' apparent use of the Septuagint at multiple times, and his textual body as a whole, shows that he either used the Septuagint continually, which would be contrary to his own written comments, or that he used a Hebraic textual form that, according to the comments of the scholar Etienne, came from the Temple in Jerusalem, which seems more likely as well as intriguing. If that was the case, then Aristeas' comment that the base text for the translation of the Septuagint came from Jerusalem would find strong supporting evidence.

Some conclusions must then be drawn that the Septuagint enjoyed a dominant and authoritative position in Judaism in the centuries prior to Christ's birth. Multiple Jewish authors saw it not as a work of mere human hands but, at minimum, as an inviable and holy work, if not directly a prophetic and inspired sister text of the Hebrew Old Testament. Though this translation began only with the Pentateuch, the priestly and royally sanctioned translated work was soon followed by complete translations of each of the remaining books, most likely as a continual effort of the original translation work in Alexandria. The complete translation of the Old Testament into Greek therefore enjoyed an authority and religious sanction which was derived from the original translation of the Pentateuch in Alexandria, which, according to the early sources, intended to include the rest of the holy Jewish books.

PART II: VETUS TESTAMENTUM IN NOVO RECEPTUM

PART II
VETUS TESTAMENTUM IN NOVO RECEPTUM
THE OLD TESTAMENT RECEIVED BY THE NEW

TEXTUAL FINDINGS AND TRANSMISSION
SEPTUAGINT FINDS IN ROMAN JUDAEA

As Professor Scott Gleaves, Pieter van der Horst, and the survey in the prior chapter about languages showed, Greek was indeed a dominant language in Roman Judaea. Large Hellenized towns such as Sepphoris, six kilometers from Nazareth, the cities of the Decapolis, Caesarea, and more made a strong presence on the surrounding landscape and cemented the Hellenic influence in Roman Judaea. It should come as no surprise that the Septuagint also had a large physical presence to which archeological finds attest. Even though the oldest fragments of the Septuagint are found in Egypt, such as the Ryland 458 fragment from the middle of the second century B.C.,[82] then Judaea, likewise, has yielded many important finds as well. The Book of the Minor Prophets from Nahal Hever, a distance from the Dead Sea, is a good example of this. In this large fragment, multiple passages from the Books of Jonah, Micah, Nahum, Habakkuk, Zephaniah, and Zechariah have survived. This manuscript is dated to around the first century B.C.[83]

The Dead Sea Scrolls, though most commonly invoking pictures of ancient Hebraic manuscripts that make up the large majority, have proven a fertile ground for physical support for the Septuagint. The Septuagint is, surprisingly to many, very well represented in the findings at the Dead Sea. Parts of Exodus, Numbers, Leviticus, and Deuteronomy, as well as the Book of Baruch, have been found dating to around the first century B.C. The Septuagint then is well represented archeologically in the area of ancient Israel. Almost all of the Pentateuch, parts of the major prophets, and parts of the minor prophets have been found. This fact was also

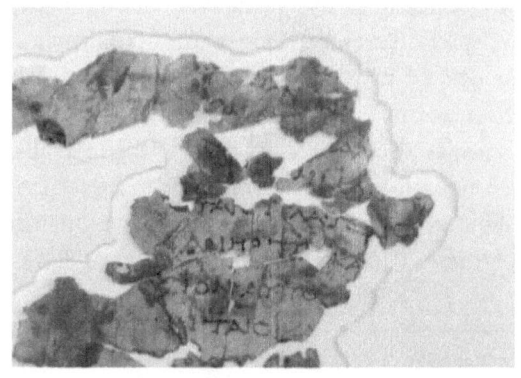

Figure 4. Here a photo of the newly found Septuagint fragment of the Book of Zachariah is seen.

---

[82] Fernández Marcos, *The Septuagint in Context*, 71.
[83] Law, *When God Spoke Greek*, 77.

underscored as recently as March 18, 2021, when the Israeli Antiquities Authority published a new *Dead Sea Scroll*. Surprisingly, this was not another Hebraic fragment, but rather a part of Zechariah from the Septuagint.[84] Thus, Greek was, along with the Septuagint, an everyday part of life in Roman Judaea.

TEXTUAL PLURALITY AT THE TIME OF CHRIST

When Christ in Mark 7:6–7 talks about the Old Testament *as it is written*, he did not refer to the total sum of all different textual material of the Old Testament in circulation. It is difficult to pinpoint exactly when, where, and how the different redactions, editions, and corruptions of the different books of the Old Testament were made or took place, and when they entered into wider circulation. It is clear that there was a plurality of different text forms of the Old Testament books available at the time of Christ.[85] These diverse editions of the different works of the Old Testament, also known as textual families or groups of manuscripts with shared variants and readings, must be acknowledged.

It is not within the scope of this present work to give a thorough exposition of the textual situation in detail, for such a picture, different relevant monographs can be referred to.[86] Here it must suffice to draw a sketch of the landscape. Three common overarching textual families can be defined, the first being a family of manuscripts whose variants reflect the readings found in the Septuagint, a second family of related manuscripts whose readings are related to, or approach, those found in the later Masoretic Text, and lastly, a third family whose readings and variants are associated with the Samaritan Pentateuch.[87] Though this picture can be criticized for being too simplistic, as Professor Tov has made note of,[88] it provides an adequate overview of the textual scene in the century around Christ, as long as it is kept in mind that each individual manuscript will only show an imperfect tendency toward a textual family when compared to one of these. Mixed types of manuscripts have also been found, sharing

---

[84] Gareth Wearne, "Cave of Horror: Fresh Fragments of the Dead Sea Scrolls Echo Dramatic Human Stories," *The Conversation*, March 18, 2021, https://theconversation.com/cave-of-horror-fresh-fragments-of-the-dead-sea-scrolls-echo-dramatic-human-stories-157423.
[85] Law, *When God Spoke Greek*, 24.
[86] E.g. the oft-quoted sources, Fernández Marcos, *The Septuagint in Context*.
[87] Fernández Marcos, *The Septuagint in Context*.
[88] Tov, *The Text-Critical Use of the Septuagint in Biblical Research*, 217.

PART II: VETUS TESTAMENTUM IN NOVO RECEPTUM

characteristics with more than one textual family, often being most closely aligned with one but having clear influence and characteristics from another.

This insight—the existence of a textual plurality somewhat summarized by the three different textual families, and the aforementioned mixed forms—eradicates the false assumption of many that there were only two text types of the Old Testament in circulation: a pure and authentic Hebraic text, often presumed to be reflected by the Masoretic Text, and a more or less faithful Greek in the translation of the Septuagint. But this is not true. The choice is not between the Septuagint on the one hand, and an *authentic* Hebraic text on the other, but between which text is to be viewed as authentic, as judged by how accurately it reflects the inspired words of the Old Testament. The existence of multiple text types contradicts the assumption, quite common in the twentieth century, that the Masoretic Text as found in the Leningrad Codex and Aleppo Codex was identical to the Hebraic text circulating during the time of Christ.[89] The belief that a single, stable, and homogenous Hebrew text was transmitted faithfully through the ages before reaching us in the medieval manuscripts of the rabbis was greatly challenged by the discovery of the Dead Sea Scrolls. For the first time, actual manuscripts from such an early era reflected the wording of the Septuagint and diverged from the Masoretic Text.

Prior to this discovery, a Hebrew Vorlage of the Septuagint had been a hypothetical entity,[90] and many scholars had sought to explain the divergence between it and the Masoretic Text either by a poor comprehension of biblical Hebrew by the translators, an imperfect knowledge of Greek, or that the Septuagint, rather than being a faithful translation, ought to be viewed more as a theological reflection on the Hebrew text or a more loose paraphrase. These notions, however, are outdated and untenable, as Professors Law,[91] Müller,[92] and Jellicoe[93] note. Yet, it must also be added that some scholars, also prior to the discovery of the Dead Sea Scrolls, had paid attention to the relationship between the Masoretic, Septuagint, and Samaritan texts.

---

[89] Law, *When God Spoke Greek*, 20.
[90] Law, *When God Spoke Greek*, 24.
[91] Law, *When God Spoke Greek*, 21.
[92] Müller, *The First Bible of the Church*, 113.
[93] Jellicoe, *The Septuagint and Modern Study*, 319.

SEVENTY-TWO SERVANTS OF THE WORD

The Samaritan Pentateuch is an edition of the Torah used by the Samaritan strand of Judaism, whose age and origin is somewhat obscure. It certainly predates the time of Christ and likely goes back even further, as manuscripts found with the Dead Sea Scrolls in Qumran bear witness to this text form. Professor Jellicoe also notes that it is difficult to place the Samaritan Pentateuch textually, because it quite often shares the readings found in the Masoretic Text in some places, though it also bears witness to many readings from the Septuagint, also those diverging from the Masoretic Text. It contains around 6,000 variants compared to the Masoretic Text, 1,900 variants of which, as shall be noted for our present survey, it shares with the Septuagint[94] and with the other variants unique to the Samaritan Pentateuch. Therefore, in the Septuagint and the Samaritan Pentateuch, there are two very different independent witnesses to a body of around 1,900 textual variants which are either wholly lacking, or worded very differently, in the Masoretic Text. This shared corpus of readings can be explained by proposing an older Hebraic Vorlage which the Septuagint and the Samaritan Pentateuch was copied from, and wherefrom this shared body of text, lacking in the Masoretic Text, was drawn. This would also corroborate the claims that the Septuagint indeed was translated from an older form of the Hebrew text of the Old Testament different from the Hebrew text as read in the Masoretic Text.

---

[94] Jellicoe, *The Septuagint and Modern Study*, 244-245.

PART II: VETUS TESTAMENTUM IN NOVO RECEPTUM

THE SEPTUAGINT AND QUMRAN

"The LXX translation [he [Orlinsky] observes], no less than the MT itself, will have gained very considerable respect as a result of the Qumrân discoveries in those circles where it has long—overlong—been necessary. And the LXX translators will no longer be blamed for dealing promiscuously with their Hebrew Vorlagen; it is to their Vorlagen that we shall have to go, and it is their Vorlagen that will have to be compared with the preserved MT.... This much, too, may be said. The theory of one original Greek translation of each of the various Books of the Hebrew Bible, which in turn gave rise to the various recensions ... has been demonstrated beyond reasonable doubt by the Hebrew and Greek materials from Qumrân. Those who have opposed this theory, notably Kahle, have received nothing but opposition from the Dead Sea scrolls. On this matter of the LXX Vorlage, the present writer's independent investigations have led him to a similar conclusion." [95]

— *Professor Sidney Jellicoe*

The discovery of the Dead Sea Scrolls was an epic event for Septuagint research. Here, for the first time, the actual physical copies of Hebrew manuscripts supporting the readings of the Septuagint were found. The differences between the Masoretic Text and the Septuagint had been noticed from the very early church onward—Exodus, 1 Samuel, the Books of Kings, Jeremiah, Isaiah, Ezekiel, Proverbs, Job, Ezra and Nehemiah (In the Septuagint, 2 Esdras), and Daniel are so different from one another, that they cannot possibly have had the same Hebraic *Vorlage*, but they must be expressions of different Hebrew texts.[96,97] The finds at Qumran also proved that there actually existed a tangible Hebraic text used by the Septuagint translators, a text which was a thousand years older than the Medieval Masoretic codex used by most current Old Testament translations.[98]

The exact identity and background of the Jewish group who inhabited the settlements at Qumran is much discussed in current scholarship. Different hypotheses exist, such as it being a theological library, an isolated sect, Essenes, etc., but each explanation is difficult to prove. It must therefore be kept in mind that the finds at Qumran cannot be understood to be a perfect representation of the textual situation of the period around

---

[95] Jellicoe, *The Septuagint and Modern Study*, 341.
[96] Müller, *The First Bible of the Church*, 103.
[97] Law, *When God Spoke Greek*, 20.
[98] Law, *When God Spoke Greek*, 24.

Christ, but neither can it be disproven. Because of the small number of manuscripts, there is a lack of sufficient material to help make any final judgment in regard to the geographical dissemination and quantitative presence of the different textual families. Although it cannot be assumed that a perfect relationship between what is found and what once was exists, these crucial findings must be taken into consideration in order to make any coherent interpretation of the data, as they provide the richest material and the closest approximation to the textual landscape that is available. Concerning the size of the findings at Qumran, which naturally only consist of a small selection of the amount of material which circulated in that time, Professor Law explains:

> At Qumran, there were roughly thirty-six copies of some portion of Psalms (though not thirty-six copies of the entire book of Psalms we now know); thirty-two of Deuteronomy; twenty-three or twenty-four of Genesis; twenty-one of Isaiah; sixteen of Exodus; fourteen of Leviticus; eight or nine of the Minor Prophets; eight of Daniel; six each of Numbers, Jeremiah, and Ezekiel; four of Samuel, Proverbs, Job, Canticles (Song of Songs), Ruth, and Lamentations; three of Judges and Kings; two of Joshua, Qoheleth (Ecclesiastes), and Ezra-Nehemiah; and one of Chronicles.[13] Esther is the only book that lacks manuscript evidence. Other books that were later called "Apocrypha" and "Pseudepigrapha" were also discovered in the Judean Desert in Hebrew and Aramaic forms (e.g., Tobit, Jubilees, Enoch, Sirach). These too were part of the textual milieu of Second Temple Judaism.[99]

The fact that Judaism at this time was rather fractured also muddies the picture. As mentioned before, a certain Pentateuchal text was in circulation among the Samaritans, and another among the Sadducees, who had a shorter canon of Scripture than the Pharisees. The Pharisees themselves seem to use a text related to the later Masoretic Text, a proto-Masoretic Text of sorts, which, though not equal to the later one, was certainly closely related to it. It is seen, therefore, that different editions of the different books were present at the time, which is a fact confirmed by the Dead Sea Scrolls. If the manuscripts of the Pentateuch found at Qumran are looked

---

[99] Law, *When God Spoke Greek*, 25.

PART II: VETUS TESTAMENTUM IN NOVO RECEPTUM

at, they reflect a text type similar to the Masoretic Text in around 48% of the finds, while the manuscripts in the remaining parts of the Old Testament reflect a Masoretic Text type in around 44% of the cases.[100] These numbers underscore the diversity of the texts circulating at the time of Christ, where no single text type can be said to have held dominance. Professor Emmanuel Tov also describes how the unexpected finds of multiple Hebraic manuscripts and fragments at Qumran, all of which reflect the wording and readings of the Septuagint, caused quite a stir. In cave four for example, scrolls have been found of the Books of Isaiah and of Ruth which equally support the Septuagint and the Masoretic Text.[101] Likewise, Hebraic fragments of Leviticus, 1 and 2 Samuel, Jeremiah, the Book of Psalms, and more have also been found, all of which reflect the wording and the characteristic features of the Septuagint,[102] and are therefore early examples of the existence of a Hebrew textual tradition undergirding the Septuagint.

Even though the Septuagint text type only makes up a minority of the finds at Qumran, it must be noted, adds Professor Tov, that the Proto-Masoretic Text was only received by certain circles within ancient Judaism, while other strands rejected it.[103] Even though the Septuagint text type is in the minority, the very oldest finds at Qumran belong to the Septuagint text type. Professor Tov comments how some of the paleographical details, such as the form and features of the style of writing, point toward a very early composition for the manuscripts sharing the text type of the Septuagint. He also notes how some of the variants in the documents seem to be caused by a misreading of the Paleo-Hebrew script. He writes, "Scholars examined the question whether we can determine the period in the development of the Hebrew alphabet to which the interchanges between the MT and LXX attest".[104] Here, Professor Tov comments that some of the differences between the Septuagint and the Proto-Masoretic Text can be explained by misreadings of the earlier Paleo-Hebrew script. Interestingly, Paleo-Hebrew scrolls, though rare, were still available at the time of the translation of the Septuagint.[105] Therefore, several scholars, such as S. Talmon, P. Casetti, and the Septuagint expert Dominique Barthelemy, have proposed

---

[100] Law, *When God Spoke Greek*, 25.
[101] Tov, *The Text-Critical Use of the Septuagint in Biblical Research*, 208.
[102] Tov, *The Text-Critical Use of the Septuagint in Biblical Research*, 208-12.
[103] Tov, *The Text-Critical Use of the Septuagint in Biblical Research*, 223.
[104] Tov, *The Text-Critical Use of the Septuagint in Biblical Research*, 163.
[105] Tov, *The Text-Critical Use of the Septuagint in Biblical Research*, 163.

that the Vorlage of the Septuagint might actually have been in the form of ancient Paleo-Hebrew scrolls. Professor Tov agrees in this point and comments that the Septuagint reflects a more ancient text type than the Masoretic Text does.[106]

CONCLUSION

The extant manuscripts of the Septuagint, which only make out a smaller subset of the available material in circulation, demonstrate the availability of the Septuagint during the time of Christ. This, combined with the extensive presence of Hellenism and knowledge of the Greek language, demonstrates that for many Jews, the Word of God was read in Greek from the Septuagint, as the ancient Hebrew manuscripts were incomprehensible for most Judaeans.[107] The Septuagint translation itself was also an authentic expression of the Old Testament text as it had deep roots in a very ancient Hebraic text form. Looking at the Samaritan Pentateuch, around 2,000 variants can be found which are either wholly lacking or very different in the Masoretic Text, yet found in the Septuagint. Assuming an ancient common Hebraic parent text as the source for both of these textual traditions explains these occurrences. Professor Tov and others seem to indicate this, in that the oldest texts found at Qumran are those which share the wording and characteristics of the Septuagint. A Paleo-Hebrew *Vorlage* as the basis of these variants also explains the differences between the Masoretic Text and the Septuagint, making it even more probable that the Hebraic text reflected by the Septuagint goes very far back indeed, much farther than any Masoretic Text.

These facts also support the claims made by the Letter of Aristeas concerning the scrolls used for the translation of the Septuagint which were given by the High Priest Eleazer from the Temple of Jerusalem. Even though this cannot be proven, these details along with the statement of Josephus concerning the use of Scripture, support the claims of Aristeas. This would mean that in the Septuagint there is a witness to an ancient Hebrew version of the text of the Old Testament as found in the Temple in Jerusalem in the early third century B.C., far earlier than any other witness to the inspired text of the Old Testament. Thus, the Septuagint began the work of translating the Old Testament into Greek beginning with the Pentateuch

---

[106] Tov, *The Text-Critical Use of the Septuagint in Biblical Research*, 223.
[107] Gleaves and Cloud, *Did Jesus Speak Greek?*, chap. 1.

PART II: VETUS TESTAMENTUM IN NOVO RECEPTUM

and in the following decades with a single translation of each Old Testament book. Scholars such as Professor Orlinsky affirm that this hypothesis "has been demonstrated beyond reasonable doubt."

The findings at Qumran have also meant that earlier speculation of the Septuagint as an imprecise translation or as a theological paraphrase must be dismissed. The difference in the wording between it and the Masoretic Text does not lie with the translators but with the Hebraic text being translated. These conclusions inevitably raise more questions. If such a divergent number of different texts were available—Aramaic Targums, Hebrew proto-Masoretic Texts, and the Greek Septuagint—and many mixed types were as well, with each of these broader groups having different editions and redactions of the Old Testament books, then it must be asked where the Word of God is to be found? The authorities of the different groups of Judaism disagreed about this. Where was it to be found, and where could it be read *as it was written*? Which textual tradition should be authoritative and why? This question, of a more dogmatic nature, will be discussed in the following section.

THE OLD TESTAMENT *AS IT IS WRITTEN*
INTERMISSION: A CONCEPTUAL FRAMEWORK

he question of the relationship between the historical Jesus, the Jesus of history, and the Gospels' portrayal of Jesus is controversial. That particular discussion is beyond the scope of this work. The conclusions drawn in the following chapters of this book, then, will assume the historical reliability of the New Testament's presentation of Jesus and of his use of the Septuagint, as narrated by the Gospels, as factual events rather than literary constructions lacking a historical precedent. That Jesus used the Septuagint will not be assumed but proven in the chapter on Christ's use of it. This assumption of the historical reliability of the New Testament, and of the Old Testament, was shared by the recipients of the Biblical writings in the early Christian church as well as being shared by the church fathers, who saw the historical events taking place in the biblical writings as coinciding with the New and Old Testaments' description of them.

When Augustine and Jerome discussed the New Testament's use of either the Masoretic Text or the Septuagint, which will be discussed later, they both shared the assumption that the New Testament text really did render the actual words and sayings spoken by the New Testament's persons. This assumption will be shared in the following chapters, though this work is conscious about the disputed nature of that claim. Augustine, though, expressing a common view of the early church, writes, "If we are perplexed by an apparent contradiction in Scripture, it is not allowable to say, The author of this book is mistaken; but either the manuscript is faulty, or the translation is wrong, or you have not understood".[108] Augustine had no doubt about the infallibility of the New Testament's writings. In a letter to Jerome he writes, "I have learned to yield this respect and honour only to the canonical books of Scripture: of these alone do I most firmly believe that the authors were completely free from error".[109] He also adds this comment in the following sentence, "this is your own opinion as well as mine." Such a conceptual approach to Scripture was far from unique to Augustine, and is representative of countless of the early Christian authors. Another such

---

[108] Philip Schaff, *A Select Library of the Nicene and Post-Nicene Fathers of the Christian Church*, trans. J. G. Cunningham, vol. 1 (Buffalo, NY: Christian Literature Company, 1886), 180.

[109] Schaff, *A Select Library of the Nicene and Post-Nicene Fathers of the Christian Church*, 350.

PART II: VETUS TESTAMENTUM IN NOVO RECEPTUM

early example is the author(s) of *First Clement*, written around A.D. 69–80, which states in chapter 45:

> You have looked into the holy scriptures, which are true, which were given by the Holy Spirit. You know that nothing unrighteous or falsified is written in them.
> (ἐγκεκύφατε εἰς τὰς ἱερὰς γραφάς, τὰς ἀληθεῖς, τὰς διὰ τοῦ πνεύματος τοῦ ἁγίου. ἐπίστασθε, ὅτι οὐδὲν ἄδικον οὐδὲ παραπεποιημένον γέγραπται ἐν αὐταῖς)

Nothing falsified (παραπεποιημένον) is written in them, but they are rather God's true word given by the Holy Spirit. This point is also picked up by Irenaeus who wrote, "We should leave things of that nature to God who created us, being most properly assured that the Scriptures are indeed perfect, since they were spoken by the Word of God and His Spirit." (*Against Heresies* 2.28.2).

It is of course true that the church fathers often employed allegorical and typological readings of Scripture and did not restrict themselves to a literalistic reading, what we may colloquially called a wooden or overly literal reading, of Scripture alone. But these different spiritual senses of Scripture—allegory, typology, and anagogy—were different depths or layers in Scripture which functioned in parallel with the literal sense of Scripture and not to the exclusion of it. This point is thoroughly discussed in Augustine's major work *The City of God* in the fifteenth book. In chapter 72, Augustine deals with two, in his view, serious errors. First, he firmly rejects those who deny the spiritual sense of Scripture and dismisses allegorical interpretations all together. Yet secondly, he just as firmly rejects those who impoverish Holy Scripture by denying its historical reality and reduce it to allegory alone. He writes:

> ...no one ought to suppose either that these things were written for no purpose, or that we should study only the historical truth, apart from any allegorical meanings; or, on the contrary, that they are only allegories, and that there were no such facts at all, or that, whether it be so or no, there is here no prophecy of the church. For what right-minded man will contend that books so religiously preserved during thousands of years, and transmitted by so orderly

a succession, were written without an object, or that only the bare historical facts are to be considered when we read them?[110]

It would thus be a great mistake to dismiss either the spiritual sense or the literal historic meaning: both are part of Holy Scripture. Therefore, Augustine could also, given his view of Scripture as inerrant and fully historically reliable, use it to count the years back to the creation of the world as having taken place 6,000 years prior to his own time, that is around 7,500 years ago as of this writing. Augustine's use of the chronology of the Septuagint rather than the Masoretic Text led to a chronology foreign to those who were used to relying on the Masoretic text. He wrote, "They are deceived, too, by those highly mendacious documents which profess to give the history of many thousand years, though, reckoning by the sacred writings, we find that not 6000 years have yet passed" (Augustine, *The City of God* 12:10).

His high view of Scripture's inerrancy is also demonstrated by the fact that Augustine wrote a whole tractate, Tractate 117 in Schaff's Edition of the *Post Nicene Fathers*, on the question of how the statement of Christ's death at the sixth hour in the Gospel of John does not contradict Mark narrating that it took place at the third hour (John 19:14 and Mark 15:25).

Such an approach to Scripture might seem naïve, or almost akin to fundamentalism, to most mainstream theologians today, many of whom would not find such seeming contradictions unsettling, nor would they in all likelihood find Augustine's young earth creationism persuasive. But these facts are central in that they illustrate an approach to Scripture which is quite unfamiliar for many today. Understanding this is helpful in better grasping the conceptual framework by which the ancient church authors approach Scripture and the lens through which they read it. Contrary to misleading statements of some contemporary theologians, such as N. T. Wright stating that "The question of errancy and inerrancy comes to us from American rationalism, from the late eighteen century onwards",[111] then this view, as outlined above, was the by far the most common and ubiquitous approach to Scripture in ancient times.

This once-common conceptual approach toward the Bible is important to understand and appreciate especially in view of the following chapter.

---

[110] Augustine, *The City of God* 15.27.
[111] Closer To Truth, "N.T. Wright - Philosophy of the Bible," YouTube, June 28, 2018, https://www.youtube.com/watch?v=ZQU83Lfdi8w.

PART II: VETUS TESTAMENTUM IN NOVO RECEPTUM

Parts of the argumentation of this work will build on the use and citation of the Biblical material by early Christian authors, and understanding their assumptions is necessary for understanding their use of the text. A belief in the inerrancy of Scripture, something to which nothing could be added and nothing could be subtracted, is demonstrated by the use of the Old Testament in the New, and the use of both of them by the early Christian authors. An author's use of a text will be contingent on his assumptions about it.

Already in ancient times authors were aware of the conceptual difference between paraphrase and citation, which they also actively distinguished between. Thus Augustine can at once place say that he has quoted Cicero "word for word, with the exception of some words omitted, and some slightly transposed, for the sake of giving the sense more readily".[112] Such a quote reveals the conceptual presence in Augustine's thought of quotation as verbatim being the true form of quotation, and that his omissions and transposition of words are *exceptions* to an otherwise loyal quotation.

This awareness does of course not originate with Augustine but goes much further back. Cicero who, in his translation of different Attic rhetoricians into Latin, does not give the Latin as a translator, *interpres*, but as a speaker, *orator*, so that the ideas and language fits the Latin style and use, rather than giving it word for word, *non verbum pro verbo*.[113] Here, Cicero again demonstrates a conceptual distinction between a looser paraphrase and a more loyal literal translation. Professor Law, too, comments on the well-developed translation tradition already present in ancient times. During the period of the Septuagint's translation other works, too, were being worked on. Among others, the Odyssey was translated into Latin by Livius Andronicus and is an example of one of antiquity's larger translation projects taking place at the time.[114]

THE USE OF THE SEPTUAGINT BY CHRIST

Theologically speaking, it must be Christ primarily, and the New Testament derivatively from Christ's authority, which directs and defines our use and approach to the Old Testament. The Gospels sets forth Christ, who takes the place of primacy with his unique statements about himself, his authority,

---

[112] Schaff, *A Select Library of the Nicene and Post-Nicene Fathers of the Christian Church*, 28.
[113] Müller, *The First Bible of the Church*, 108.
[114] Law, *When God Spoke Greek*, 34.

and his role. He points us toward the Holy Scriptures in the Old Testament, which bear witness to him and his work. Thus, Christ is the chief cornerstone who upholds the Holy Scriptures, in this case the Old Testament, by his authority. They in return point us toward Christ as his own faithful witness, such as in Luke 24:27 which states, "And beginning at Moses and all the Prophets, He expounded to them in all the Scriptures the things concerning Himself."

This must not be understood so as to make Scripture *secondary* in any way with regard to authority, but rather it is to say that we must consider how the authority of Scripture flows out from the authority of Christ. Christ is first and foremost, and is himself properly, the Word of God (John 1:1) yet Scripture, as it is breathed out by God and reveals his words, is then derivatively also God's word, as Christ himself also testifies (Matthew 15:6 and Mark 7:13) where Scripture is rightly noted as being the Word of God.

Therefore, it is Christ, the incarnate Word of God, who is himself the living guide pointing to the written Word of God. The Scriptures are alive and powerful on account of Christ, who vivifies and bestows it to the church by the Holy Spirit. Christ is the touchstone for the reception of the Old Testament by the Church, and Christians' reception of these writings must go through him. He is the chief cornerstone, the foundation of the faith (1 Peter 2:6 and 1 Corinthians 3:11). The Latin maxim of Saint Augustine, *Vetus Testamentum in Novo receptum (The Old Testament received in the New)*, captures this sentiment accurately. The New Testament is hidden within the Old Testament and the Old Testament is made clear by the New Testament. This insight clarifies which of the competing editions and textual traditions of the Old Testament must be received by the church. Christ himself then, is the chief shepherd who leads the flock toward the Holy Scriptures, pointing toward them asking, "have you not read?" In other words, Christ is the final revealer of the Old Testament, not only in regard to its content, but also in regard to its being, how to read it, and *where* to read it.

As anticipated earlier, Jesus himself used the Septuagint at multiple occasions. In the Gospel of Mark 7:6–8, Christ reads a passage from the Book of Isaiah *as it is written*. As can be seen in the table below, the passage recited by Christ contains multiple differences between the Masoretic Text and the Septuagint. Though the differences are not theological in character, they are important in so far as they indicate that Jesus did not use nor read from the Masoretic Text but from the Septuagint, especially considering

PART II: VETUS TESTAMENTUM IN NOVO RECEPTUM

that the quote is described as presenting the text *as it is written* (ὡς γέγραπται).

Mark 7:6–7	
Greek	Οὗτος ὁ λαὸς τοῖς χείλεσίν με τιμᾷ, ἡ δὲ καρδία αὐτῶν πόρρω ἀπέχει ἀπ' ἐμοῦ. ⁷Μάτην δὲ σέβονταί με, διδάσκοντες διδασκαλίας ἐντάλματα ἀνθρώπων.
English	This people honor me with lips, but their heart is far from me, in vain they worship me teaching doctrines, precepts of men
Isaiah 29:13	
Koine Greek LXX	ὁ λαὸς οὗτος τοῖς χείλεσιν αὐτῶν τιμῶσίν με, ἡ δὲ καρδία αὐτῶν πόρρω ἀπέχει ἀπ' ἐμοῦ, μάτην δὲ σέβονταί με διδάσκοντες ἐντάλματα ἀνθρώπων καὶ διδασκαλίας
English From LXX	This people honor me with their lips, but their heart is far from me, in vain they worship me teaching precepts of men and doctrines
English From MT	This people honor me with their mouths and with their lips, but have removed their hearts far from me, and their fear toward me is taught by commandments of men

Table 1 – Comparison of Mark 7:6-7 with Isaiah 29:13

Another important example of Jesus' use of the Septuagint can be found in Luke 4:18–19. Here, Luke narrates how Jesus was handed the scrolls of Isaiah in the Synagogue in Nazareth, whereafter he read a passage from Isaiah before commenting that the words which were just heard "have been fulfilled in your ears (*hearing*)" (verse 21). The passage Jesus quotes is a verbatim rendition of the text of Isaiah as read in the Septuagint's Book of Isaiah chapter 61, with an addition of a passage from Isaiah 58:6 also from the Septuagint, shown in turquoise beneath. The passage in brackets in yellow is not witnessed to by all New Testament manuscripts but has very early support and is witnessed to by Irenaeus,[115] Codex Alexandrinus, and the Byzantine Majority Text, among others.

---

[115] Irenaeus, *Against Heresies* 4.23.

SEVENTY-TWO SERVANTS OF THE WORD

Luke 4:18–19	
Greek	Πνεῦμα κυρίου ἐπ' ἐμέ, οὗ εἵνεκεν ἔχρισέν με εὐαγγελίσασθαι πτωχοῖς· ἀπέσταλκέν με [ἰάσασθαι τοὺς συντετριμμένους τὴν καρδίαν] κηρύξαι αἰχμαλώτοις ἄφεσιν, καὶ τυφλοῖς ἀνάβλεψιν, ἀποστεῖλαι τεθραυσμένους ἐν ἀφέσει, κηρύξαι ἐνιαυτὸν κυρίου δεκτόν.
English	The Spirit of the Lord is upon me, because he has anointed me to preach the gospel to the poor, he has sent me [to heal the brokenhearted] to proclaim liberty to the captives and recovery of sight to the blind, to set at liberty those who are oppressed, to proclaim the acceptable year of the Lord.
Isaiah 61:1–2	
Koine Greek LXX	Πνεῦμα κυρίου ἐπ' ἐμέ, οὗ εἵνεκεν ἔχρισέν με, εὐαγγελίσασθαι πτωχοῖς ἀπέσταλκέν με, ἰάσασθαι τοὺς συντετριμμένους τῇ καρδίᾳ, κηρύξαι αἰχμαλώτοις ἄφεσιν καὶ τυφλοῖς ἀνάβλεψιν, καλέσαι ἐνιαυτὸν κυρίου δεκτὸν [ἀπόστελλε τεθραυσμένους ἐν ἀφέσει]
English From LXX	The Spirit of the Lord is upon me, because he has anointed me to preach the gospel to the poor, he has sent me to heal the brokenhearted, to proclaim liberty to the captives and recovery of sight to the blind, to call* the acceptable year of the Lord. [to set at liberty those who are oppressed] *Synonym with κηρύξαι/to proclaim
English From MT	The Spirit of the Lord is upon me, for the Lord has anointed me to bring good tidings to the poor, he has sent me to bind the brokenhearted, to proclaim liberty to prisoners, and an opening to those imprisoned, to proclaim the acceptable year of the Lord.

Table 2 – Comparison of Luke 4:18–19 with Isaiah 61:1–2

PART II: VETUS TESTAMENTUM IN NOVO RECEPTUM

Jesus' use of the Septuagint, considering the actual presence of the Septuagint in Galilee and Judaea at the time of Christ, as shown prior, underscores the central role of the Septuagint. The New Testaments' presentation, taken at face value, is made historically plausible by the archeological record which shows the availability of the Septuagint in that time and era. Moreover, the alternative that he had recourse to a form of the Hebrew Text, which is rather unlikely, as few understood spoken or written Hebrew at that time, and even less in the north of Israel than in the south. Secondly, the comment about how the recited passage says "today this Scripture is fulfilled in your hearing" [literally *in your ears*, ἐν τοῖς ὠσὶν ὑμῶν] lends itself to a direct correlation between that which was read and that which was heard.

Unlike the table comparing the renderings of the text used in Mark 7, Table 1, the differences in Table 2 are of theological relevance. The statement about the recovery of sight to the blind is lacking in the Masoretic edition of the Book of Isaiah, but is of major importance to the ministry of Christ. Both in the Synoptic Gospels, Mark 8 and Luke 7, but especially in the Gospel of John chapter 9, this part of Christ's ministry plays a major role, where physical and spiritual blindness, and the healing thereof, are theologically significant in Christ's acts.

That Jesus himself used the Septuagint and read and preached from it is not a novel insight. Professor of New Testament Studies Stanley Porter explains this quite modestly when he says, "*I would even go so far as to posit that the evidence from the Gospels indicates that Jesus himself may well have used, at least on occasion, the Septuagint when he wished to cite Scripture*".[116] This comment is supported by the actual data, as shown above. Much earlier this was also noticed, not only in the ancient church, which will be discussed at length later, but the early biblical scholar Edward Grinfield, who died in 1864, wrote extensively on this subject. His work specialized in the Septuagint and its use in the New Testament, as well as the New Testament's more general use of the Old Testament. He also published multiple editions of the Greek New Testament and lectured on the Septuagint at the University of Oxford.[117] By comparing the wording of Christ's quotations of the Old Testament, he counted 37 such quotations, he found that 33 were verbatim, or almost

---

[116] Porter, "The Septuagint: A Greek-Text-Oriented Approach," 414.

[117] N. D. F. Pearce, "Grinfield, Edward William (1785–1864), Biblical Scholar," in *Oxford Dictionary of National Biography*, ed. Sinéad Agnew (Oxford University Press, September 23, 2004), https://www.oxforddnb.com/.

verbatim, citations of the Septuagint, while two reflected the wording of the Masoretic Text and not the Septuagint. One quotation matched neither and the last one was ambiguous.[118] Not all of these examples will be examined here, but some of the more illustrative examples are given beneath. In Matthew 13:14–15, Christ gives a longer quotation from Isaiah 6:9–10.

---

[118] Edward William Grinfield, *An Apology for the Septuagint* (London: William Pickering, 1850), 30.

PART II: VETUS TESTAMENTUM IN NOVO RECEPTUM

Matthew 13:14–15	
Greek	ἀκοῇ ἀκούσετε καὶ οὐ μὴ συνῆτε, καὶ βλέποντες βλέψετε καὶ οὐ μὴ ἴδητε. ἐπαχύνθη γὰρ ἡ καρδία τοῦ λαοῦ τούτου, καὶ τοῖς ὠσὶν βαρέως ἤκουσαν καὶ τοὺς ὀφθαλμοὺς αὐτῶν ἐκάμμυσαν, μήποτε ἴδωσιν τοῖς ὀφθαλμοῖς καὶ τοῖς ὠσὶν ἀκούσωσιν καὶ τῇ καρδίᾳ συνῶσιν καὶ ἐπιστρέψωσιν καὶ ἰάσομαι αὐτούς
English	"Hearing you will hear and shall not understand, and seeing you will see and not perceive. For the heart of this people have grown dull. And with their ears they are hard of hearing, and with eyes they have closed, lest they should see with the eyes and hear with the ears, lest they should understand with the hearts and turn, so that I should heal them."
Isaiah 6:9–10	
Koine Greek LXX	Ἀκοῇ ἀκούσετε καὶ οὐ μὴ συνῆτε καὶ βλέποντες βλέψετε καὶ οὐ μὴ ἴδητε, ἐπαχύνθη γὰρ ἡ καρδία τοῦ λαοῦ τούτου, καὶ τοῖς ὠσὶν αὐτῶν βαρέως ἤκουσαν καὶ τοὺς ὀφθαλμοὺς αὐτῶν ἐκάμμυσαν, μήποτε ἴδωσιν τοῖς ὀφθαλμοῖς καὶ τοῖς ὠσὶν ἀκούσωσιν καὶ τῇ καρδίᾳ συνῶσιν καὶ ἐπιστρέψωσιν καὶ ἰάσομαι αὐτούς
English From LXX	"Hearing you will hear and shall not understand, and seeing you will see and not perceive. For the heart of this people have grown dull. And with ears they are hard of hearing, and with eyes they have closed, lest they should see with the eyes and hear with the ears, lest they should understand with the hearts and turn, so that I should heal them."
English From MT	"Hearing you shall hear, but you do not understand Seeing you shall see, but not perceive Make the heart of this people dull! And make their ears heavy, and shut their eyes, lest they see with their eyes, and hear with their ears, and understand with their heart, and return and be healed"

Table 3 – Comparison of Matthew 13:14–15 with Isaiah 6:9–10

As demonstrated above, this quotation is a one-to-one rendering of the text as found in the Septuagint, with the exception of a single processive pronoun *theirs*. This example is interesting because of the plain differences in the text. The Septuagint and the New Testament describes the people as having their hearts covered by fat and that their ears are heavy, whereas the Masoretic Text describes how God supposedly commands Isaiah to cover their hearts with fat and make their ears heavy, which seems to presuppose that their hearts were not yet covered nor were their ears yet heavy. This difference alters the meaning significantly in that either the people are already in this state presently, as Christ teaches, or, according to the Isaiah of the Masoretes, it is something which is not yet actualized but something which the prophet must bring about.

But it is not only with the Book of Isaiah that Jesus uses the Septuagint, he also uses it at places where its wording differs from the Masoretic Text. Another shorter example can be found in Matthew 21:16 where Jesus quotes the eighth Psalm. He quotes the third verse in his confrontation with the Pharisees and adds an interesting rhetorical question to the quotation, "*have you not read?*" This is important, as the questions impose a presupposition to the hearers that they ought to be familiar with the passage.

Matthew 21:16	
Greek	Ἐκ στόματος νηπίων καὶ θηλαζόντων κατηρτίσω αἶνον
English	Out of babes' and infants' mouth have you perfected praise
Psalm 8:3	
Koine Greek LXX	ἐκ στόματος νηπίων καὶ θηλαζόντων κατηρτίσω αἶνον
English From LXX	Out of babes' and infants' mouth have you perfected praise
English From MT	Out of babes' and infants' mouths have you ordained strength* *or possibly *defense, guard*.

Table 4 – Comparison of Matthew 21:16 with Psalm 8:3

Jesus quotes the text of the Septuagint verbatim here, though there is a significant difference which cannot be grounded semantically in the translation. In other words, Matthew clearly presents Jesus as speaking the words of the Book of Psalms from the Septuagint or, which is much less likely given the linguistic landscape, a Hebraic text belonging to the Septuagint textual family. Whichever text was used, the fact is that the authoritative text is that of the Septuagint. This is clear on account of the context, namely the songs of praise of the small children (νηπίων) are the reason for Christ's use of the passage to correct the Pharisees, who were angered by the praise given to Christ by the children (παῖδας) at the Temple (Matthew 21:15) while the Masoretic variant would not fit the context.

Given the plurality of text types and editions at the time of Christ, as discussed earlier, these examples help to establish which text ought to be the authoritative one. On account of Christ's persistent use of it, the Lord himself presented the Septuagint as *the* Old Testament that ought to be used. This conclusion is supported by his use of passages whose wording differs strongly from the Masoretic Text, even to the degree of containing significant theological differences.

Jesus underscores the authority of the Septuagint by adding comments to his quotations of it – such as "as it is written" and "have you not read" – comments which assume *prima facie* that the normative status of the Septuagint and that the text given in that source is indeed faithful. Christ's use of it is neither confined to a single book nor is Christ presented as using the Septuagint in a single Gospel alone. Rather, clear examples can be provided from multiple books, such as Isaiah and Psalms, and presented by both Mark, Matthew, and Luke. More examples could have been provided though, such as his verbatim citation of Deuteronomy 8:3 from the Septuagint in Matthew 4:4, the quotation in Matthew 19:18–19 from Exodus 12–16, or the quotation in Mark 12:10–11 from Psalm 118:22–23. This list is not exhaustive, but only illustrative of Jesus' use of the translation of the Seventy-Two which, as the evangelists' presentation shows, is put forth as the authentic Old Testament.

Grinfield also proposes another, quite intriguing, reason for Jesus' frequent use of the Septuagint. For, as shown earlier, the Greek language was in no way an unknown language, but an intimate and common part of Jewish daily life in Roman Judaea. Grinfield argues that Jesus not only used the Septuagint as an adult, but that it was also the text of the Old Testament he had grown up with. For just as he himself in his adulthood would read from it in the Synagogue, likewise it would have been the one he had been taught with and had grown up hearing as a child. It is rather unlikely that either the Virgin Mary or Joseph were able to read Hebrew well, as they did not belong to any of the social segments where a good knowledge of ancient Hebrew, which required some education, were necessary. Rather, they were likely familiar with the Greek Septuagint as Joseph and the Holy Family lived only six kilometers (3.7 miles) from Sepphoris, a large, Greek-speaking

Hellenized town. It is very plausible that Joseph would have done business there as a skilled craftsman (τέκτων) (Mark 6:3). Thus, use and knowledge of the Septuagint seems to have been much more likely than an equivalent knowledge of the Hebrew Proto-Masoretic Text.

The Magnificat of Mary in Luke 1:46–56 also lends strong support to such an interpretation, in that it is in tone and style literarily dependent on the Septuagint. Its particular phraseology and allusions taken therefrom, as is also noted by Grinfield,[119] and by modern biblical scholars.[120] Mary calls God ὁ δυνατός (*the strong one*) in verse 49, a title which is never used elsewhere in the New Testament about God, yet is used about God in the Septuagint in Zephaniah 3:17, the context of which also uses some of the same themes found in the Magnificat. More phraseology of the Septuagint that is not found elsewhere in the New Testament, can be found in the Magnificat—for example, διανοίᾳ καρδίας (*the heart's thoughts*) from verse 51 is taken from 1 Chronicles 29:18 and Baruch 1:22, and ὕψωσεν ταπεινούς (*he has lifted up the humble*) in verse 52 is found in Ezekiel 21:31 and Job 5:11. This, along with the aforementioned circumstances, indicates an active use of the Septuagint by the Virgin Mary which again, prima farcie, points toward her having an intimate knowledge of it.

The Hebrew culture and social environment was highly influenced, even saturated, by the Septuagint. Its phrases and terminology impacted the religious language of the believers, as can be seen by the New Testament texts. Mary's own use of the Septuagint in the Magnificat is also considered by Grinfield who says, "I arrived at the conviction, that Jesus, when a child, was instructed in the knowledge of the LXX [the Septuagint]" [121] and "we may fairly, I think, deduce from these facts (circumstances such as those mentioned before), that our Lord was instructed by his parents, in the Hellenistic version [the Septuagint]".[122]

THE USE OF THE SEPTUAGINT BY THE APOSTLES

There is a broad consensus that, when the New Testament authors cite the Old Testament, it is the Septuagint that is being relied on, as noted by

---

[119] Grinfield, *An Apology for the Septuagint*, 184.
[120] James T Forestell, "Old Testament Background of the Magnificat," *Marian Studies* 12, no. 12 (2016): 205–44, https://ecommons.udayton.edu/marian_studies/vol12/iss1/12.
[121] Grinfield, *An Apology for the Septuagint*, 183.
[122] Grinfield, *An Apology for the Septuagint*, 186.

PART II: VETUS TESTAMENTUM IN NOVO RECEPTUM

Professor Marcos[123] and Professor Gleaves.[124] Not only the Gospels preferred the Septuagint, but "the consensus is now that when he [Paul] quotes from the Jewish scriptures he most often, perhaps always, preferred the Greek [Septuagint]".[125] Providing an exhaustive exposition of all citations cannot be given here, as that would require far too many pages, but some interesting and illuminating examples must be brought forth.

The closest one can come to an exhaustive list of examples is the praiseworthy work done by Ph.D. R. Grant Jones in his *Notes on the Septuagint*, which is to be highly recommended to anyone interested in the topic. In this work, the author goes through around 320 citations of the Old Testament by the New Testament's authors, and he compares the wording found in the New Testament with the Masoretic Text and with the Septuagint. In his comparisons, Dr. Jones deals with different grades of overlap ranging from perfect/near perfect quotation (verbatim), perfect in meaning (a word might be exchanged with a synonym, or with a word or a couple of words might be dropped though the rest of the quote overlaps), and lastly, if there be further differences though there still remains an overlap in meaning.

Some examples will be helpful here. In Matthew 13:14–15, an example of a verbatim quotation is found where only one word has been dropped in Matthew's quotation of the Septuagint. Thus, 48 out of the 49-word long quotation is given precisely and in the same order. An example of overlap in meaning, though there is a difference in the wording, can be found in in the following table.

---

[123] Fernández Marcos, *The Septuagint in Context*, 326.
[124] Gleaves and Cloud, *Did Jesus Speak Greek?*, chap. 4.
[125] Law, *When God Spoke Greek*, 105.

Matthew 1:23	
Greek	Ἰδοὺ ἡ παρθένος ἐν γαστρὶ ἕξει καὶ τέξεται υἱόν, καὶ καλέσουσιν τὸ ὄνομα αὐτοῦ Ἐμμανουήλ
English	See, the virgin will receive in her womb*, and she will birth a son, and you will call his name Emmanuel. *Literal translation, here meaning *will become pregnant*
Isaiah 7:14	
Koine Greek LXX	ἰδοὺ ἡ παρθένος ἐν γαστρὶ λήμψεται καὶ τέξεται υἱόν, καὶ καλέσεις τὸ ὄνομα αὐτοῦ Ἐμμανουήλ
English From LXX	See, the virgin will receive* in her womb*, and she will birth a son, and you will call his name called Emmanuel. *Literal translation, here meaning *will become pregnant*
English From MT	See, the maiden is with child*, and she brings forth a son, and she will call him Emmanuel *The verbs here are participles and the tense of them must be supplied from the context, which here seemingly is present, thus reads also <u>Tanakh: The Holy Scriptures</u>, Jewish Publication Society, 1985

Table 5 – Comparison of Matthew 1:23 with Isaiah 7:14

PART II: VETUS TESTAMENTUM IN NOVO RECEPTUM

Book	P&O
Matthew	61.1
Mark	55.6
Luke	69.2
John	46.4
Acts	60
Romas	73.8
1 Corinthians	47
2 Corinthians	50
Galatians	80
Ephesians	80
1 Timothy	100
2 Timothy	50
Hebrews	71.6
James	75
1 Peter	58.3

Matthew	83.3
Mark	88.9
Luke	92.3
John	92.9
Acts	100
Romas	94.3
1 Corinthians	88.2
2 Corinthians	100
Galatians	100
Ephesians	100
1 Timothy	100
2 Timothy	100
Hebrews	97.3
James	100
1 Peter	91.7
2 Peter	100
Total	93.0

Figure 5 – Comparison Chart over Textual Overlap

Here, a difference is seen between the wording of the New Testament and of the Septuagint, though the meaning and sense of the text is the same. Λαμβάνω means *to take or receive* and ἔχω means *to have*, though it can also be used in the sense of *to receive*, such as in Matthew 19:16. Λαμβάνω in the future tense is often used in the Septuagint in place of ἔχω in the future tense, the words are therefore synonyms. The Septuagint also differs from the New Testament in that it uses καλέω (*to call*) in the second person plural future tense rather than the third person plural future tense. There is an overlap in meaning compared to the Masoretic Text, which gives a different text. This quotation, then, is an example of this middle category, wherein there is an overlap in meaning though there is no exact correspondence word for word.

With these more methodological considerations in mind, these two graphs from Ph.D. R. Grant Jones' work can be given[126]. The numbers in the column to the left provide the percentage of verbatim or near-verbatim quotations of the Septuagint as a total of the Old Testament quotations found in each New Testament book, one example of which is the use of Isaiah 29:13 in Matthew 13:14–15, where 48 words out of 49 words were the same. The numbers show that 73.8% of all the Old Testament quotations used in Romans are perfect or near-perfect quotations of the Septuagint. In the right column, the numbers are given for how many quotations from the Old Testament overlap in their meaning with the Septuagint per each New Testament book, an example of such would be Matthew 1:23 and Isaiah 7:14 as shown above. The book of Roman's use of the Old Testament reflects the Septuagint in 94.3% of all cases. These numbers should be seen in contrast to the overlap between the New Testament citations of the Old Testament with the Masoretic Text. Here is found an overlap in only 58.2% of all cases. If one compares across all of the New Testament books, a total overlap is found between the New Testament's quotations of the Old Testament with the Septuagint in 93% of all cases, compared to an overlap with the Masoretic Text in 68.3% of all cases.[127]

It is therefore ably demonstrated that the Old Testament of not only Christ and the Gospel authors, but also of Paul and the authors of the General Epistles, was the Septuagint and not the Masoretic Text, though one has to be conscious of slight differences caused by subjective judgements, differences in the biblical manuscripts, and that the New Testament authors might have had slightly different manuscripts of the Septuagint in front of them than what is presently available. Though there is not a 100% overlap, as shown by the numbers above, these last differences between the New Testament's wording and the wording of the Septuagint, a difference at around 7%, can be explained by different factors.

Text-critical issues have to come into consideration as well, as some strands of the transmission of the Septuagint in the centuries following A.D. 1 underwent revisions—though the textual instability of the Septuagint has been vastly overstated by many including *Theodotian*, *Kaige*, and the *Lucian recension*, among others, which will be discussed later. Likewise, the New

---

[126] R. Grant Jones, "Notes on the Septuagint" (2006), 22, 31–32, https://www.scriptureanalysis.com/wp-content/uploads/2016/09/Grant-Jones-LXXNotesFeb06.pdf.

[127] Jones, "Notes on the Septuagint", 26.

PART II: VETUS TESTAMENTUM IN NOVO RECEPTUM

Testament manuscripts themselves also differ at times in their exact wording given, as the New Testament itself also comes to the present day with some text critical issues at hand through a few different transmitted textual families—the *Western Text, the Byzantine Majority Text, the Alexandrian Text*, and more. Some of the differences in the wording of the Old Testament as provided by the Septuagint and the New Testament may also be due to a more dynamic citation rather than literal at times. But to provide a detailed examination of each case of difference and to propose an explanation would take up too many pages and is, though an important task, far beyond the scope of this present work. But it is naturally important to be aware of these remaining differences and not to brush them aside too quickly.

Regardless, these final differences do not alter the significant fact that an overlap between the Septuagint and the New Testament's quotations of the Old Testament occur in more than 9 out of 10 cases, that is a 93% overlap compared to 68% for the Masoretic Text. This chief conclusion remains firmly established and is crucial to keep in mind when considering which text ought to be the authoritative basis for the Old Testament.

To summarize, the demonstrable textual dependence of the New Testament on the unique wording, phraseology, and particular variants, though a strong argument for the case of the Septuagint as *the* Old Testament of the New, is not the only argument. The case for the Septuagint is equally strengthened by the fact that the New Testament does not only depend on the special wording, but also on distinct features of the Greek language which are not present in the Hebrew text.

None of the New Testament's authors address the Septuagint explicitly, so their presuppositions and approach to it must be gleaned by the implications of their choices and use of it. Thus, one of the strongest arguments in favor of the Septuagint is not just its use, as one could theoretically explain that by the use of a hypothetical Hebrew Vorlage matching the Septuagint, but rather it is the New Testament's use of the Septuagint in dogmatical questions where the reasoning is contingent on features of the Greek language that could not possibly be made on the basis of the Hebrew text. The best example of this is Paul's use of Genesis 22:18 in Galatians 3:16.

SEVENTY-TWO SERVANTS OF THE WORD

Galatians 3:16	
Greek	τῷ δὲ Ἀβραὰμ ἐρρέθη-σαν αἱ ἐπαγγελίαι καὶ τῷ σπέρματι αὐτοῦ. οὐ λέγει, καὶ τοῖς σπέρμασιν, ὡς ἐπὶ πολλῶν, ἀλλ' ὡς ἐφ' ἑνός, Καὶ τῷ σπέρματί σου, ὅς ἐστιν Χριστός.
English	Now to Abraham and his Descendant were the promises made. He does not say, "*and to descendants*" as of many, but as of one, "*and to your descendant*" who is Christ
Genesis 22:18	
Koine Greek LXX	καὶ ἐνευλογηθήσονται ἐν τῷ σπέρματί σου πάντα τὰ ἔθνη τῆς γῆς
English From LXX	And in your descendant will all the peoples of the earth be blessed
English From MT	And in your offspring will all the peoples of the earth be blessed.

Table 6 – Comparison of Galatians 3:16 with Genesis 22:18

Language-wise this argument is simply invalid if made on the basis of the Hebrew text. The blessing of the peoples of the world through the descendant, singular, of Abraham, and the dogmatic implication drawn from this in regard to Christ's status as the promised offspring, is directly contingent on the authority of the Greek text of the Septuagint. Such a use of the Septuagint presupposes a view of the Septuagint as an inspired and authoritative text providing a valid basis for binding exegesis. Notice that Paul is not making some appeal to a new proclamation on account of his inspired authority as an apostle. Rather, by justifying the reading in the text itself, he presupposes the validity of the reading and grounds his argument in the text itself, hinging in on the validity of the Septuagint.

The Masoretic Text uses the word זֶרַע for *descendant/seed/offspring*, while the Greek term is σπέρμα. In Hebrew, the word זֶרַע is a mass noun or an *uncountable noun* and does not have a plural form but only a singular form. Though one can speak about *more or less offspring* (זֶרַע), the noun itself is uncountable and thus only has one form whether one intends to denote a plurality of offspring or a single one, just as we in English might talk about an extraordinary *sheep* as well as many mediocre *sheep*. The word זֶרַע appears around 230 times in the Masoretic Text, and always in the same singular form, whether denoting one or many offspring.

PART II: VETUS TESTAMENTUM IN NOVO RECEPTUM

Yet Paul says that "and to your descendent (*singular*) Scripture does not say, and to your descendants (*plural*)." Had Paul made this argument from the Hebrew text it, would at best have been naïve language-wise and quite unfounded, and at worst very misleading and fraudulent. But assuming ignorance of Hebrew on Paul's side would be mistaken. According to Acts 22:3, he was trained by the rabbi Gamaliel and knew the Law thoroughly. Thus, as a well-trained Pharisee, Paul would have had a thorough knowledge of the Old Testament Scriptures in Hebrew as well as in Greek. Such an explanation must therefore be rejected. Yet on the other hand, Greek does differ between descent in singular (το σπέρμα) and in plural (τὰ σπέρμᾰτᾰ) descendants,[128] as the Greek text of Paul itself also acknowledges—the contrast between τῷ σπέρματι and τοῖς σπέρμασιν in Galatians 3:16—here in the dative case. Neither is Paul making some sort of interpretive move either, for he clearly presents this as is the authoritative written promise, which can be seen by his appeal to the written nature of the promise given, "it [Scripture] does not say 'to your offspring [plural]' but ... ." His appeal is therefore not made to some sort of hypothetical interpretation of the vague Hebrew term, which is compatible with either a plural or singular meaning, but rather to the written Greek text employing the term in singular.

Looking at the Greek of the Septuagint, therefore, it is significant that Genesis 22:18 says ἐν τῷ σπέρματί σου rather than ἐν τοῖς σπέρμασιν σου (singular rather than plural). Paul's argumentation would be very problematic if one assumed that the Hebrew text was the only infallible text from which dogmatic and exegetical conclusions could be drawn and that the Septuagint was, albeit useful, then just a secondary translation useful for preaching among Greek-speaking Jews and Pagans, but only valid insofar as it agreed with the Hebrew text. Yet Paul's use of the Septuagint here, and other places, supposes a much higher view of the Septuagint wherein the Greek text of the Septuagint itself is viewed as inspired, authoritative, and useful for valid dogmatic and exegetical conclusions, even where it differs from the Hebrew text, and also where it states something which could not be stated by the Hebrew text.

Looking at the Jewish context and reception of the Septuagint, it can be seen that such an interpretation of Paul's fits nicely within his

---

[128] Though το σπερμα is also at times used as a collective noun in some texts then Paul's argument is quite reasonable and well founded, insofar as το σπερμα is often used in the plural in contemporary texts; see, for example, Josephus, *Antiquities of the Jews* 8.7.6; 4 *Maccabees* 18:1; Plato, *Laws* 9.

contemptuous Jewish context, where such a high view of the Septuagint was already present in theologians such as Philo, who died only around 14 years prior to Paul. This view, as will be shown in the following chapters, was also the received position of the early Christian Church, which shared Paul's high view of the Septuagint. This interpretation of Paul and his use of the Septuagint fits squarely both with the period before him as well as subsequent to him. Nor did he develop this view in isolation, as it was common among many Jews prior to the writing of the New Testament and was, as argued above, the position of Christ himself, whose Old Testament was nothing else than that of the Seventy-Two.

CONCLUSION

The primacy of the Septuagint flows out as a result of the primacy of Christ as the final guide to the Old Testament. As he led his disciple on the road to Emmaus, so he still leads his flock today, *through* the Old Testament, teaching how we ought to read and understand what God so long ago spoke to the patriarchs and prophets of Israel, now finally revealed in the fullness of truth by Christ and his apostles. But Christ does not only lead his flock *through* the Old Testament but also *to* it. It is Christ that points toward the authority of the prophets and the sacred writings, and it is by his authority that their authority is affirmed. Jesus is, therefore, the Scriptural paradigm of the church.

Through his ministry, the incarnated Word of God shone his light on the written Word of God, bringing clarity to both what once lay hidden therein but also on the right path toward it. For in the confusion of different editions, books, translations, versions, and the like, Christ himself cut through, lifting up the Septuagint Scroll, and read the Word of God as it was written. He was taught the same as a child and did himself teach the same to his disciples who passed it on in return. They were also ubiquitous in their use of the Septuagint, which explains why the early translations of the Old Testament Scriptures, whether in the High North, African South, Latin West, or Armenian East, were made on the basis of the Septuagint.

Paul's own use is particularly clear as he draws doctrine from the Greek text itself based on exegetical arguments which could not even be made from the Hebrew text alone. This shows the assumptions lying behind the inspired apostle's use, which serves as an example for us, as we imitate Paul as he imitated Christ (1 Corinthians 11:1).

PART III: THE RECEPTION OF THE SEPTUAGINT BY THE CHURCH

PART III
THE RECEPTION OF THE SEPTUAGINT BY THE CHURCH

THE EARLY ECCLESIAL AND CONCILIAR RECEPTION OF THE SEPTUAGINT
THE EARLY RECEPTION

As the analysis of the New Testament shows, the Septuagint simply was the Old Testament of Christ, the four evangelists, and the rest of the apostles. In it, they found the very wording of the Scriptures "as they are written," and this tradition was passed down in the church and became the approach throughout the early church. As some have put it, the Septuagint was the Bible of the church and the source of her preaching and doctrine.[129] It was *the* Bible which was copied and used as the source for translations into the many languages of the peoples who were evangelized early on.[130]

These two facts are strengthened by a quick look at all the great codices containing the Old Testament which have survived from late antiquity. First, the Old Testament of Codex Vaticanus, of Codex Sinaiticus, of Codex Alexandrinus, and of Codex Ephraemi all have the Septuagint as their Old Testament. Secondly, it was also the text of the Septuagint, and not a Hebrew text, which was used as the source text, or Vorlage, for the many early Bible translations made in antiquity. Such observations provide a strong implicit argument for the view that the early church considered the Septuagint as the authoritative Old Testament.

When the Old Testament was translated into other languages, the Septuagint provided the textual basis. The earliest translation was the Vetus Latina—the Old Latin translation of the Septuagint—which quickly became popular in the Latin-speaking West and remained in common circulation until around the eighth century, when Jerome's translation finally supplanted it[131]. But this was not restricted to the Vetus Latina alone. By looking at the wording and the phrases differing between the Masoretic Text and the Septuagint, it can be discerned whether a translation used one or the other as the textual basis.

---

[129] Jellicoe, *The Septuagint and Modern Study*, 342.
[130] Fernández Marcos, *The Septuagint in Context*, 338.
[131] Fernández Marcos, *The Septuagint in Context*, 338.

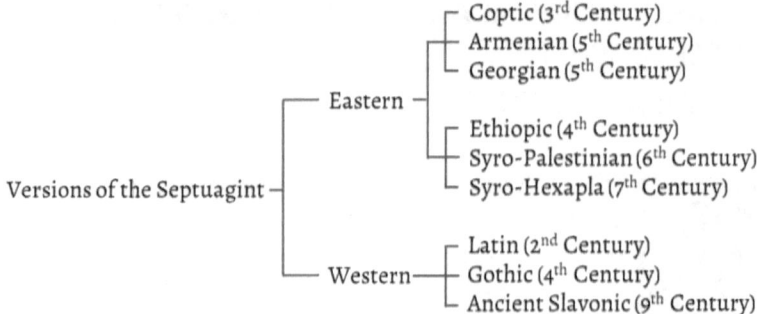

Figure 6 – Geneological Chart of Translations of the Septuagint

Here, the Septuagint indeed served the church as the global mother text for its translations. The Septuagint was the church's Bible, whether directly in its Greek form or indirectly through translation. Slavs, Germanics, Copts, Ethiopians, Armenians, Syrians, Italics, Barbers, and Celts all prayed, sung, and heard their Scriptures from the Septuagint, the words of which resounded from the High North of Germania to the South in Ethiopia, from the Atlantic Ocean in the West to the East in the Caucasus and beyond. The catholicity, the *universality*, of the Septuagint was witnessed to, not just by the Hellenized Mediterranean, but by the church catholic herself.

THE LOCAL SYNODS AND THE ECUMENICAL COUNCIL

The Septuagint scholar Marcos, building on these insights and others, even goes as far as concluding that the Septuagint was "adopted as the official Bible of the Church".[132] This conclusion seems warranted when looking at the common reception of it by the church, but the case can find further support when considering the ecclesiastical decisions of the different early synods, the early canon lists of the church, and even when looking at the great First Ecumenical Council of Nicaea. Though Jerome's Vulgate followed the categorization and structure of the Septuagint in regard to its ordering of the Old Testament books, its wording and text type are unmistakably Masoretic. This poses a challenge, insofar as canon lists alone cannot determine whether the Vorlage of the text in question is taken from the Septuagint or the Masoretic Text. So how can it be deciphered whether an ancient canon list canonized the Septuagint or the Masoretic Text? Jerome's novel choice of the Masoretic Text rather than the Septuagint shows that the

---

[132] Fernández Marcos, *The Septuagint in Context*, 338.

PART III: THE RECEPTION OF THE SEPTUAGINT BY THE CHURCH

Septuagint was the standard textual basis for the Old Testament prior to the Fifth Century A.D., and the books of 1 and 2 Esdras were also helpful in showing this.

In the Masoretic Text, two historical books are present—though sometimes grouped as one—known as Ezra and Nehemiah. These books are combined, with some additions and alterations, as one work in the Septuagint, known as 1 Esdras. 1 Esdras, then, is a unique composition found only in the Septuagint whose Hebrew Vorlage, if it had one, is lacking in the Masoretic Text. This insight is especially helpful in regard to the ancient canon lists provided by the early church fathers and by conciliar synods as an explicit mentioning of 1 and 2 Esdras in relationship to the canon demonstrates a reliance on, and confirmation of, the Septuagint. Thus, by looking for these two works, one can exclude a reliance on the Masoretic Text because that text type simple lacks 1 and 2 Esdras and instead splits 1 Esdras into Ezra and Nehemiah.

Jerome, who translated a Hebrew text closely related to the Masoretic Text, was aware of this and correctly wrote in his forward to the book of Ezra in the Vulgate that this book was *liber Ezrae* (the book of Ezra). But looking at the Latin fathers prior to Jerome, as well as the earlier councils, all that one finds are references to books of Esdras, i.e. Libri Esdrae or Hesdrae, of which two books are mentioned, namely 1 and 2 Esdras of the Septuagint. This can also be demonstrated when, for example, Augustine quotes from *Esdrae liber* (the book of Esdras) in *The City of God* 18:36, then he quotes a passage from 1 Esdras, a book absent from the Masoretic Text, for which reason the quoted passage cannot be found in the Masoretic Text though it is in the copies of the Septuagint.

Additional support is also seen when looking at Augustine's *totus canon Scripturarum* (the whole canon of Scripture) given in his work *On Christian Doctrine* 28:13, where he gives two books of Esdras, *Esdrae duo [librii]*. The same inclusion is also found in earlier canon lists, for example in Codex Claromontanus from the first half of the fourth century, which mentions the book of Esdras (*liber Esdra*) where the books are referred to as one[133]. In canon 36 of the Breviarium Hipponense, which contains the decrees of the Synod of Carthage in A.D. 393, a canon list including two books of Esdras (*esdrae librii II*), is given.[134] This latter source is important insofar as it provides a

---

[133] Edmon L. Gallagher and John Daniel Meade, *The Biblical Canon Lists from Early Christianity: Texts and Analysis* (Oxford: Oxford University Press, 2017), 184.
[134] Gallagher and Meade, *The Biblical Canon Lists from Early Christianity*, 224.

conciliar statement reflecting a much broader North African tradition in comparison to comments made by individual ecclesiastical authors.

In his book *The Biblical Canon Lists from Early Christianity*, Professor Gallagher also mentions that, though the naming conventions of these books would later change, then *"when the ancient canon lists, whether Greek or Latin, mention two books of Esdras, they must have in mind the books known in the LXX and VL* (Vetus Latina, i.e. the Old Latin translation of the Septuagint) as Esdras A and Esdras B (1 and 2 Esdras)." [135] This is also seen in the Gelasium Decree from the fifth century, which transmits an older text from a local council in Rome in A.D. 382 during Bishop Damasus I. Here, too, the canon list includes *Hesdrae librii duo* (two books of Esdras). Though the precise age of the document is disputed, its reliability finds support in a canon list provided by Bishop Innocent I of Rome from A.D. 405, which likewise gives *Hesdrae libri II*.[136] It is therefore amply shown, through individual authors such as Augustine, as well as the conciliar statements, that the canonical text affirmed was the Septuagint and, as shown by the use and inclusion of 1 and 2 Esdras, not the Masoretic Text.

LEX CREDENDI LEX ORANDI

It was not only singular individuals or locale synods which received and professed the use of the Septuagint, but also Christendom itself in the broadest manner in which it could express itself concretely. For weightier than the local synods, is the consideration that the ecumenical creed of Nicaea, edition of A.D. 381, itself flows from the words of the Septuagint. The confession of the First Ecumenical Council itself is drawn from the wording of Genesis as found in the Septuagint, including parts differing from the Masoretic Text.

Nicene Creed, First Article	
Greek	Πιστεύομεν εἰς ἕνα Θεὸν Πατέρα παντοκράτορα, ποιητὴν οὐρανοῦ καὶ γῆς, ὁρατῶν τε πάντων καὶ ἀοράτων.
English	I believe in one God, the Father Almighty, Maker of heaven and earth, and of all things visible and invisible.

---

[135] Gallagher and Meade, *The Biblical Canon Lists from Early Christianity*, 269.
[136] Gallagher and Meade, *The Biblical Canon Lists from Early Christianity*, 233.

PART III: THE RECEPTION OF THE SEPTUAGINT BY THE CHURCH

Genesis 1:1	
Koine Greek LXX	Ἐν ἀρχῇ ἐποίησεν ὁ θεὸς τὸν οὐρανὸν καὶ τὴν γῆν. ἡ δὲ γῆ ἦν ἀόρατος καὶ ἀκατασκεύαστος
English From LXX	In the beginning God created the heavens and the earth, and the earth was formless and void
English From MT	In the beginning God created the heaven and the earth, and the earth was unseemly and unformed

Table 7 – Comparison of Nicene Creed, First Article with Genesis 1:1

The Nicene Confession cites the Septuagint directly, which is plain to see when comparing the original Greek of both texts. The Nicene Creed calls God *creator* (ποιητὴ) of Heaven, singular, compared to the Masoretic plural, Heavens, though it is properly a collective noun which does necessarily change the meaning. The creed further lends from the Septuagint where God *creates* (ποιέω), which is the same word in the form of a noun that the creed uses to describe God. The Nicene Creed uses Genesis 1 as its conscious choice of context, describing further how God is the creator of not only *Heaven* (οὐρανὸς) but also *earth* (γῆ).

This backdrop becomes important as it helps explain the, for many, somewhat surprising description of God as creator of all things visible (Heaven and earth) but also invisible (ἀόρατος). The Masoretic Text of Genesis 1 lacks any kind of language describing visible and invisible creation, but the Septuagint, on the other hand, describes the world as ἀόρατος, which literally means invisible but here denotes unseemliness or incompleteness; yet it is the same word that the Nicene Creed uses. The special vocabulary of the Septuagint has thus been formative for the church's most universal creeds and prayers, the Nicene Creed being one pivotal example of this. Doctrinally, one could here make the appeal to the general concept of *lex orandi lex*, which is what is or ought to be prayed and ought to be believed, or less literally, the rule of prayer is the rule of faith. Appeal to the authority of the Septuagint can thus be drawn from its basis as the liturgical and canonical text for both synods and ecumenical councils.

Following this line of reasoning, the Book of Psalms, in particular, holds a place of honor. Historically, it has served as a chief cornerstone in the devotional life of both lay and ordained Christians. From it, the daily office with its prayers and worship throughout the day sprung. The close relationship between the Book of Psalms and the Septuagint is further highlighted by the fact that, even as Jerome's Latin Vulgate began to supplant the Septuagint-based Old Latin Bible in the West, Jerome's translation of the Psalms from the Masoretic Text, the so-called *Juxta Hebreos*, never managed to replace the Septuagint-based Latin edition, the so-called *Versio Gallicana*.[137] Different reasons could be used to explain this, but one important factor was the laity's attachment to the wording and phraseology of the Septuagint's Book of Psalms, causing its abandonment to be much harder and much more impactful than the rest of the Old Testament books.

THE PATRISTIC RECEPTION OF THE SEPTUAGINT: A DIGRESSION ON THE EXTENT OF THE CANON

The question of the extent of the canon—which and how many books are included in the Old Testament—is often coupled with the question of the use of the Septuagint. That is to say, it is often assumed that use of the Septuagint results in a broader canon, and use of the Masoretic Text necessarily leads to a smaller canon. But this assumption must be wholly rejected. Among the church fathers who confessed the supremacy of the Septuagint, who will be examined on the following pages, there were a wide divergence in views regarding the exact size of the canon. Melito of Sardis, Origen, Eusebius, Gregor of Nyssa, Hilary of Potiers, Cyril of Jerusalem, Epiphanius of Salamis, Athanasius the Great, etc., all used the Septuagint yet held to a smaller canon, rejecting the deuterocanonical books[138]. Augustine and many others, however, confessed the supremacy of the Septuagint and viewed the deuterocanonical books as canonical.

Which view one takes on the role, authority, and canonicity of the deuterocanonical/apocryphal books simply has no bearing on which position one takes on the primacy of the Septuagint. As stated above, one could affirm the primacy of the Masoretic Text while affirming the equality of the deuterocanonical books, as do current Roman Catholic Bibles, one could also affirm the Septuagint text and affirm the deuterocanonical books, as do many Eastern Orthodox, and again, as did many of the early church fathers. It is likewise possible to embrace a shorter canon while affirming the supremacy of the Septuagint. This should help to underline the importance of keeping these questions distinct, as the size of the canon simply does not touch on the question of the textual basis for the canon.

---

[137] Law, *When God Spoke Greek*, 55.
[138] Gallagher and Meade, *The Biblical Canon Lists from Early Christianity*, 78, 83, 98, etc.

PART III: THE RECEPTION OF THE SEPTUAGINT BY THE CHURCH

Reception or rejection of the Septuagint as Old Testament is a question of which *text* to use, not which canon to use.

A PRESENTATION OF THE PATRISTIC RECEPTION OF THE SEPTUAGINT

In the following collection of patristic comments on the canon, the relationship between the early church fathers and the Septuagint will be examined. The fathers, it will be shown, did not just use the Septuagint because of simple accessibility, rather it was an active choice on their account and a conscious rejection of the Masoretic Text, as they confess the first to be the inspired text of Scripture while the latter was viewed as noticeably corrupted.

Importantly, the discussion between Jerome and Augustine must be examined, as this central controversy marked the beginning of the Western Church's later departure from the Septuagint. The discussion between Jerome and Augustine will therefore serve as the backdrop for this patristic journey, as their debate in many ways sums up the whole controversy. In comparison to the pre-Christian Jewish reception of the Septuagint, two additional traits that were not explicit among the Jews became common for the Christian view of the Septuagint.

First of all, the whole Old Testament, regardless of the exact canonical boundaries, were viewed as an inspired work of the Seventy-Two translators. This illustrates, as discussed at length earlier, that the authority, legitimacy and prestige of the original work of the translation of the Pentateuch had come to be shared in a derived sense with succeeding translated works of the rest of the Old Testament books in Alexandria. The books were viewed as one, a whole, and inspired work encompassing the full extent of the Old Testament. Secondly, the terms *Seventy* and *Seventy-Two* became fully synonymous and were used interchangeably—though the term *Seventy*, in Latin *Septuaginta*, became the predominant term. Some falsely attribute this to a confusion on account of the church fathers in regard to the actual number of translators, but this is not at all likely. The number *Seventy* functioned as a so-called synecdoche, which was a common rhetorical figure. Thus, Paul can talk about *The Twelve* to denote the 11 remaining disciples, as Judas had died (1 Corinthians 15:5) which was known as a *totum pro parte*. Likewise, Augustine also discusses the Seventy-Two Translators, six from each of the 12 tribes of Israel, who translated the Septuagint in his work *The City of God* (18:42), yet just afterward, in the next paragraph (18:43), he talks about them as "seventy learned men", underscoring the commonality of this rhetorical device and again showing that one should not confuse the use of *Seventy* with an ignorance of the actual number of translators on the part of Augustine.

1. Clement, circa late 60s, early date, or around 90s, late date, A.D.
This letter enjoyed an extensive circulation and popularity in the ancient church. It was most likely penned by a group of ecclesiastical leaders from the congregations in Rome and sent to the church in Corinth. The letter quotes often from Isaiah and the Book of Psalms from the Septuagint, though there is some uncertainty, as most quotations are paraphrases and few are verbatim.[139]

Justin Martyr, circa A.D. 100–165
Justin Martyr was an early Christian apologist and was one of the first authors from whom multiple works have survived. He is especially interesting in regard to the question of the Septuagint, since one of his works, *Dialogue with the Jew Trypho*, contains a longer discussion concerning the Septuagint itself. As will be shown later in the chapters concerning the Masoretic Text, the Masoretic Text has a demonstrable tendency of omitting messianic prophecies found in the Septuagint, a tendency also noted by the church fathers. Justin Martyr, commenting on these, writes:

> But I am far from putting reliance in your teachers, who refuse to admit that the interpretation made by the seventy elders who were with Ptolemy of the Egyptians is a correct one; and they attempt to frame another. And I wish you to observe, that they have altogether taken away many Scriptures from the translations (ἀπὸ τῶν ἐξηγήσεων) effected by those seventy elders who were with Ptolemy, and by which this very man who was crucified is proved to have been set forth expressly as God, and man, and as being crucified and as dying.
>
> — *Dialogue with the Jew Trypho*, chapter 71 and following

This quotation is illustrative of the developments in post-second temple Judaism which increasingly distanced itself from the Septuagint in the

---

[139] Fernández Marcos, *The Septuagint in Context*, 265.

PART III: THE RECEPTION OF THE SEPTUAGINT BY THE CHURCH

period after the destruction of Jerusalem, a development many scholars see as a result of the conflict with the early Christian church, which had appropriated the Septuagint as their own text.[140]

It is therefore also not surprising that it was only after this increasing conflict and divide that the next great translation of the Old Testament by the Jews commenced, this time through an individual effort by Aquila of Sinope. Though the Jews still relied on a Greek Old Testament, this development further fueled the chasm between rabbinic Judaism and the Septuagint and began the slow journeying by rabbinical Judaism toward what would later become the Masoretic Text. This development was a break with the earlier Jewish tradition, as shown previously, where the Septuagint had been eagerly received and used.

Justin's comment is also important, because he provides a reason for the lack of certain messianic passages in the Masoretic Text by stating that these had been removed by the Jews. This is an accusation that finds strong support in some passages such as Psalms 22, as will be shown later. Justin Martyr further discusses more examples of this in chapter 72 and 73 of the same work, and his testimony is relevant as it provides one of the earliest Christian explanations for the church's conscious choice of using the Septuagint as the authentic text and rejecting the Masoretic Text as corrupt or, more precisely in the time of Justin Martyr, the Proto-Masoretic Text.

Cohortatio ad Graecos, early Second Century A.D.
This anonymous apology was often attributed to Justin Martyr, though this view is now commonly rejected as most scholars date the work to a later period[141]. The work contains the origin story of the Septuagint in chapter 13, where the inspired status of it is underscored. The *Cohortatio* states that the Septuagint was a translation done by *divine power* (θεία δύναμις). Like the Letter of Aristeas, the *Cohortatio* also mentions how the translators carried out their work in tranquil surroundings but, unlike Aristeas' work, the author here adds further details such as that each translator received his own small hut on the island of Pharos, which the author himself states to have seen the remainders of during his visit to Alexandria. During this visit, the local populace likewise shared their oral traditions concerning the Septuagint with him. The work is, despite its anonymous character, an important witness to the early Christian view of the Septuagint and, if its

---

[140] Fernández Marcos, *The Septuagint in Context*, 109.
[141] Müller, *The First Bible of the Church*, 72.

statements are taken as truthful, also to the oral traditions concerning the Septuagint as they circulated in Alexandria in the early second century. He states:

> And having, as was natural, marveled at the books, and concluded them to be divine, he consecrated them in that library. These things, ye men of Greece, are no fable, nor do we narrate fictions; but we ourselves having been in Alexandria, saw the remains of the little cots at the Pharos still preserved, and having heard these things from the inhabitants, who had received them as part of their country's tradition, we now tell to you what you can also learn from others, and specially from those wise and esteemed men who have written of these things, Philo and Josephus, and many others. But if any of those who are wont to be forward in contradiction should say that these books do not belong to us, but to the Jews, and should assert that we in vain profess to have learnt our religion from them, let him know, as he may from those very things which are written in these books, that not to them, but to us, does the doctrine of them refer.
>
> — *Cohortatio ad Graecos*, chapter 13

The alleged existence of living oral traditions in second century Alexandria should not be quickly dismissed, as these traditions already fit well with what is known. As stated above in the chapter on the Jewish reception of the Septuagint, Philo, himself a native of Alexandria, likewise bears witness to the existence not only of a living memory of the Septuagint in Alexandria during the middle of the first century A.D., but also to a yearly solemn festivity commemorating its translation.

Irenaeus, circa A.D. 130–203
From the hand of Irenaeus is preserved the large work *Against Heresies*. In this work, like in Justin Martyr before him, a strong self-conscious affirmation of the Septuagint and a rejection of the Jewish proto-Masoretic Text is clearly present. Irenaeus, affirming the inspiration and divinity of the Septuagint, writes:

> The Scriptures [here Septuagint] were acknowledged as truly divine. For all of them [i.e. the Seventy-Two] read out the common

PART III: THE RECEPTION OF THE SEPTUAGINT BY THE CHURCH

> translation in the very same words and the very same names, from beginning to end, so that even the Gentiles present perceived that the Scriptures had been interpreted [ἡρμηνευμέναι, translated] by the inspiration of God. And there was nothing astonishing in God having done this (...) Since, therefore, the Scriptures have been interpreted with such fidelity, and by the grace of God, and since from these God has prepared and formed again our faith towards His Son, and has preserved to us the unadulterated Scriptures in Egypt.
>
> —*Against Heresies* 3:21

God thus preserved His words in Egypt, and Irenaeus draws a comparison between the origin of the Septuagint and the disappearance and reappearance of Scripture during the time of Ezra. Here Irenaeus is borrowing from an oral tradition also found in the apocryphal work of 4 Ezra, wherein Ezra in chapter 14 writes down the whole Old Testament under the inspiration of God as, according to this tradition, all the books of the Old Testament had been lost during the reign of King Nebuchadnezzar.[142] The themes of the uncertain transmission and availability of Scripture during the latter days of the Israelite kingdoms, the connection between the origins of God's written word in Egypt, Jeremiah's arrival in Egypt, and its final inscripturation in Egypt by the hands of the Seventy-Two, provides credence to the Septuagint's unique role in salvation history, even if one were to reject Ezra's rewriting the Old Testament. According to Irenaeus, the Septuagint is the final revelation of the Old Testament, which served to *prepare and form* (*praeparavit et praeformavit*) faith in God's Son (Book 3, 3:21). Irenaeus also notes how the authority of the Septuagint has been affirmed by the apostles' use of it and reconfirmed by the church's preaching from it. He writes:

> For the apostles, since they are of more ancient date than all these [heretics], agree with this aforesaid translation; and the translation harmonizes with the tradition of the apostles. For Peter, and John, and Matthew, and Paul, and the rest successively, as well as their followers, did set forth all prophetical [announcements], just as the interpretation of the elders contains them. For the one and the

---

[142] Müller, *The First Bible of the Church*, p. 73.

same Spirit of God, who proclaimed by the prophets what and of what sort the advent of the Lord should be, did by these elders [i.e. the Seventy-Two] give a just interpretation of what had been truly prophesied; and He did Himself, by the apostles, announce that the fulness of the times of the adoption had arrived.

—*Against Heresies*, Book 3, 3:23

Therefore, says Irenaeus, one should also view as suspect any later Greek translation of the Old Testament, because such a translation would not be inspired by God, unlike the Septuagint.[143] In the first paragraph of chapter 21, Irenaeus notes how the prophecy concerning the virgin with child from Isaiah 7:14 has been translated by the Jews in his time, such as Aquila, as "a young woman will be with child." He thus raises the same issue as Justin Martyr did before him, albeit a bit less directly, that the Jews have changed or twisted the text. Irenaeus concludes that the Septuagint is the authoritative Old Testament, not just because it is inspired by God Himself, but also because it is more ancient than the text of the Christ-rejecting Jews, and finally, because it is translated by the learned and inspired Jews themselves.[144]

Clement of Alexandria, circa A.D. *150–215*
Clement of Alexandria presents the origin story of the Septuagint much akin to Irenaeus,[145] though he more expressively underscores the divine inspiration of the translation. He writes:

And each having severally translated each prophetic book, and all the translations being compared together, they agreed both in meaning and expression. For it was the counsel of God carried out for the benefit of Grecian ears. It was not alien to the inspiration of God, who gave the prophecy, also to produce the translation, and make it as it were Greek prophecy.

—*Stromata*, Book 1:23

---

[143] Irenaeus, *Against Heresies* 3.21.4.
[144] Irenaeus, *Against Heresies* 3.21.4.
[145] Müller, *The First Bible of the Church*, 75.

PART III: THE RECEPTION OF THE SEPTUAGINT BY THE CHURCH

Clement likewise uses, as noted by Professor Gallagher, the Septuagint as the authoritative basis for his Old Testament exegesis. An example of this is seen in his allegorical interpretation of Genesis 14:14, wherein Clement understands the 318 servants in the household of Abraham as a reference to Jesus. In Greek, the number 18 is written with the two Greek letters *iota* (ι) and *eta* (η), which are the first two letters in the name *Jesus* (Ἰησοῦς), and the number 300 is denoted with the letter *tau* (τ), which bears resemblance to a cross.

> They say, then, that the character representing 300 is, as to shape, the type of the Lord's sign, and that the Iota and the Eta indicate the Savior's name; that it was indicated, accordingly, that Abraham's domestics were in salvation, who having fled to the Sign and the Name became lords of the captives, and of the very many unbelieving nations that followed them.
>
> — *Stromata*, Book 6:11

Unsurprisingly, Professor Gallagher concludes, "This sort of interpretation could not have occurred to a reader of Hebrew".[146]

Tertullian, circa A.D. 160–220
Tertullian was the first prominent church father to write in Latin, and his reception of the Septuagint therefore helped to shape the approach of the Latin-speaking Western Church. He is the first church father to name Aristeas by name, and in his work *Apologeticum* he refers to the Letter of Aristeas. He writes:

> The same account is given by Aristaeus. So the king left these works unlocked to all, in the Greek language. To this day, at the temple of Serapis, the libraries of Ptolemy are to be seen, with the identical Hebrew originals in them. The Jews, too, read them publicly. Under a tribute-liberty, they are in the habit of going to hear them every Sabbath. Whoever gives ear will find God in them; whoever takes pains to understand, will be compelled to believe.

---

[146] Edmon L. Gallagher, "The Septuagint in Patristic Sources," in *T&T Clark Handbook of Septuagint Research*, ed. William A. Ross and W. Edward Glenny (New York: Bloomsbury Publishing Plc, 2021), 303.

SEVENTY-TWO SERVANTS OF THE WORD

—*Apologeticum*, chapter 18

It is interesting that Tertullian adds the detail about how the Hebrew originals used for the translation were still publicly available in Alexandria during his time. Tertullian himself also used the Old Testament in its Septuagint form, though it was through a Latin translation made on the basis of the Septuagint.

Origen, A.D. 184–253
Origen takes a distinguished and pre-eminent role with regards to the Septuagint among all the church fathers. He was one among a very tiny minority of church fathers who learned Hebrew, the list being possibly restricted to only him, Jerome, and a few Syriac fathers.[147] His knowledge of Hebrew enabled him to access and use the Hebrew text which circulated in his time. This resulted in Origen being aware, to a much higher degree than Justin Martyr and Irenaeus, of just how great the difference was between the Septuagint and the Proto-Masoretic Text which was common among Rabbinic Jews of his time. Interestingly, though, this did not lead Origen to view the Hebrew text as the authoritative one. In a reply to a letter Origen had received from another Christian, called Africanus, Origen provides a humorous and deeply ironic rebuff to Africanus' questioning of the Septuagint's superiority with regards to the Hebrew texts found in the synagogues. Origen writes, answering Africanus' question about whether one should not rather follow the Hebrew text than the Septuagint when the former differs from the latter:

> And, forsooth, when we notice such things are we forthwith to reject as spurious the copies in use in our churches, and enjoin the brotherhood to put away the sacred books current among them, and to coax the Jews and persuade them to give us copies which shall be untampered with, and free from forgery? Are we to suppose that that Providence which in the sacred Scriptures has ministered to the edification of all the churches of Christ, had no thought for those bought with a price [1 Cor. 6:20], for whom Christ died [Rom. 14:15]; whom, although His Son, God who is love spared not, but gave Him up for us all that with Him He might freely give us all

---
[147] Fernández Marcos, *The Septuagint in Context*, 204.

PART III: THE RECEPTION OF THE SEPTUAGINT BY THE CHURCH

> things [Rom. 8:32]. In all these cases consider whether it would not be well to remember the words, "Thou shalt not remove the ancient landmarks which thy fathers have set."
>
> — *Epistola ad Africanum*, chapter 4

Origen argues that God's divine providence would not allow the Christian church to be without the Word of God, and thus it would therefore also be a fruitless endeavor to go to the synagogue to search for it there when God undoubtedly had preserved Scripture in the church, and not among those who have rejected Christ and been cut off from the olive tree. This motif also seen with Justin Martyr and Irenaeus, of the Jews altering Scripture, is also plainly asserted by Origen.

Origen's credentials for making such statements were much better than for the previous church fathers. For through his knowledge of Hebrew, Origen began a pioneering effort of textual criticism hitherto unseen in the early church. Origen began collecting countless Septuagint manuscripts, Hebrew scrolls, and other Greek translations of the Old Testament, and compared them with a goal of finding different textual variants and readings of the Old Testament Scriptures. The result of this exceptional effort was the Hexapla, which in size and uniqueness is without any parallel in all of antiquity. The work, of which a few fragments have been found, was divided into six large columns, one having the Hebrew consonantal text, the second having a transcribed Greek version of it, including vowel sounds to aid the reading and understanding of the Hebrew consonantal text, and then followed four different Greek editions. First of them, in the third column, was Aquilas' translation, then Symmachus', then the Septuagint itself, and lastly was found the Theodotian translation. The Septuagint's column was equipped with a series of text-critical signs, developed by Alexandrian philologists in the second century B.C., to denote words and passages either found in the Septuagint and lacking in the Masoretic Text, or found in the Masoretic Text and lacking in the Septuagint.

This enormous work of Origen's served many different purposes, as noted by professor Orlinsky. First of all, it enabled the Christian church to learn Hebrew, which the transliterated text greatly helped with as it gave the vowels to the Hebrew consonantal text. Secondly, it also equipped the church in her polemics against the Jews, as the Christian author could now challenge the Jews on the basis of their own Synagogal texts, as well as receiving an overview of the textual variants between the texts,[148] a point which Origen himself is also explicit about, *Epistulam ad Africanum*, in chapter 5.

There has been much controversy as to whether Origen altered or edited the text of the Septuagint as part of his text critical work. This notion should be rejected, however, as Origen himself explicitly denies such a proposition. He writes, "I paid particular attention to the interpretation of the Seventy, lest I might to be found to accredit any forgery to the Churches which are under heaven".[149] In the same text he also adds the following with regard to the purpose of the *Hexapla*, "an effort not to ignore the ones belonging to them; so that when we converse with the Jews, we do not quote to them what is not found in their manuscripts, and so that we can use what they [in turn] show even though not found in our books".[150] The Septuagint scholar Soininen concurs and concludes that the text of the Septuagint left Origen's hands without change *"sowohl inhaltlich als auch sprachlich (both with regard to content and with regard to language)"*.[151] This is also supported by the historical witnesses in the generations following Origen. Rufinus of Aquileia, who translated many of Origen's works from Greek into Latin, said concerning Origen's *Hexapla*:

> Just in the same way, Origen pointed out by certain marks of his own, namely, the signs of asterisks and obeli, which words had been, so to speak, killed by other translators, and those which had been superfluously introduced. But he put in no single word of his own, nor did he make it appear that the certainty of our copies was in any point shaken.
>
> —*Apology against Jerome*, 2:36

Even though Origen knew Hebrew, or maybe because he did, the Septuagint remained as the authoritative and inspired Old Testament text, even when it differed from the Hebrew Text of his time, which he repeatedly states in many of his works, for example in his commentary on Romans.[152] The fame

---

[148] Jellicoe, *The Septuagint and Modern Study*, 108-109.
[149] Origen, *Epistula ad Africanum*, chap. 5.
[150] Origen, *Epistula ad Africanum*, chap. 5.
[151] Jellicoe, *The Septuagint and Modern Study*, 141.
[152] Origen, *Commentary on the Epistle to the Romans*, trans. Thomas P. Scheck, vol. 2, *Fathers of the Church* 104 (Washington, D.C.: Catholic University of America Press, 2002), 8.6–7.

PART III: THE RECEPTION OF THE SEPTUAGINT BY THE CHURCH

of the Hexapla endured long after Origen passed away, and for good reason. The work is calculated, on the basis of the few fragments of it which have been found, to have filled up 6,500 pages divided into 50 volumes[153]. Origen began his work on the Hexapla in Alexandria and finished it around 15 years later in Caesarea[154], where it was accessible in the large library found there. How long it survived is unknown, Jerome himself saw the work and used it when he visited Caesarea in the end of the fourth century, but it most likely perished during the advent of Islam when Kalif Omar ordered the large library of Caesarea to be burned in A.D. 651.[155]

Eusebius of Caesarea, circa A.D. 260–340
Like Origen, Eusebius saw the providence of God as central for the advent of the Septuagint and for its role in preserving the Scriptures in the church since, as he says, God has promised to preserve his word. Eusebius is most widely known for being the first real church historian, and thus he naturally also provides a detailed account of the history of the Septuagint. He is one of the most important sources for our knowledge of the early Jewish reception of the Septuagint, and he shows that he is well acquainted with these early Jewish sources as well. In his work *Praeparatio evangelica* 8:2–15:9 (*Preparation for the Gospel*), he supplies the reader with a paraphrase of large parts of the Letter of Aristeas, which he takes as an eyewitness account of the Septuagint's origin. Eusebius also understands the Septuagint as playing a vital role in salvation history, as it served as a tool of preparation for the arrival of the Gospel, as it was an embodiment of Hellenized Jewish monotheism.[156] He writes:

> When the time was close at hand in which, under the Roman Empire, the salutary preaching concerning our Saviour was destined to shed forth its light upon all men, and there was thus an exceptional and imperative reason why the prophecies concerning Him and the life of the divinely favoured Hebrews of old and the lessons of their pious teaching, which for long ages had been veiled in their country's language, should now at length be transmitted to all the nations, who were to be introduced to the privileges of a

---

[153] Jellicoe, *The Septuagint and Modern Study*, 100-101.
[154] Jellicoe, *The Septuagint and Modern Study*, 100-101.
[155] Jellicoe, *The Septuagint and Modern Study*, 124.
[156] Law, *When God Spoke Greek*, 128.

knowledge of God, God Himself, the author of these benefits, anticipating that future with divine foreknowledge, providentially ordained that the predictions about Him Who was shortly to appear as Saviour of all men and to become for all nations under sun the Teacher of pious worship of the one supreme God, should, by means of an accurate version deposited in public libraries, be revealed to the world and come to the light.

— *Praeparatio Evangelica*, Book VIII, 1

Thus, the Septuagint served as the divinely-ordered instrument by which the promises and prophecies of God were revealed to the Gentiles in preparation for the coming of the Messiah. These prophecies, hitherto hidden in Hebrew robes, were laid bare for all to hear and receive so that they could recognize the Christ, foretold to them by the Seventy, when they met him. In seeing the relevance of the work, Eusebius did not restrict it to some mere utility, but also affirmed it to be more than just a precise translation, as said above, but one directly inspired by God himself.[157]

Cyril of Jerusalem, circa A.D. *313–386*
Cyril of Jerusalem was an important early Greek-speaking father in the East. He served as bishop and patriarch of Jerusalem and is especially known for his 24 preserved *Catechetical Lectures*. In his fourth catechetical lecture, he provides his catechumens with the origin story of the Septuagint, much akin to the one given by the Letter of Aristeas. The divine inspiration of the Septuagint itself is also explicitly affirmed by Cyril, who says that it was not, "contrivance of human devices: but the translation of the Divine Scriptures, spoken by the Holy Ghost, was of the Holy Ghost accomplished" (4:34). The Septuagint itself simply is what Cyril understands by the term Scripture, "Read the Divine Scriptures, the twenty-two books of the Old Testament, these that have been translated by the Seventy-two Interpreters." He also lists all of the canonical books of the Old Testament including 1 and 2 Esdras, which underscores his view of the Septuagint as canonical Scripture (4:35).

Hilary of Poitiers, circa A.D. *315–367*
Hilary was a bishop in Central France and became known as the hammer of the Arians during his lifetime on account of his importance in that

---

[157] Gallagher, "The Septuagint in Patristic Sources," 302, Eusebius, *Church History* 5.8.7.

Christological controversy. He made use of the Latin translation of the Septuagint, the so-called Vetus Latina, though he was also fluent in Greek. In his commentary on the Psalms, he notes that the *"complete authority of the Seventy* [translators] *endures (perfecta horum septuaginta interpretum auctoritas manet)"* (*Tractatus super Psalmos* 2:3). He grounds its authority not only in its age, as it far predates the arrival of Christ, but also in the fact that its authors, the Seventy-Two, were fully taught by Moses in the hidden doctrines of Scripture, *"per Moysen quoque doctrina secretiore perfecti (through Moses, too, the secret doctrine was perfected)."* This last comment, though not explicit, might point toward the Septuagint's role in not only making the Hebrew Scriptures accessible for Greek speakers, but also in explicating vague and ambiguous passages, an issue that will be delved into later. Hilary also presents a canon list in the same work including 1 and 2 Esdras, thus affirming the Septuagint as canonical text.

Epiphanius of Salamis, circa A.D. *315–403*
Epiphanius was a bishop of the Greek island of Cyprus, just north of Egypt, and an author from whom multiple works have survived. In his large, semi-encyclopedic work, *De mensuris et ponderibus*, he provides an extensive exposition of many biblical topics. The Septuagint plays a large role and its origin are described with great detail. In chapters 3 through 11 he provides the, now well known, origin story of the Septuagint, but also adds more details, some of which are unique to Epiphanius. Some of these are less significant, such as that translators apparently had servants available to tend to their earthly needs for food, but some of them are very interesting. Epiphanius writes, to give one example, on the variants in the Hebrew compared to the Septuagint. He says:

> It was such an amazing work of God that it was recognized that these men possessed the gift of the Holy Spirit, because they agreed in translation. And wherever they had added a word all of them had added the same, and where they had made an omission all alike had made the omission. And there was no need for the omitted words, but for those they added there was need.
>
> — *De mensuris et ponderibus*, chapter 6

These comments are interesting insofar as they show that Epiphanius is conscious about the differences between the Hebrew text and the

Septuagint's, yet Epiphanius is explicit about the validity and authority of words found in the Septuagint yet lacking in the Hebrew, sometimes for clarity, sometimes for explanation. Regardless, Epiphanius notes that, insofar as the translators added these words in unison, those words were inspired and added by the Holy Spirit himself.[158] Concerning these additions, he further clarifies in chapter 3, "This may be surprising, but we should not be rash to bring censure, but rather praise that it is according to the will of God that what is sacred should be understood." Thus, like Paul in his exegesis in Galatians, Epiphanius also considers the Septuagint to be inspired and authoritative in itself, even where its exact wording could not be grounded in the Hebrew text alone. This fits well with Epiphanius and other church fathers' view of the Septuagint not just as a translation but also as a revelation and explication of the Hebrew text.

Epiphanius' strong defense of the Septuagint also led him to view the Hebrew texts circulating in his time with skepticism. He directly accuses Aquila of having perverted and altered the text in his translation of the Old Testament (chapter 15), but it is not clear whether Epiphanius thought that only the newer Jewish translations were corrupted or whether he also viewed the Hebrew text circulating among the Jews itself to have suffered corruption.

Philastrius of Brescia, circa A.D. *330–397*
Philastrius was Bishop of Brescia in Northern Italy, and some letters from his hand have survived. In one of them, he complains about the fact that certain Jews and heretics "*spit* [reject] *out the Seventy-two most wise and holy men's translation*" and in its stead use another.[159] In the same letter he also describes that, "it is heretical to again receive the translation of Aquila's thirty men rather than [the translation] of the Seventy-two most blessed men, who, perceiving rightly and inviolately concerning the trinity, handed on the most assured foundation of the catholic church as they interpreted the Scriptures".[160] The Septuagint, then, far from being a mere translation, was the foundation of the church, the rejection of which was rebuked as heretical as it tampered with the ground of the very church itself.

---

[158] Müller, *The First Bible of the Church*, 78.
[159] Filastrius Brixiensis, *Liber Diversarum Hereseon*, ed. Friedrich Marx, vol. 38 of *Corpus Scriptorum Ecclesiasticorum Latinorum* (Vienna: F. Tempsky, 1898), 113.
[160] Brixiensis, *Liber Diversarum Hereseon*, 115.

PART III: THE RECEPTION OF THE SEPTUAGINT BY THE CHURCH

Gregory of Nyssa, circa A.D. *325–394*
This famous Eastern church father, one might naturally add at this point, also used the Septuagint. But he is also worth mentioning as he bears witness to the patristic tradition concerning the alterations of Scripture by the Jews. In his commentary on Psalms 2:8–9, he notes how the Jewish scribes have removed certain Messianic characteristics from the Hebrew text[161]. One should rather follow the unaltered text of the Septuagint than the adulterated Jewish one (*On the Inscriptions of the Psalms* 2:8).

Rufinus of Aquileia, circa A.D. *345–412*
Rufinus was a monk, theologian, historian, and well-known translator of Greek works of theology into Latin. He also used the Septuagint and was an avid defender of it. This led him to sharply rebuke the contemporaneous writer Jerome, who was the first major figure who tried to break with the patristic consensus regarding the Septuagint.

Rufinus argued for the superiority of the Septuagint in many ways. He pointed out that the large number of Jews that converted to Christianity in the earliest days of the church had all used the Septuagint, as did the ancient church itself, which they would not have done had they viewed the proto-Masoretic text as the inspired and more authoritative one (*Apology against Jerome* 2:33). Rufinus likewise states that this is not true only of Jews in former times, but also among those of his own and Jerome's time, for he writes that in:

> Jerusalem, a plentiful supply of men who being born Jews have become Christians; and their perfect acquaintance with both languages and their sufficient knowledge of the law is shown by their administration of the pontifical office. In all this abundance of learned men, has there been one who has dared to make havoc of the divine record handed down to the Churches by the Apostles and the deposit of the Holy Spirit?
> —*Apology against Jerome* 2:33

In the same chapter he also adds, directed against Jerome:

---

[161] Gallagher, "The Septuagint in Patristic Sources," 307.

SEVENTY-TWO SERVANTS OF THE WORD

The seventy translators, each in their separate cells, produced a version couched in consonant and identical words, under the inspiration, as we cannot doubt, of the Holy Spirit; and this version must certainly be of more authority with us than a translation made by a single man under the inspiration of Barabbas.

— *Apology against Jerome* 2:33

In these poignant words, and in the following paragraphs, Rufinus argues against the efforts of Jerome and his solo project.

Jerome wished to translate the Old Testament into Latin from the Hebrew texts he had received from the Synagogue, where he had also acquired his skills in Hebrew that "under the inspiration of Barabbas." Could the abilities of this one private individual best the wisdom of Seventy-Two learned Jews, chosen by the High Priest of Jerusalem, and inspired by the Holy Spirit himself? Rufinus thought not. He also pointed to the great work done in Rome by Peter and Paul during the apostolic time. Rufinus asks, could not these two men, who had received the gift of tongues and languages, have made a reliable translation of the Old Testament, as Jerome himself had claimed that he had done, if the two apostles had found the Septuagint wanting? As Jerome had accused it of being. The fact that they did not do so, but that they rather committed the Septuagint to the church in Rome, is a strong reminder to all the churches under heaven to listen to the holy apostles rather than the novelties of the solitary monk Jerome. Rufinus sharply asks:

Is it conceivable that they could not foresee through the Spirit that a time would come, after nearly four hundred years, when the church would find out that the Apostles had not delivered to them the truth of the old Testament, and would send an embassy to those whom the apostles spoke of as the circumcision, begging and beseeching them to dole out to them some small portion of the truth which was in their possession: and that the Church would through this embassy confess that she had been for all those four hundred years in error?

— *Apology against Jerome* 2:35

PART III: THE RECEPTION OF THE SEPTUAGINT BY THE CHURCH

Further criticizing the novelties of Jerome's break with the church's tradition, Rufinus points out the danger and the audacity Jerome possesses when he tries to teach contrary to the universal witness of the church, even calling Jerome's move a crime against Scripture and the church,

> Perhaps it was a greater piece of audacity to alter the books of the divine Scriptures which had been delivered to the Churches of Christ by the Apostles to be a complete record of their faith by making a new translation under the influence of the Jews (...) And what are we to do when we are told that the books which bear the names of the Hebrew Prophets and lawgivers are to be had from you in a truer form than that which was approved by the Apostles? How, I ask, is this mistake to be set right, or rather, how is this crime to be expiated? We hold it a thing worthy of condemnation that a man should have put forth some strange opinions in the interpretation of the law of God; but to pervert the law itself and make it different from that which the Apostles handed down to us,—how many times over must this be pronounced worthy of condemnation? To the daring temerity of this act we may much more justly apply your words: Which of all the wise and holy men who have gone before you has dared to put his hand to that work? Which of them would have presumed thus to profane the book of God, and the sacred words of the Holy Spirit? Who but you would have laid hands upon the divine gift and the inheritance of the Apostles?
>
> —*Apology against Jerome* 2:32

Finally, Rufinus also beseeches Jerome to consider how the non-Christian world of Pagans and Jews would ridicule the Christians if they were to discard the Scriptures used for 400 years and exchange it for a new text. The confusion and scandal caused by such a change would be a grave blow to the credibility of the church. Rufinus writes:

> But this emendation of the Seventy, what are we to think of it? Is it not evident, how greatly the grounds for the heathens' unbelief have been increased by this proceeding? For they take notice of what is going on amongst us. They know that our law has been amended, or at least changed; and do you suppose they do not say among themselves, These

people are wandering at random, they have no fixed truth among them, for you see how they make amendments and corrections in their laws whenever they please, and indeed it is evident that there must have been previous error where amendment has supervened, and that things which undergo change at the hand of man cannot possibly be divine. (...) Now therefore after four hundred years the truth of the law comes forth for us, it has been bought with money from the Synagogue.

— *Apology against Jerome* 2:35

John Chrysostom, circa A.D. 349–407

The famous church father John Chrysostom served as bishop and patriarch in Constantinople and left us a written corpus far exceeding that of all other Eastern church fathers. He also taught and preached from the Septuagint, which he saw as a product of God's salvific providence. In his commentary on Genesis 4:4, he writes that the Septuagint was the exposition of the words of God so that the whole world might be able to read them,[162] and that the translation carried out under Ptolemy was a "work of divine providence".[163] In his commentary on Matthew 5:2, he also notes that the Jews altered the Hebrew text so as to be able to deny the prophecy concerning the virgin birth from Isaiah 7:14.[164] In his work *Adversus Judaeos* 1:6, he shortly summarizes the origin of the Septuagint, which he is aware of, though he does not describe it at length.

Jerome, circa A.D. 347–420

With the arrival of the monk, priest, and translator Jerome, the groundwork began to be laid by which the replacement of the Septuagint by the Masoretic Text would be built on, thereby breaking one of the few broad consensuses of the early church. His translation of the Old Testament, based on a Jewish Synagogal text very closely related to the Masoretic Text, would, in the centuries following, replace the Septuagint in the Western church and in the end become the sole text type during the Medieval era up until the advent of the Reformation almost 1,000 years later.

This radical break with the received tradition was a result of developments in the thought of Jerome. In his early career as an

---

[162] Müller, *The First Bible of the Church*, 77.
[163] Robert C. Hill, *Fathers of the Church: Saint John Chrysostom: Homilies on Genesis 1-17* (Washington, D.C.: Catholic University of America Press, 1986), 56.
[164] Hill, *Fathers of the Church*, 56.

PART III: THE RECEPTION OF THE SEPTUAGINT BY THE CHURCH

ecclesiastical writer, he supported the use of the Septuagint, which he viewed as a *truthful interpretation (vera interpretation)* that had been used by the apostles themselves.[165] But as time progressed, he began to view the Hebrew text more positively, which he denoted as the *true Hebrew/authentic Hebrew (hebraica veritas)*. This change of mind was caused by different misunderstandings embraced by Jerome. He judged the Septuagint to have translated many passages of Scripture mistakenly and even to have purposefully hidden away or obscured messianic prophecies on account of King Ptolemy.[166] This first misunderstanding could possibly have been caused by an assumption, which was and still is quite common, that there was a one-to-one relationship between the Synagogical text of the Jews of his time and that of the Hebrew texts used by the Seventy-Two, an assumption now known to be grossly mistaken. He also arrived at the belief that the apostles and Christ himself had cited and used the Masoretic Text and not the Septuagint,[167] a belief which is demonstrably false.[168] Lastly, he regarded the origin story of the Septuagint as mythical, pointing toward how certain details in the story common in his day were lacking in the earlier historical sources.[169] Jerome began viewing the Seventy-Two merely as knowledgeable translators but not as prophets. There was thus nothing inspired about the Septuagint.[170]

This profound attitude shift would have a revolutionary impact on Jerome's role as a Bible translator. In the early A.D. 380s, Jerome was commissioned by Damasus, the Bishop of Rome, to make a new translation. This translation was to be either of the Gospels and the Psalms or of the whole Scriptures, both the Old and New Testaments[171]—the sources differ somewhat on this point. The Bishop of Rome commissioned Jerome to make a new translation because there were major issues with the Latin Scriptures in circulation. The textual transmission was rather unstable, which had led to many different variants appearing in both Testaments. The style and language of the Latin translations of the New Testament and of the Septuagint, the so-called *Vetus Latina*, left much to be desired.

---

[165] Müller, *The First Bible of the Church*, 83.
[166] Müller, *The First Bible of the Church*, 84-85,
[167] Müller, *The First Bible of the Church*, 85.
[168] Law, *When God Spoke Greek*, 158.
[169] Müller, *The First Bible of the Church*, 86.
[170] Jellicoe, *The Septuagint and Modern Study*, 46-47.
[171] Law, *When God Spoke Greek*, 156.

Thus, Jerome began his great enterprise, at first as a faithful custodian of the received tradition, for which reason he used the Septuagint as the textual basis for his new translation. He continued studiously and dutifully in his effort, eventually completing a new Latin translation of the whole Book of Psalms as well as of the book of Job. As discussed earlier, his translation of Psalms quickly became popular both on account of its beauty in style and its faithfulness to the Septuagint text, and though he would later finish a translation of the Book of Psalms based on the Synagogal text, this translation never managed to replace his earlier translation of the Septuagint, which remained in use as part of the Latin Vulgate throughout the medieval era and beyond.

It was in all likelihood during his translation work that Jerome started to doubt the validity of using the Septuagint. As he gathered different manuscripts of the Septuagint to translate from, he was met with different variants in some passages. Frustrated by this, he thought that this issue could be solved if he acquired Hebrew manuscripts with which he could compare them, using the Hebrew as a touchstone by which the Septuagint manuscripts could be tested. This was the concept of the *hebraica veritas*.

Thus, he made the cardinal error of equating his contemporaneous Synagogal manuscript with the original Vorlage of the Septuagint, an error many following him would likewise make. But unknown to him, these manuscripts were much unlike the ancient Hebrew texts, as discussed earlier. Interestingly, he also moved far beyond his commissioned task, which was to make a new translation of the Septuagint, yet Jerome would in the end finish a translation of a text he was not ecclesiastically sanctioned to do.

Around A.D. 385, Jerome was cast out of Rome after being found guilty of uncanonical behavior, though it should be added that some sources have disputed the justice of the judicial process.[172] Jerome, embittered over his involuntary exile from Rome, took residence in Bethlehem where he would in time acquire a knowledge of Hebrew.[173] Here he also began, having become self-aware of his unique abilities, of boasting "about his unrivaled knowledge of Palestine, and that put him in a unique position over those who could only read of the place".[174] Jerome took on the role of a teacher, whose unique insight and knowledge of Hebrew, his access to the Hebraic

---

[172] Law, *When God Spoke Greek*, 156.
[173] Law, *When God Spoke Greek*, 157.
[174] Law, *When God Spoke Greek*, 156.

PART III: THE RECEPTION OF THE SEPTUAGINT BY THE CHURCH

manuscripts, and his knowledge of the Judaic context enabled him to reject the authority of the Septuagint. He believes that he could do so because it did not agree with the Hebrew texts he had received from the Synagogues in Roman Palestine. These were texts which he alone could access, and no one could examine him on his judgments because his knowledge of Hebrew was so unique in his time, thus giving him an extraordinary position of power in the ancient church. Professor Law describes it this way, *"to Christians who could not read Hebrew, it was an argument that would have won Jerome favor as one who possessed the key to a mysterious treasure."*[175] Therefore Jerome, after having used the Septuagint as his translation basis for a couple of years, changed his mind and exchanged it for a Synagogal text sometime during the A.D. 390s.

The text that he received was given to him by the religious communities of Rabbinical Jews, and his translation also bears witness to having been carried out by one taught by the Rabbinical Jews. The style and phrasing bears strong resemblance to contemporaneous Rabbinical exegesis. One of the more well-known examples of this is found in Jerome's translation of Exodus 34:29, which describes Moses' descent from Mount Sinai where "the appearance of the skin of his face was made glorious" according to the Septuagint, yet Jerome translated it as "his face having been horned".[176] The Hebrew consonantal text is actually compatible with both readings as the root ק-ר-נ (Q-R-N) can be read as either *qaran (shining with glory)* or *qeren (horned)*. Thus, in all likelihood, Jerome was taught by the Rabbinical Jews, whose own knowledge of Hebrew had deteriorated during the centuries after Hebrew ceased to be a commonly spoken language. This meant that many words had been forgotten, among them being the more uncommon gloss of ק-ר-נ as *shining* rather than *horned*. Thus also the Jew Aquila, translating around 300 years after the Seventy-Two, and around 270 years before Jerome, also translated it "his face skin became horned".[177] Jerome thus followed in the footsteps of his Jewish teachers and repeated their mistakes. Had he read Origen's rhetorical question to Africanus, it would seem likely that he would have answered with an unabashed *yes*.

In this manner, then, Jerome became the great innovator who—with the exception of some Syriac-speaking Christians—on account of having

---

[175] Law, *When God Spoke Greek*, 159.
[176] Law, *When God Spoke Greek*, 160.
[177] John William Wevers, *Notes on the Greek Text of Exodus*, Septuagint and Cognate Studies Series 30 (Atlanta, GA: Scholars Press, 1990). 383.

mastered Hebrew, was unilaterally emboldened to push the Septuagint from off its time-honored throne in the church and to put the Masoretic Text of the Synagogue, dressed in beautiful Latin robes, in its place. The discontinuity this break with tradition caused can hardly be exaggerated. Professor Law described the change in this way, "it was the first time in Christian history that a Bible other than or not based on the Septuagint was promoted for use in the church. For four hundred years most Christians had heard and read from the Septuagint and its daughter translations".[178] Such a bold move would not pass by without great controversy, and, far from being alone, many church fathers other than Rufinus raised their voices in objection against Jerome's departure from the Christian consensus.

Augustine of Hippo, A.D. 354–430
The Roman and North African theologian and bishop Augustine stands, in all likelihood, only second to Paul himself as the most influential Christian theologian. In the enormous textual corpus preserved from his productive literary activity, one finds a broad range of topics treated. The issue of the Septuagint, its role with regard to canonicity, and the effects of Jerome's new translation were also treated with great consideration by Augustine himself. In Augustine's authorship, a well-developed synthesis of Origen's and Eusebius' view of the Septuagint can be found. Like Origen before him, Augustine too, was keenly aware of the differences between the Septuagint and the Hebrew text.

> We are right in believing that the translators of the Septuagint had received the spirit of prophecy; and so if, with its authority, they altered anything and used expressions in their translation different from those of the original, we should not doubt that these expressions also were divinely inspired.
>
> — *City of God* 15:23

Augustine clearly confessed not only the divine inspiration of the Septuagint but likewise affirmed its authority, even where it was thought to deviate from the Hebrew text. In his work *On Christian Teaching* he lays out the same idea:

---

[178] Wevers, *Notes on the Greek Text of Exodus*, 161.

PART III: THE RECEPTION OF THE SEPTUAGINT BY THE CHURCH

> Wherefore, even if anything is found in the original Hebrew in a different form from that in which these men [the Seventy-Two] have expressed it, I think we must give way to the dispensation of Providence which used these men to bring it about, that books which the Jewish race were unwilling, either from religious scruple or from jealousy, to make known to other nations.
>
> — *On Christian Teaching* 2:15,25

Here, the theme of the role of the Septuagint as part of the providential plan of salvation is presented, as seen also with Eusebius, with both notions working together to underscore the pre-eminent position of the Septuagint.

In his later works, a development in Augustine's thought with regard to the Septuagint comes forth. Not that anything is taken away from his high view of the Septuagint, yet the role of the Hebrew texts is made more noteworthy. Augustine remained firm that no alterations could be made to the Septuagint, yet he considered the Hebrew text to be able to shed light in the Christian's understanding of the Septuagint, thus providing the Hebrew text with a form of peculiar importance. This duality is aptly demonstrated in Augustine's commentary on Zechariah 12:10, which in the Septuagint reads, "they shall look upon me because they have mocked me," yet in the Masoretic Text reads, "They shall look upon me whom they have pierced." Here Augustine notes that the text of the Septuagint is most fitting as *"they have mocked me"* encompasses the whole passion of Christ, from his arrest, interrogation, torture, crowning with thorns, crucifixion, and more, yet he also points to the usefulness of the Hebrew text, which *"more plainly"* indicates the crucifixion of Christ (*City of God* 20:30,3).

This dual approach to the Old Testament can be seen in different places within Augustine's writings, and thus he concludes that both are divine and inspired (*City of God* 18:44,1). This being said, it is difficult to ascertain to what degree Augustine was aware that the Hebrew text circulating in his time, the proto-Masoretic Text, did not reflect the earlier Hebrew texts, such as those used by the Seventy-Two, or possibly those circulating earlier than the second century B.C. and prior. Augustine does not draw any explicit conclusion as to whether or not the Hebrew text contemporaneous with him correctly matched that used by the Seventy-Two, yet he is aware that different "copyist's error[s]" are present. Despite the usefulness of the Hebrew text, then, the Septuagint itself remains the gold standard by which these differences are settled and doctrine is made.

SEVENTY-TWO SERVANTS OF THE WORD

> But that discrepancy of numbers [here discussing the different ages in the genealogies of Genesis] which is found to exist between our own and the Hebrew text does not touch the longevity of the ancients; and if there is any diversity so great that both versions cannot be true, we must take our ideas of the real facts from that text out of which our own version has been translated [i.e. the Septuagint, from which Augustine's Old Testament, the Vetus Latina, was translated]. However, though any one who pleases has it in his power to correct this version [I.d. the Old Latin], yet it is not unimportant to observe that no one has presumed to emend the Septuagint from the Hebrew text in the many places where they seem to disagree. For this difference has not been reckoned a falsification; and for my own part I am persuaded it ought not to be reckoned so.
>
> — *City of God* 15:14.2

Augustine, though appreciating and using the Hebrew text many times, constantly reminds his readers of the unrivaled authority and lofty pre-eminence of the Septuagint. This text was simply *the* text of the church according to Augustine. Though there also were other texts and translations, "the Church has received this Septuagint translation just as if it were the only one" (18:43.1), and again, though being fully aware of Jerome's new translation, he writes admonishingly:

> The churches of Christ judge that no one [having just mentioned Jerome's individual translation] should be preferred to the authority of so many men [the Seventy Two], chosen for this very great work by Eleazar, who was then high priest; for even if there had not appeared in them one spirit, without doubt divine, and the seventy learned men had, after the manner of men, compared together the words of their translation, that what pleased them all might stand, no single translator ought to be preferred to them; but since so great a sign of divinity has appeared in them, certainly, if any other translator, of their Scriptures from the Hebrew into any other tongue is faithful, in that case he agrees with these seventy translators, and if he is not found to agree with them, then we ought to believe that the prophetic gift is with them. For the same Spirit who was in the prophets when they spoke these things was

PART III: THE RECEPTION OF THE SEPTUAGINT BY THE CHURCH

> also in the seventy men when they translated them, so that assuredly they could also say something else, just as if the prophet himself had said both, because it would be the same Spirit who said both.
>
> — *City of God* 18:34

The clarity of Augustine's exhortation is hard to miss as "no single translator ought to be preferred to them" cannot be read as anything but a warning against Jerome's novel endeavor, which ventured away from the Septuagint that, according to Augustine, was the very touchstone for translation precision and Scriptural truth.

Jerome, however, ignored Augustine's pleas. *City of God* was begun around A.D. 410 and published around A.D. 426, when Jerome's Vulgate had been in circulation for some time. Jerome, though, did not take up the glove thrown him by Augustine. This was not the first time he had warned Jerome against his troubling endeavor. Already around A.D. 394, Augustine had tried to write him a personal letter beseeching him to cease his work with the Masoretic Text.[179] In this letter, he expresses his deep skepticism to Jerome who, if he wanted to make a new translation, ought to follow Origen's method and translate the Septuagint and, at most, mark those words or variants present in the Hebrew text but lacking in the Septuagint with text-critical signs. Changing the text of the Septuagint was not an option at all for, Augustine asks rhetorically, could a sole translator dare to interpret the Hebrew text alone and conjure up a different meaning than the inspired Seventy-Two authors? Augustine says that the Hebrew texts are "either obscure or plain: if they were obscure, it is believed that you are as likely to have been mistaken as the others; if they were plain, it is not believed that they [the Seventy-Two] could possibly have been mistaken".[180]

Jerome never replied to Augustine's letter. So, Augustine tried again and sent one more letter, yet to no avail. Jerome kept ignoring him. Augustine however, aware of the importance of the question, did not relinquish trying. Some years later, around A.D. 403, he tried again and wrote a third letter to Jerome and attached the first letter to it in case Jerome had failed to receive the original letter. Here he warned with even larger letters writing, as a bishop to a monk, "I would much rather that you would

---

[179] Wevers, *Notes on the Greek Text of Exodus*, 163.
[180] Jerome, *Epistula* 28, chap. 2.

furnish us with a translation of the Greek version of the canonical Scriptures known as the work of the Seventy translators" (*Epistula* 71,4).

Ever mindful of charity, Augustine bolstered his entreaty with multiple arguments. First of all, he warned that Jerome's choice to depart from the Septuagint, which was the text of the whole church, would give cause to scandal and division between the Latin and the Greek-speaking churches since, if Jerome's translation became common, then the Latin-speaking church would have a different Old Testament text than the East. Secondly, Augustine pointed toward how suspect it was to use a translation made by a single individual from a language virtually unknown. The Septuagint, said Augustine, was made by Seventy-Two learned men guided by the Holy Spirit, yet Jerome's solo project could only be as good as his Jewish teachers taught him to make it. His translation would be a mere human endeavor which could not be verified by anyone in the church. Augustine strongly cautioned Jerome against placing himself into such a powerful position, "it will seem as if your presence were indispensable, as being the only one who could refute their view [if someone challenged the translation]; and it would be a miracle if one could be found capable of acting as arbiter between you and them" (*Epistula* 71,4).

Thirdly, Augustine shares a story about how Jerome's novel translation had alienated the laity, as its choice of words was foreign to the Septuagint's words, which were "old familiar to the senses and memory of all the worshipers, and had been chanted for so many generations in the church" (*Epistula* 71,5). This had angered the congregation, who rejected Jerome's Vulgate as false since it strayed from the Septuagint. The bishop, who had used the translation during the service, then had to go—with great shame it is implied—to the Jewish Synagogue to coax the Jews to validate the truthfulness of the translation. This was, as Origen had written centuries before, unacceptable. That the Word of God should thus be submitted to the approval and validation of the Synagogue's Jews was unacceptable. Quite surprisingly, in this case though, they actually replied that the Septuagint was more precise than Jerome's Vulgate, though Augustine, underscoring the repugnant situation, doubts whether the Jews replied "from ignorance or from spite." The damage had been done, and Augustine rhetorically asks, "what further need I say?"

Christian unity and the church's guardianship of the divine Scriptures cannot stand subject to Synagogal sanctioning. This view found explicit expression among Origen and Rufinus and, implicitly, among many other

PART III: THE RECEPTION OF THE SEPTUAGINT BY THE CHURCH

church fathers. Augustine ends his letter by praising the quality of Jerome's translation of the New Testament "because in almost every passage we have found nothing to object to, when we compared it with the Greek Scriptures", and with a repetition of his request to "confer upon us (...) an exact Latin translation of the Greek Septuagint."

The debate continued with Jerome finally replying after having received a third letter. He writes, rather irately, and complains about having received hostile questions from Augustine. When beginning to reply to Augustine he, surprisingly and quite groundlessly, accuses him of not knowing the issue at hand, writing to him "that you seem to me not to understand the matter." Jerome, rather than dealing Augustine's concerns, goes on the offensive, calling Augustine a "partisan of the Seventy translators" and, in a roundabout way, criticizes him for not using a better Latin manuscript of the Septuagint. Quite an odd reply, given that Augustine requested a faithful translation of the Septuagint exactly because he wished to receive a better text of the Septuagint superior to the less stable Vetus Latina he was relying on. The debate did not end there and continued, however the chance for a constructive and thoughtful discussion of Jerome's unparalleled choice of action most likely did end there.

CONCLUSION

Certain important clues prove decisive when trying to ascertain the ancient Scriptural canon. In many English translations of the church's ancient canon, the phrase *Liber Esdrae/Hesdrae* is often translated as *the Book of Ezra*. This is not correct, though, and is at best mistaken and at worst highly anachronistic and misleading. As noticed above, exemplified by Augustine and affirmed by Professor Gallagher, the book of Ezra and the books of Esdras cannot be equated. This is further proved by Jerome himself who, in his preface to his Biblical books translated out of the Masoretic Text, distinguishes between them. Noting this detail helps decipher the ancient witnesses of the church with regard to support for either the Masoretic Text or the Septuagint.

The early councils of the church ought also to be emphasized as the church collectively, when either in local or provincial unity, such as North Africa or Italy, the views of the attending bishops from that area are expressed. Above that of the local councils, great consideration must be given to the wording of the Ecumenical Council of Nicaea, being the first declaration of conjoined Christendom. Here the council shows a clear dependence on the Septuagint, not just in general but also in particular when there is divergence from the Masoretic Text. The old rule of *Lex credenda lex orandi* (*the law of prayer is the law of belief*) thus also plays a supportive role notably in the West even after the publication of the Vulgate. The Book of Psalms, being the beating heart of most Christian's devotional life, largely formative for the liturgy, and important for the personal spiritual life of the believer, remained fixed through the ancient and medieval church and was never supplanted by Jerome's Hebrew psalter.

The supremacy of the Septuagint and its role as authoritative and ecclesiastical text for the whole Christian church is further supported by an examination of the patristic witnesses, who affirm its pre-eminence as *the* authoritative Old Testament. This is an agreement that is so demonstrable that it seems to be one of the few patristic consensuses found in the first half millennium of the ancient church. Here, the famous dictum of Tertullian should be quoted, "*iam hinc praeiudicatum sit id esse, verum quodcunque primum, id esse adulterum quodcunque posterius*",[181] that is, "what is first must be true, and what is afterward, false," and, first of all Scriptures, presented by the apostles and Christ, was the Septuagint.

---

[181] Tertullian, *Adversus Praxean* 2.

AN OUTLINE OF THE EARLY MODERN RECEPTION OF THE SEPTUAGINT

he Reformational zeal for the Scriptures and the need for vernacular translations ushered in a renewed interest in the Septuagint. Not so much on account of a perceived superiority in regard to textual issues, but rather for its invaluable role in clarifying Greek semantics and grammar. As Melanchthon wrote, "Scripture cannot be understood theologically if one has not first understood it grammatically".[182] Here, the Septuagint stood as a fountain spring in the scholarly and theological movement *ad fontes* (*to the primary sources in their original languages*) and toward this end the Septuagint served as a gateway to the Greek of the New Testament.

But the eagerness for a renewed return to the original sources sadly brought some less than useful consequences with it as well, chief of which was the reaffirmation of the supremacy of the Masoretic Text which by far was, and still continues to be, the majority position among the different Roman Catholic traditions—whether through the Clementine Vulgate or newer translations made directly from the Masoretic Text—and Protestant traditions. This choice was made on a quite mistaken assumption, as Professor Law writes:

> When the Reformers and their predecessors talked about returning to the original Hebrew (ad fontes!!), and when modern Christians talk about studying the Hebrew because it is the "original text," they are perpetuating in those statements several mistaken assumptions. The Hebrew Bible in the editions we now use is often not the oldest form of the Hebrew text, and in fact it is not a singular text at all but an amalgamation of similar though not identical sources. In many cases the Septuagint provides the only access we have to the oldest form. Our modern editions of the Hebrew Bible contain a text that was more or less established in the second century CE.[183]

---

[182] Fernández Marcos, *The Septuagint in Context*, 16.
[183] Law, *When God Spoke Greek*, 6.

Though this continued to be the most common approach undergirding most Lutheran, Anglican, Reformed, and Roman Catholic biblical scholarship, as it will be shown, the patristic viewpoint never became fully extinguished, though it mostly remained a marginal viewpoint. One such indirect manner is seen in the Lutheran tradition, where the Septuagint served as the textual basis for the translation of the deuterocanonical books which remained in the German vernacular Bible translated by, among others, Luther himself. Luther even kept parts of the canonical books, such as Daniel, which were found in the Septuagint but lacking in the Masoretic Text, such as the Song of the Three Children from Daniel.

For the Old Testament text in general, Luther made use of a printed edition of the Hebrew Masoretic Text published in Brescia around 1494, and thus followed the precedent set by Jerome and the Medieval Church. Yet Luther did not do so consistently, as is clearly seen in his translation of the Book of Psalms. Here, Luther drew heavily on the text of the Septuagint, with one scholar noting how, out of the Hebrew text, the Latin Vulgate, and the Septuagint, it is:

> ...exceedingly difficult to assign to any of these three the position of basis, subordinating thereby the others to the rank of auxiliary. Nor is it possible to say that any one of the three was consistently used as a check, or that the revision was undertaken at the hand of one or the other. The original draft and the revised manuscript as it went to press were moreover the result of a collating of the three versions before the translator. After a comparison of the three, the author accepted those readings which appeared to him the true ones regardless of the Psalter in which they happened to be found. Luther's resulting Psalter is not a translation of the Hebrew Psalter, nor is it a translation of the Hebrew Psalter corrected from the Vulgate, nor vice versa.[184]

Luther's use of the Septuagint resulted in a final translation of the Psalms which often reflected the wording of the Septuagint rather than of the Masoretic Text. It should also be noted that, during the translation work of the Old Testament carried out by Luther, Melanchthon, Bugenhagen, Justus Jonas, Creutziger, Aurogallus, and Rörer, that Melanchthon would bring his

---

[184] Edward Henry Lauer, "Luther's Translation of the Psalms in 1523-24," *The Journal of English and Germanic Philology* 14, no. 1 (1915), https://doi.org/10.2307/27700635, 15.

PART III: THE RECEPTION OF THE SEPTUAGINT BY THE CHURCH

copy of the Septuagint along every time they met as a resource for clarifying and understand the Hebrew text.[185] Melanchthon was actually partly himself involved in the publication of the Septuagint. The Aldine Septuagint—the first whole Greek Bible in Western Europe since the ancient church—was edited by Aldus Manutius, with Erasmus' New Testament and the Septuagint as the Old Testament. It was quickly picked up by the Protestants and became popular in many Reformational centers. Thus the Aldine Septuagint was printed in Strasbourg in 1526, in Basel in 1545, and again in Frankfurt in 1597 It was to this second edition that Melanchthon himself had written the preface.[186]

Thus, though Luther's German Bible was translated from the Hebrew Masoretic Text, it cannot be said that it was consistently only translated from the Masoretic Text, and the influence of the Septuagint is seen through both Old and New Testament. This influence is seen sometimes indirectly through style by explication of the Hebrew, or directly in following the very wording of the Septuagint's readings that are absent from the Masoretic Text, not only in the Book of Psalms but also in other books.[187] It should also be noted that Luther chose to follow the book ordering and naming conventions of the Septuagint, shared too by the Vulgate, rather than using those of the Masoretic Text.[188] A bit digressive but worth mentioning is the fact that Luther himself rejected the Masoretic vowel points and signs as later rabbinical additions,[189] though this view was almost wholly given up during the period of Confessional Orthodoxy. Perhaps this helps to explain Luther's openness to the correction of the vague Hebrew consonantal text

---

[185] Magne Sæbø et al., *Hebrew Bible / Old Testament: The History of Its Interpretation* (Vandenhoeck & Ruprecht, 2008), 400.

[186] Alison G. Salvesen and Timothy Michael Law, eds., *The Oxford Handbook of the Septuagint* (Oxford University Press, 2021), 38.

[187] Erik T Lundeen, "Luther's Messianic Translations of the Hebrew Bible," *Lutheran Quarterly* 34, no. 1 (January 1, 2020), https://doi.org/10.1353/lut.2020.0004, 33/

[188] Sæbø et al., *Hebrew Bible / Old Testament*, 400.

[189] Møgens Müller, "Septuaginta Som Udfordring Til Den Bibelske Kanon," *Religionsvidenskabeligt Tidsskrift* 73, no. 73 (June 22, 2022), https://doi.org/10.7146/rt.vi73.132568, 100, who quotes the following passage, "Zu Luther's Zeiten, ja eine geraume Zeit nachher, war es gar nicht bedenklich, die hebräischen Vocale und Accente nicht mit dem übrigen Text für gleichzeitig, sondern für eine spätere Erfindung der Rabbinen zu erklären, die also als ein bloß menschliches Werk zu betrachten, und als solches der Prüfung zu unterwerfen, und danach zu billigen und beizubehalten, oder zu mißbilligen, und im Fall der Noth abzuändern wäre". From Meyer, Gottlob Wilhelm, 1804 Geschichte der Schrifterklärung seit der Wiederherstellung der Wissenschaften 1-5, bind 3, Göttingen: Johann Friedrich Röwer.

The early Reformation figure Ulrich Zwingli, 1484–1531, who, chiefly through his successor Bullinger, would influence Reformed thought and theology, must also be mentioned. Though many of Zwingli's thoughts and ideas would become common among later Reformed theologians, his view of the Septuagint would not. He had a peculiarly high view of the Septuagint, sometimes even embracing its supremacy against the Masoretic Text. An example of this is seen in his preface to the book of Isaiah, where he states that the Septuagint is a more reliable witness to the words of Isaiah than the Masoretic Text is, which had been corrupted by the Jews.[190]

THE SEPTUAGINT AND TEXT CRITICISM AMONG THE PROTESTANTS

The famous early Reformed Dutch scholar Johannes Drusius, 1550–1616, in following the dictum of Melanchthon, that Scripture cannot be understood theologically if one has not first understood it grammatically, helped popularize the Septuagint as an interpretative key to the Greek of the New Testament. He relied on its peculiar use of Greek and its idiom in tracking down the source from which the apostles were quoting the Old Testament, and how their vocabulary was to be understood.[191]

In the second generation of Reformers, a thorough knowledge of the Septuagint was prerequisite to the polemical debates across confessional lines. The Septuagint served as an anchor-point for clarifying the meaning and semantic range of different terms and concepts employed in the New Testament. Thus, the Septuagint was referred to and quoted extensively by John Calvin in his work, *Institutes of the Christian Religion*, to explain and to gain the exact sense of vital concepts such as to justify, to worship, and more.[192] Calvin did view the Masoretic Text as the authoritative one, yet the Roman Cardinal Robert Bellarmine, whose view will be examined later, points out some interesting examples where Calvin corrects the Hebrew text with reference to the Septuagint and the New Testament's quotations.[193]

---

[190] Sæbø et al., *Hebrew Bible / Old Testament*, 485.
[191] William A. Ross and W. Edward Glenny, *T&T Clark Handbook of Septuagint Research* (Bloomsbury Publishing, 2021), 351.
[192] John Calvin, *Institutes of the Christian Religion*, trans. Henry Beveridge (Grand Rapids, MI: Christian Classics Ethereal Library, 1845), 675.
[193] Müller, "Septuaginta Som Udfordring Til Den Bibelske Kanon," 99, and Robert Bellarmine, *De Controversiis Christianae Fidei* (Book II, chap. 2).

PART III: THE RECEPTION OF THE SEPTUAGINT BY THE CHURCH

Likewise in the Lutheran tradition, important figures like Martin Chemnitz, 1522–1586, made use of the Septuagint in defining terms multiple times in many of his works.[194] In his writings, a deep awareness of the Septuagint and an acknowledgement of its importance is also explicitly displayed. Chemnitz affirmed that it was the edition of the Old Testament used by the apostles themselves, though he does reject it having authority over the Masoretic Text.[195] He brings forth the example of the use of the Septuagint as a proof of the usefulness and ancient pedigree of vernacular translations:

> The apostles made very much use of the Greek translation of the Old Testament. Therefore the custom of translating the sacred books into other native and popular languages was approved by the Son of God Himself and by the apostles. Indeed, God did not so set apart only one certain language for the Holy Scripture that it is a sin to translate it into other native and popular languages, so that whatever of the heavenly doctrine God wanted written down in either Hebrew or Greek could be read and understood by all. For God wants all men to be saved and to come to the knowledge of the truth. Thus the eunuch of the queen of Ethiopia in Acts 8 read the prophet Isaiah not in the Hebrew language but in the Greek translation.[196]

Johan Gerhard, 1582–1637, though agreeing with Chemnitz on the status of the Masoretic Text as the authoritative text of the Old Testament, presents a more positive view of the Septuagint. He includes a longer discussion of it in his large tome *On Interpreting Sacred Scripture*, the first section of his massive work *Loci Theologici*. Here, Gerhard includes a large amount of the patristic witnesses praising the Septuagint and presents Augustine's commentary on the inspired status of the Septuagint, without adding any criticism or further clarification.[197] In his discussion of the Septuagint, an interesting window into Gerhard's thought process is given.

---

[194] Such as *Examination of the Council of Trent*, *Theological Commonplaces*, etc.

[195] Martin Chemnitz, *Examination of the Council of Trent*, trans. Fred Kramer (Concordia Publishing House, 1971), vol. 1, First Topic, sec. 7.

[196] Martin Chemnitz, *Examination of the Council of Trent*, trans. Fred Kramer (Concordia Publishing House, 1971), 197.

[197] Johann Gerhard, *On Interpreting Sacred Scripture and Method of Theological Study*, ed. Benjamin T. G. Mayes, trans. Joshua J. Hayes (St. Louis, Missouri: Concordia Publishing House, 2017), 247.

SEVENTY-TWO SERVANTS OF THE WORD

Gerhard grapples with the fact that the ancient witnesses are universal in their appraisal of the accuracy and preciseness of the Septuagint's translation. He says "Aristaeus (in his Historia of this translation) and Philo (De vita Mosis, book 2) testify that the Seventy Translators very faithfully and literally translated everything verbatim, that their translation was diligently examined by many before it was placed in the king's library, and that everyone praised it for its fidelity and accuracy".[198] Yet Gerhard struggles with how to make sense of this fact when he sees that in many places the Septuagint omits, or differs strongly, from what is found in his Hebrew, and from this he concludes that the Septuagint must have suffered corruption through the ages.

These comments exemplify the false assumptions undergirding the Reformers' rejection of the Septuagint. They simply did not imagine that there was any other Hebrew text than that of the Synagogue, and since the Old Testament was originally written in Hebrew, then a divergence from the Synagogal text must be a divergence from the Hebraica veritas. It is therefore worth pondering whether the Reformers would have made the same choices had they had access to the vast amount of textual resources we now have and had known their copies of the Hebrew Text, the Masoretic Text, did not necessarily reflect the original wording of the ancient Hebrew documents any better than the Septuagint.

That being said, there does seem to be some tension in Gerhard's view, for he, like Chemnitz and Luther before him, often relies heavily on the Septuagint in his understanding and explanation of the Hebrew, which would appear to presuppose its trustfulness and exactness. On such example is Gerhard's comment on Psalm 103:6, where he praises the Septuagint translators as *"very wise men"* and uses their translation to exegete the text. He writes, "For example, when Lot said to the angel (in the Hebrew): "You have magnified Your mercy [Gen. 19:19], the Septuagint translators rendered it "righteousness." Again, when David had said, 'The Lord works righteousness" (Ps. 103:6), the Septuagint has "mercies." (Compare similar passages in Ps. 103:6; Gen. 20:13; 21:23; 32:10.) These very wise men would not have taken such license had they not known that "the righteousness of God" sometimes indicates His mercy by which He does good to those who believe".[199] This conclusion seems to presuppose the stability of the Septuagint's textual transmission as well as its quality of translation.

---

[198] Gerhard, *On Interpreting Sacred Scripture and Method of Theological Study*, 250.

[199] Gerhard, *On Interpreting Sacred Scripture and Method of Theological Study*, 77.

PART III: THE RECEPTION OF THE SEPTUAGINT BY THE CHURCH

CROSS-CONFESSIONAL PROTESTANT APPRAISAL OF THE SEPTUAGINT

It can safely be concluded that, though Jerome's view won out in the Reformation traditions over all, the Septuagint was never dropped but was picked up by the Reformer and actively used. Yet not all were content with this approach to the Septuagint, and different voices argued for a much more prominent role for the Septuagint.

Louis Cappel, a famous French Reformed theologian in his day, was born October 15, 1585, and became Professor of Hebrew at Saumur, France, at the tender age of 28. Even at this age, he had already engaged thoroughly in the study of the Semitic languages. Here, he became one of the earliest proponents of a critical view of the Masoretic additions to the Hebrew text. Through a skillful examination of earlier rabbinical authors, as well as of ancient writers such as Josephus and Philo, he concluded that the vowel points and the different signs added to the clarity of the text, the so-called *qere* were "invented by the Masoretes and added to the sacred text around 500 AD and at least after 400 AD".[200] He also pointed out, as discussed earlier, how radical were the changes that the Hebrew Scriptures underwent, such as its complete overhaul and rewriting from the paleo-Hebrew characters, used by the ancient Israelites, into the Aramaic square alphabet used by the Babylonian Empire. These new insights led Cappel to treat the Masoretic Text as no more valuable or useful than the Septuagint, which he saw as an equally authoritative witness to the Old Testament.[201]

Later on, Isaac Vossius, 1618–1689, followed and concurred with Cappel. He was a famous Dutch Protestant scholar who worked on a new critical edition of the Septuagint from the different circulating Greek manuscripts.[202] He began this awesome project at the Royal Library in London, where he had firsthand access to one of the most important and early manuscripts of the Septuagint, the Codex Alexandrinus, the crown jewel of the Royal Library. This manuscript had been a gift to the English King Charles I from the Patriarch of Constantinople himself, Cyril Lucaris, 1572–1638, who had studied in Western Europe and was, seemingly, a secret

---

[200] Sæbø et al., *Hebrew Bible / Old Testament*, 748.
[201] Eric Jorink and Dirk van Miert, *Isaac Vossius (1618-1689) between Science and Scholarship* (BRILL, 2012), 91.
[202] Jorink and van Miert, *Isaac Vossius (1618-1689)*, 87.

convert to Protestantism.[203] He tried to reform the Greek Orthodox Church along Protestant lines but was later deposed and subsequently condemned after his death at the Eastern Orthodox Council of Jerusalem in 1672.

Vossius' interest in the Septuagint had been caused by his work as a historian, which increasingly made him doubt the chronology of the Masoretic Text as much too short, placing the creation around 2,000 years later than the Septuagint.[204] This later led him to argue that "the only solution to the Hebrew text's and post-Second Temple Jewish tradition's weaknesses was recourse to an entirely alternative set of Hellenistic Jewish works, chief among them the Septuagint".[205] And that "Vossius countered that his sole ambition was to prefer the univocal Christian truth of the Septuagint to the uncertainty of the mute Hebrew codex".[206] Indeed, Vossius, after having worked to prove his view by examining the circulating Hebrew manuscripts critically, came to the conclusion that the Septuagint had been translated from a better Hebrew text than the text reflected by the Masoretic Text and, indeed, that the Septuagint was divinely inspired.[207]

This debate quickly erupted and spread across confessional lines, with representatives of both schools of thought—both those defending a Jerome-type view of Masoretic supremacy and those supporting the Septuagint, in varying degrees, over and against the Masoretic Text. The scholar Twining writes how this led to:

> A new scholarly field in which it was possible to think and argue about the text and history of the Bible in a new way, whether one was Catholic or Protestant. This had important consequences for one specific version of the Old Testament. (...) the scepticism with which an array of Catholic and Protestant scholars had come to regard the Masoretic Hebrew text of the Old Testament. This had even spurred some Protestant scholars, such as Henry Thorndike, to see Vossius's turn to the Septuagint as an entirely viable option.[208]

---

[203] This topic and the whole controversy regarding the patriarch and his confessional standpoints are, though extremely interesting, beyond the scope of this work.
[204] Jorink and van Miert, *Isaac Vossius (1618-1689)*, 92-93.
[205] T. Twining, "Richard Simon and the Remaking of Seventeenth-Century Biblical Criticism," *Erudition and the Republic of Letters 3*, no. 4 (October 24, 2018), https://doi.org/10.1163/24055069-00304003, 4.
[206] Twining, "Richard Simon and the Remaking of Seventeenth-Century Biblical Criticism," 50.
[207] Müller, "Septuaginta Som Udfordring Til Den Bibelske Kanon," 102.
[208] Müller, "Septuaginta Som Udfordring Til Den Bibelske Kanon," 5.

PART III: THE RECEPTION OF THE SEPTUAGINT BY THE CHURCH

TRIDENTINE CATHOLICISM'S RELATION TO THE SEPTUAGINT

This renewed focus on original languages sources was not only found north of the Alps, but was mirrored in many Roman Catholic Churches as well. Leading up to the Council of Trent, biblical humanism exerted its influence on Roman Catholicism as well. One famous example was Erasmus of Rotterdam, who edited and collected new editions of the original Greek New Testament from the best manuscripts available. The Old Testament was not exempt either from this renewed focus on original language sources, an example of such being the Hebrew Old Testament used by Luther, which was printed in 1494.

This emphasis on original texts was also found among some of the higher hierarchs of the Roman Catholic church, where especially Cardinal Francisco Ximenes de Cisneros, 1436–1517, must be mentioned. Under his auspice, the University of Alcala, known in Latin as *Complutum*, undertook the herculean work of, for the first time, printing an accurate, textually sound, polyglot Bible. This Bible included not only the text of the Latin Vulgate, but also the Aramaic Targum Onkelos as well as the Greek Septuagint all laid out side-by-side. This enormous work, known as the Complutensian Polyglot consisted of a six-volume set. A massive number for the time—600 copies—were printed in 1520 with papal approval.[209]

This also marked the earliest attempt at providing Europe with a text-critical edition of the Septuagint. In this work, they followed the method of using one principal manuscript as the base text, while correcting and amending its errors using a host of other reliable sources. But because of slightly different approaches among the editors themselves, this resulted in a somewhat uneven text for some parts of the Septuagint, though on a whole it was a faithful rendition[210] which till this day serves as a good witness to many ancient Septuagint readings.[211] This work proved highly influential and helped equip theologians all over Europe with a good and precise Septuagintal text. Later on, more biblical polyglots including the Septuagint would follow, the most important of which were the Polyglot of Antwerp in 1572, of Paris in 1645, and of London in 1657.

But the Septuagint was more than a helpful textual tool for the Roman Catholic Church, and among some of its foremost theologians the old

---

[209] Sæbø et al., *Hebrew Bible / Old Testament*, 288 and 291.
[210] Sæbø et al., *Hebrew Bible / Old Testament*, 290.
[211] Sæbø et al., *Hebrew Bible / Old Testament*, 290.

patristic idea of the divine inspiration of the Septuagint survived even in a time where the Latin Vulgate of Jerome stood supreme. One factor in this development was the renaissance that the study and use of Greek had enjoyed in the century prior to the Reformation. With its rise, the study of the Septuagint became common once again, and the Letter of Aristeas began recirculating in Western Europe, especially after having been attached as a kind of preface to multiple early printed Bibles, among which were the Roman Bible of 1471, the first printed Bible in Rome.[212] The importance of this should be underscored, for one of the main reasons for the Septuagint's decline in the West had been the almost total eclipse of the study and teaching of Greek in early medieval Europe. This had now changed, and with the reassertion of the importance of Greek, the prominence of the Septuagint again rose and, along with it, appreciation of its importance, which was also helped by the availability of the Aristeas' letter.

The Reformation-era bishop and cardinal John Fisher, 1469–1535, is one example of a theologian who encapsulates both the love of Greek as well as the re-embodiment of the patristic ideal of the Septuagint. Around 1527, Fisher wrote a longer treatise on the Septuagint as a defense against the churchman Richard Pace,[213] who had argued for a revision of the Book of Sirach of the Latin Vulgate because it was based on the Septuagint rather than the Hebrew version of the book.[214] In his treatise, Cardinal Fisher chiefly argues for the inspired status and authority of the Septuagint on the grounds of the historicity of its origin story—that it was commissioned under the authority of the Jewish High Priest, that it was translated faithfully by Seventy-Two skilled translators, and that the story of their miraculous identical translation was a true account witnessed to by many historical sources.

Secondly, he also argues, akin to the ancient church fathers, that providence would not have left God's church without a reliable, infallible, and untampered edition of the Word of God in a common language, such as Greek, so that the Gentiles themselves would know the prophecies that Christ fulfilled. From this, Fisher argues that this translation would necessarily need to be, first of all, translated prior to the advent of Christ, so that the Gentiles would not doubt that the prophecies were written post-

---

[212] Richard Rex, "St John Fisher's Treatise on the Authority of the Septuagint," The Journal of Theological Studies 43, no. 1 (1992), https://doi.org/10.2307/23965451, 63.

[213] Rex, "St John Fisher's Treatise on the Authority of the Septuagint," 56.

[214] Rex, "St John Fisher's Treatise on the Authority of the Septuagint," 57.

PART III: THE RECEPTION OF THE SEPTUAGINT BY THE CHURCH

hoc, and secondly, that it needed to be divinely inspired as the Hebrew original so that it could be as faithfully believed as the Hebrew, and so that the ambiguities and unclarities of the Hebrew could be clearly revealed.[215] Lastly, Fisher argued that these considerations were affirmed by the reception and the use of the Septuagint by Christ and the apostles as well as the universal church in the first four centuries of its history, writing:

> For there can be no doubt for anyone that the ancient church had the Sacred Scriptures with which she relied on and consulted whenever it was necessary to establish the faith or to refute heresies or to corroborate the mysteries which the apostles preached about Christ. Certainly, Peter would never have left the church, whose care-taking he received after Christ spoke, "feed my sheep" so naked that the Gentiles, who converted to Christ and were ignorant of the Hebrew language, had no translation of the Scriptures.[216]

A decade after Cardinal Fisher's death, he was executed by the English crown for his refusal to recant his loyalty to the Pope. the Roman Catholic Church summoned the Council of Trent to provide an official response to the Reformation as well as to institute church reforms. The council, convoked in 1545, worked in three sessions with years of pause in between, and ended finally in 1563, having also dealt extensively with the question of the canon and the textual basis of the Bible. The council fathers declared the extent of the canon and that, crucially, out of all the Latin translations of the Bible then in circulation, Jerome's Vulgate was to be considered as the only authoritative translation. Jared Wick writes, discussing the proceedings among the council fathers, and he notes how this was not meant to be an exclusion of the Septuagint, though the Vulgate did take pride of position.

> In the same meeting, Bishop Tommaso Caselli, O.P., spoke to the issue of multiple Latin versions in a manner that proved decisive, calling for the designation of one translation as authoritative on doctrine, which should be a corrected version of the Vulgate, to be approved because of its long service in transmitting the faith of the Church. The commission on abuses and remedial measures submitted a draft formulation to the Council on March 17. First,

---

[215] Rex, "St John Fisher's Treatise on the Authority of the Septuagint," 65 and 93.
[216] Rex, "St John Fisher's Treatise on the Authority of the Septuagint," 110.

confusion should be reduced by receiving only one Latin version as authentic, that is, authoritative, in the public sphere of the Church. But the Septuagint retains its authority and other Latin versions can help one understand the Vulgate. Second, the Vulgate should be revised to give the Catholic world a "pure and genuine" edition.[217]

The reception of the Tridentine decrees and the council's theology found a skillful treatment under the pen of Cardinal Robert Bellarmine, 1542–1621, who was arguably the greatest Roman Catholic theologian of the century. He bears the title of *doctor ecclesiae* (doctor of the church) in the Roman Catholic Church as one of only 37 theologians. His *magnum opus*, the massive *Disputationes de Controversiis Christianae Fidei* sets forth a thorough defense of the claims and doctrines of Roman Catholicism against the arguments of the Reformers in 17 volumes. In Volume I, book 2 he treats the topic of Holy Scripture, its different editions, its translations, and related questions. The work includes a longer discussion of the Septuagint, which Bellarmine held in very high regard, like Fisher before him, and which the comments by Bishop Tommaso Caselli at the Council of Trent also echoed, though not to the same extent. Bellarmine places a large emphasis on the patristic support for the Septuagint and viewed the Letter of Aristeas as a truthful, historical witness to its origin, and he argued that the Seventy-Two translators were responsible for the translation of the whole Old Testament rather than just the Pentateuch.

In this discussion, Bellarmine also had to deal with Jerome's dismissive view of the Septuagint. On account of his authorship of the Latin Vulgate, Jerome was, along with Augustine, the two church fathers who enjoyed the highest authority and standing in the Christian West. Bellarmine's approach to this question was quite creative for, while affirming that Jerome rejected the Septuagint as anything more than a mere translation, and a somewhat unprecise one at that, Bellarmine was able to use other positive statements made by Jerome about the Septuagint against Jerome's negative statements. Thus, having blunted Jerome's criticism of the Septuagint with Jerome's praises of the Septuagint, Bellarmine presents the broad patristic consensus of the authority and divinity of the Septuagint. He writes:

---

[217] Sæbø et al., *Hebrew Bible / Old Testament*, 627.

PART III: THE RECEPTION OF THE SEPTUAGINT BY THE CHURCH

Yet nevertheless it should be very certain that the Septuagint translators translated very well, and had in a special way the assistance of the Holy Spirit lest they err in anything, so that they seem to have been not so much translators as Prophets. This is proved in the first place by common opinion. For this is constantly asserted by all the cited authors, Aristaeus, Philo, Josephus, Justin, Irenaeus, Eusebius, Clement of Alexandria, Epiphanius, Chrysostom, Cyril, and from the Latins Tertullian and Augustine, again Hilary in his preface to the Psalms, and all the others.[218]

Bellarmine likewise affirms that the Septuagint served as the text used by the apostles themselves, but, though granting this as well as the inspired and inerrant status of the Septuagint, Bellarmine stops short of setting forth the Septuagint as the textual basis of the Old Testament. Bellarmine defends his position first by expressing doubt about the stability of the textual transmission of the Septuagint as, he states, it is clearly seen that it diverges from the Masoretic Hebrew Text of his day, which does not fit with the witness of the ancients. The earliest of these ancient witnesses, such as Philo and others, explicitly claimed precise overlap between the Septuagint and the Hebrew text.

From this, Bellarmine concludes that the Septuagint must have suffered corruption, the alternative being that the Latin Vulgate, which is based on a text much closer to the Masoretic Hebrew than to the Septuagint and was the version sanctioned by Rome as the authentic edition of Holy Scripture, was the corrupt one. It cannot therefore be judged as erroneous, Bellarmine writes, "nor should Catholics admit it, lest they be compelled to confess that the Latin Vulgate edition, which the Catholic Church has used already for so many centuries and which the Council of Trent judged to be authentic, is also wholly corrupted. For with the exception of the Psalter, the Latin edition agrees more with the Hebrew codices than with the Greek." [219] Bellarmine's final rejection of the Septuagint was strongly tied to a precommitment to the Latin Vulgate. Though this was the case, Bellarmine's view shows nuance as he fits the patristic view of the inspired status of the Septuagint into the post-Tridentine textual paradigm. And indeed, should the same argument not be raised in favor of the Septuagint,

---

[218] Bellarmine, *Controversies of the Christian Faith*, Book II, chap. 6.
[219] Bellarmine, *Controversies of the Christian Faith*, Book II, chap. 6.

which the *Church has used already for so many centuries and which the Councils judged to be canonical?*

CONCLUSION

The advent of Jerome's Latin Vulgate coincided with the beginning of a long and sharp decline in Greek learning in Western Europe, a development which strengthened and reinforced the Vulgate's trajectory toward the position as Latin Christendom's sacred Scripture. Use and knowledge of the Septuagint almost wholly vanished in this period, until the effects of the increasing contact with the Greek-speaking East sowed the seeds for new developments. One of the few positives of the destructive Fourth Crusade was that a large influx of Greek manuscripts and Greek education flowed into Europe from the states partitioned out of the Byzantine Empire. The rediscovery of Aristotle and Greek thought and literature helped the seeds germinate and, with the large influx of Byzantine scholars and intellectuals in the periods surrounding the fall of Constantinople in 1453, the harvest was finally ready.

The Renaissance, the flourishing of biblical humanism, and the invention of the printing press around 1440 changed the intellectual European landscape drastically. Much larger amounts of firsthand sources had become available at much lower prices to many more scholars thanks to the large number of new European universities being founded in the fifteenth and sixteenth centuries. The Reformation-era synthesis would depart from the view of the Medievals, not in the rejection of Jerome's Vulgate, which as written above was seen as the authoritative Scripture for public discourse for Rome, but in a return to the methodology of Jerome. Both north and south of the Alps, it became necessary for Protestants and Roman Catholics alike to learn Hebrew and delve into the study of the ancient Hebrew manuscripts. Yet in this the error of Jerome was repeated as they, like Jerome a thousand years before, assumed the Masoretic Text, copied and transmitted by the Rabbinic Judaism, was a faithful witness to the ancient original texts.

Somewhat accidentally, though, the difficult and often vague nature of the Hebrew helped cause a resurgence of interest and study of the Septuagint. As shown above, the Septuagint was received as an important, and for many vital, tool in understanding and accessing the Hebrew text. This was true not only linguistically for interpretation and translation but

PART III: THE RECEPTION OF THE SEPTUAGINT BY THE CHURCH

also textually, as no one, regardless of how high his view of the Masoretic Text was, was willing to follow it consistently.

Western Christianity, though now fractured, retained agreement on this point. But not among all, for the new interest in the Septuagint led some scholars to re-embrace the patristic ideal of the Septuagint as inspired and inerrant. This was a position, though a minority one, found in both Protestant and Roman Catholic camps. From its position in almost obscurity during the Medieval era, the Septuagint was dusted off and taken down from the shelves where its place, more or less, has remained ever since—that is, mostly as an important tool and resource for theologians, academics, and clergy, and as a clarifying source of light for translators.

PART IV
THE SEPTUAGINT IN THE THIRD MILLENNIUM CHURCH

A SKETCH OF THE SEPTUAGINT'S TEXTUAL TRANSMISSION

"On this topic I remind you briefly of this: you should know that there is one edition [Of the Septuagint], which Origen, Eusebius of Caesarea, and all the writers of Greece call the κοινά, that is, the common and popular edition."

— Jerome, Letter 106.

THE ANCIENT COPYISTS

When approaching the question of the textual reliability of the Septuagint, an extreme and quite unfounded position of wild skepticism is sometimes encountered. At popular levels, much misinformed and even fantastical positions are shared. With this chapter, the goal is to give a short summary of the transmissional history of the Septuagint, to shed light on the question of its text's stability, or lack thereof, and to explore how this should impact how the Septuagint is viewed.

The topic of textual criticism is a very complicated one, so some simplification and summaries are to be expected. Yet the goal here is to provide an adequate and representative discussion regarding the text of the Septuagint which fairly represents modern scholarship. As has been concluded from the earlier chapters, the Septuagint was the result of translation work which began with the Pentateuch but included, and finished with, the translation of the whole Old Testament, though the exact guidelines regarding which of the deuterocanonical books were included are a bit fuzzy.

Regardless of where exactly this line was drawn, the whole translation was understood to be a divine work under the direction of the Seventy-Two translators, at least from the second and first centuries onward (for example, in the Prologue of Sirach and Philo's comments). As defined earlier, this authoritative origin also best explains the fact that only one translation of each book was made and entered into circulation until the time Aquila would make his new translation around four hundred years later.

Yet some scholars have strongly challenged the notion of a single, uniform, and well-defined collection of books identified by the label *Septuagint*. Unlike the astonishing criticisms often found at popular levels on blogs and the general theological internet sphere, a few thoughtful and thorough critics have raised their voices as well. One such witty example would be that of Dr. Peter J. Williams' critique. Dr. Williams serves as the principal of Tyndale House, which is a Cambridge-based biblical research institute. In 2016, he provided a short summary of such a criticism in a speech at the ETS Septuagint Conference, which is available to watch online.[220] Dr. Williams is known for his sometimes-harsh criticism of the Septuagint, whose very existence he, tongue-in-check, doubts, as he explains in one lecture he gave under the title *Why I don't Believe in the Septuagint*.[221]

Dr. Williams problematizes the term *Septuagint* for being a very misleading and even anachronistic term imposed on a diverse range of different translations and editions of an ever-shifting number of books. Thus, though the language is somewhat bombastic, Dr. Williams' point is not so much that there does not exist a Greek translation of the Old Testament—this truth he actually affirms. Rather, he claims it is nonsensical to talk about *one* translation or even *the one* translation. The diversity, editorial recensions, and the span of time during which the translation work supposedly took place was much too long to be meaningfully grouped under one clear heading, such the *Septuagint*. Another, though less impactful, problem Dr. William raises is how much development the term *Septuaginta* itself has gone through. From being the title of the actual group of Seventy-Two translators, the term slowly shifted and lost its meaning as a heading for a plurality of persons and changed into a single, proper noun denoting a collection of texts.

Those who have read so far in this present book to have arrived at this paragraph will hopefully have noticed how the older scholarship has had a tendency of exaggerating the textual plurality of Greek translations, such as with Kahle's hypothesis, and how adequate grounds there are to posit the existence of a single authoritative translation arising from the work of the Seventy-Two in Alexandria. Secondly, one should also ask if this kind of deconstructive criticism would not effect the term *Bible* or *New Testament* as much as it does *Septuagint*. The term *Biblia* was originally a plural designation of a collection of books or, if one ventures back far enough,

---

[220] fleetwd1, "On the Invention and Problem of the Term Septuagint - Peter Williams - ETS 2016," YouTube, December 12, 2016, youtube.com/watch?v=xhmMKwl3KeE.

[221] Run2Christ, "Why I Don't Believe in the Septuagint - Dr. Peter Williams, PhD," YouTube, September 8, 2015, https://www.youtube.com/watch?v=RmpnJ1cgh58.

PART IV: THE SEPTUAGINT IN THE THIRD MILLENNIUM CHURCH

scrolls. *Biblia* was derived from the Greek word βιβλίον, or, scroll. One can naturally point how far the term Bible has progressed from the Medieval Latin, *biblia sacrae* (*the Holy Books, the inspired library*), from its original τὰ βιβλία (*the books*), an appellation used by some of the church fathers, but which before that could denote any unspecified collection of scrolls, whether it was the dialogues of Plato or a collection of writings of Hebrew prophets.

But does this change somehow make the current use of the term *Bible* problematic? One can naturally talk about an Ethiopian Orthodox Bible or a Lutheran Bible, but though the amount of included works differs, the meaning of the term remains clear—namely the collection of divinely inspired writings, which is a clear category even when people disagree about the exact amount of included books. How much more is Dr. Williams' criticism also not true for the term *New Testament* which, used by Christ himself at the Last Supper, draws from the Septuagint's translation of the Hebrew word for *covenant* or *pact* (בְּרִית) into *testament* (διαθήκη), which later, around two centuries or so, ended up denoting a set group of 27 inspired books, though there remained doubt around its edges for centuries. Should we believe in the "New Testament"?

Thus, Dr. Williams is not really raising any questions which could not be raised equally as forcefully for the perfectly useful denominator *Bible* and *New Testament*. But to bring this comparison home, it would be fruitful to examine closer whether the term Septuagint also historically has been understood clearly as referring to any and all Greek versions and translations of the Old Testament, or to just one particular and distinguishable translation.

THE COMMON SEPTUAGINT

By the nature of the case, it is difficult to prove the nonexistence of something, yet the view of the Septuagint as a coherent and distinct text type will be examined. The term Septuagint is here understood as the Old Greek translation of the Old Testament—of all the books of the Hebrew Bible, including the proto and deuterocanonical books, though leaving aside the question of the canonical boundaries for this moment.

Though challenged by some scholars, there is an increasing awareness that this authoritative translation consisted of one single translation of each Old Testament book. Eugene Ulrich, professor emeritus of Old Testament Hebrew studies states, "the LXX, now generally exonerated and shown to be basically a faithful translation of one ancient Hebrew text form of each book, sometimes earlier than or superior to the MT [Masoretic Text]".[222] Although this translation underwent textual changes during transmission, as did the New Testament, it never underwent such a degree of alteration that there was any doubt about what constitutes the original Septuagint, the Old Greek translation, and its transmission in the ancient church. These changes will be examined more closely in the following chapter.

Many ancient witnesses testify to the intactness of the original Septuagint. As discussed in the chapter about Origen, the very existence of an independent Septuagint column presupposes that a well-defined and identifiable Septuagint text existed in the third century, and that this text was clearly distinguishable from the other Greek translations of the Old Testament, such as Aquilas', Theodotian's, and more. Indeed, Origen equates this Septuagint translation as the one of which *"copies [are] in use in our churches"*,[223] in distinction to the other Greek texts. A fact also noted by Professor Sidney, who writes:

> There is, however, an important point to be gleaned. His isolation of the 'version of the Seventy' in the passage cited above—a distinction not confined in his writings to this passage—has a significant bearing on the question of the LXX Vorlage, as indicating the recognition of a 'standard' text, 'found in every Church of Christ in that Greek copy which the Greeks use' (Ad Afr., para. 2) and traceable backwards through the Fathers to the pre-Christian era.[224]

Nor did this reality change substantially in the following centuries, for the existence of a common and widespread text of the Septuagint is explicitly affirmed by Augustine and by Jerome, whose critical view of the Septuagint only adds credibility to this observation.

In his work *On Christian Doctrine*, Augustine includes a chapter where he discusses the different editions and translations of Scripture then in circulation—Book II chapter 15. Here, he recommends a so-called Italian edition of the Old Latin translation of the Septuagint, yet, on account of textual variants present in the Latin, he says that:

---

[222] Salvesen and Law, eds. *The Oxford Handbook of the Septuagint*, 455.
[223] Letter to Africanus, chap. 4.
[224] Jellicoe, *The Septuagint and Modern Study*, 111-12.

PART IV: THE SEPTUAGINT IN THE THIRD MILLENNIUM CHURCH

> To correct the Latin we must use the Greek versions, among which the authority of the Septuagint is pre-eminent as far as the Old Testament is concerned; for it is reported through all the more learned churches that the seventy translators enjoyed so much of the presence and power of the Holy Spirit in their work of translation, that among that number of men there was but one voice.[225]

Notice here how Augustine mentions the existence of a plurality of Greek versions one could correct the Latin from, yet among these, *in quibus (in which)*, he points to a singular edition, namely the Septuagint, which is to be followed to the exclusion of the others. Such an approach presupposes a clear delineation between these different editions, which was clear and taken for granted by the ancients. It is remarkable how this text, written in the A.D. 410s, reflects the clarity of the situation during this time, a time, indeed, generations after the period from which the first complete surviving manuscripts of the Septuagint were entered into circulation. Some of these survive to this very day, such as the Codex Vaticanus and the Codex Alexandrinus, which were both written in the A.D. 300s.

Jerome also bears strong evidence to the circulation of a common Septuagint text. Indeed, he simply calls this edition the *Septuaginta communis*[226] that is the *common* or *universal Septuagint*. Around A.D. 391, Jerome received a letter from two Gothic clergymen who had written what must have been a very extensive letter asking questions about the exact wording, textual variants, and translation details for almost every single psalm in the whole Book of Psalms. Jerome's answer, which runs around 42 pages, meticulously goes through each of the approximately 178 questions posed by these two evidently diligent readers of Scripture. Indeed, these questions concerned the Book of Psalms *only*. The letter is a goldmine of insight into the textual history of the Septuagint and provides many interesting considerations. The text is somewhat complicated because of the many different versions and editions of texts being discussed. The Gothic clergymen were reading a manuscript of Jerome's Gallican Psalter which, as discussed earlier, is mostly a translation of the Septuagint. However, this Psalter still differs from the text found in their own Greek Septuagint, which

---

[225] Augustine, *On Christian Doctrine*, Book II, chap. 15.
[226] Jerome, *Epistulae*, ed. Isidor Hilberg, vol. 55 of *Corpus Scriptorum Ecclesiasticorum Latinorum* (Leipzig: G. Freytag, 1922), letter 106.

reflects the *common* text of the Septuagint. Jerome refers in the letter to his own translation of the Latin, the Gallican Psalter, as well as other differing Latin editions, the Hebrew text, different editions of the Greek Old Testament, and even Origen's text-critical edition of the Septuagint found in the Hexapla. Yet, when one cuts through this entangled presentation, a clear picture is found amidst the complexity.

The discussion is illuminating, for Jerome himself bears witness to the existence of single, common, and widespread edition of the Septuagint. He writes:

> On this topic I remind you briefly of this: you should know that there is one edition, which Origen, Eusebius of Caesarea, and all the writers of Greece call the κοινά, that is, the common and popular edition, and which now adays is referred to by most as Lucianic (Λουκιάνειος); and there is another edition of the Seventy Translators that is found in the hexaplaric (ἑξαπλοῖς) codices, which I faithfully translated into the Latin language and which is recited both in Jerusalem and in the churches of the East.[227]

Jerome, like Augustine, refers matter-of-factly to the existence of one, common version of the Septuagint, which is called *communis* and *vulgatus* (*universal* and *common*). Indeed, Jerome refers to this viewpoint as one with a long history, being the opinion not only of himself but also that of Origen, Eusebius, and of *"all the writers of Greece"*. Now Jerome himself did not have too high of a view of the common Septuagint which he saw as inferior to the Hexaplaric edition of Origen, which he again viewed as inferior to the synagogal Hebrew text. This must be kept in mind when interpreting Jerome's comments, for his higher view of the Hexaplaric Septuagint was not at all due to it being a better or more faithful rendition of the original Septuagint.

Rather, Origen had included, under certain text-critical signs, the words and passages found in the Hebrew text in circulation in the third century, so that his Hexaplaric text contained both the original text of the Septuagint, which he did not alter, as well additional readings from the Proto-Masoretic Text, as marked in the text by signs. Hexaplaric editions is here meant as copies of the Septuagint which had been corrected toward the

---

[227] Michael Graves, *Jerome, Epistle 106 (on the Psalms)* (The Society of Biblical Literature, 2022), 81.

wording of the Hebrew on account of the carelessness of scribes, who had failed to copy the textual signs of Origen and therefore included words and phrases not found in the Septuagint. This will be explained further in the following chapter.

This meant that Jerome could come closer to his veritas Hebraica when using Origen's Hexapla compared to the common Septuagint, because with the Hexapla he allowed himself to not only translate the words of the Septuagint itself but also the additional words and passages of the Hebrew text, included by Origin merely for apologetical purposes with explicit signs showing they were not part of the Septuagint's text. Yet Jerome, here early in his career, increasingly allowed the Masoretic Text to dictate his translation, first by letting it direct his translation when he thought the Greek did not capture what he understood by the Hebrew, and later by adding in what was found under these text-critical signs. Thus, Origin's work became the means by which Jerome could draw closer to the proto-Masoretic Text, a pursuit which ultimately, as discussed earlier, resulted in his wholesale abandonment of the Septuagint, common or Hexaplaric, in favor of the Synagogue's text.

That text which Jerome calls *common* is the same text that is found in current copies of the Septuagint. Professor Michael Graves, who has written a whole monograph on this intriguing letter of Jerome, comments on the manuscripts and codices of the common Septuagint that have survived, such as the uncials. On the common text of the Septuagint, he notes that "In other words, Jerome claims that this edition is the most widely available, and he implies that calling this text type 'Lucianic' is a recent phenomenon".[228] Indeed, the common Septuagint employed by the text diligent Goths "Jerome calls the "popular" Septuagint upon which Sunnia and Fretela base their questions".[229] Professor Gleaves notes that the general trend is that it is the text of the Goths, which Jerome denotes as the common type, that matches the text of the Septuagint that survives today rather than the Hexaplaric text used by Jerome.[230] Though some differences still remain, sometimes due to copyist errors being present in particular manuscripts available to the two enquirers, the trend is clear, "The fact that the uniform (or almost uniform) Septuagint readings tend to agree with Sunnia and

---

[228] Graves, *Jerome, Epistle 106 (on the Psalms)*, 32.
[229] Graves, *Jerome, Epistle 106 (on the Psalms)*, 150.
[230] Graves, *Jerome, Epistle 106 (on the Psalms)*, 34.

Fretela more often than with Jerome lends support to Jerome's claim that the text employed by Sunnia and Fretela was 'popular'".[231]

One last interesting witness to the commonality of one distinguishable Septuagint text in opposition to other Greek editions is found within Imperial Roman law itself. Emperor Justinian the Great, who reigned A.D. 527–565, published many law codes during his reign, including a collection of *Novellae Constitutiones* (*new regulations*). The 146th Novellae sought to regulate the use of the Old Testament by the rabbinical Jewish communities of the Roman Empire. The law mandated that the Jews should read the Old Testament in the native language of the populace attending the services in the Synagogue. This was done with an aim toward converting the Jews to Christianity, supposing that, when they heard and understood the prophecies concerning Christ in the Old Testament, they would convert. Though at this point in history, Hebrew was a language understood only by a tiny minority of people. An excerpt of the first chapter of the Novellae reads:

> We do not, however, allow the Hebrew translators to corrupt the text, and conceal their fraud because of the ignorance of many persons. Those who read the Sacred Writings in Greek shall make use of the Septuagint, which is considered the most correct, and the best; as the authors, although separated from one another and residing in different localities, nevertheless, all agreed in the version which they made. And, indeed, who would not be surprised to learn that these men, having lived a long time before the beneficent appearance of Our Lord Jesus Christ, predicted the events mentioned in the Sacred Books, just as if they had been witnesses of them, and had been enlightened by the grace of prophesy? Without intending to exclude the other versions, We also permit the Hebrews to make use of that of Aquilea, even though it is foreign, and does not in some points agree with the Septuagint. We, however, absolutely forbid the use of the one which the Hebrews call the second edition, for it does not form a part of the Sacred Books, it was not handed down to Us by the prophets, and is an invention devised by men who only speak of earthly things, and who had in them nothing that was divine.[232]

---

[231] Graves, *Jerome, Epistle 106 (on the Psalms)*, 35.
[232] S. P. Scott, *The Civil Law*, vol. 17 (Cincinnati: Central Trust Company, 1932), 264.

The text acknowledges the existence of a commonly recognizable Greek translation of the Old Testament, called the Septuagint, which is viewed as superior to all other Greek translations. These other translations are noticeably different from it, such as Aquila's, and the unspecified number of "other versions". The so-called "second edition" mentioned by the law is not a translation of the Old Testament, but rather a technical term (δευτέρωσις) employed by some ancient Christians to denote Jewish rabbinical teachings.[233]

Thus, from the translation of each particular book of the Hebrew Old Testament in the centuries prior to Christ, these works were published and received as the translation of the Seventy-Two, a translation which was copied and handed down through the ages in a stable and recognizable form, which is witnessed to by authors from as early as A.D. 230, like Origen, and onward. The case made against the Septuagint's textual transmission has been greatly exaggerated, sometimes even to comical proportions. Yet one must also not fall into the opposite extreme, though it is difficult to find anyone defending such a view, that would wholly deny the existence of any text-critical issues of the Septuagint. Just like the case of the New Testament, the abundance of manuscripts and textual witnesses have resulted in different variants and readings arising, as well as, given the span of time these witnesses date from, some particular developments in the text. These will be examined in the following chapters.

RECENSIONS AND TEXTUAL VARIANTS

An overview of the text-critical landscape of the Septuagint and some concrete examples of the textual issues faced by the reader of the Septuagint should be presented. When these topics are discussed in headlines—such as the existence of many Septuagints, multiple recensions, or other issues—some scholars greatly magnify these issues into larger problems. Many terms, too, are often thrown around without sufficient clarifications, which greatly muddy the waters even for well-read laymen wanting to delve into the topic. *Kaige, Lucianic, Hexaplaric, Symmachus, Theodotian,* and *Hesychian* are all terms often associated with the text-critical discussion of the Septuagint. Jerome, whose witness is rightly given a weighty emphasis on account of his text-critical work and knowledge of the three languages of Latin, Greek, and Hebrew, counts three textual families of the Septuagint in

---

[233] Salvesen and Law, eds. *The Oxford Handbook of the Septuagint*, 460.

circulation during his time, around the early fifth century. He comments on these three in his preface to his translation into Latin of the book of Chronicles.

One of these three textual families is the Hexaplaric, which was a Septuagint text that suffered some alterations that brought it into closer conformity with the Masoretic Text, on account of the many scribes that did failed to learn Origen's system of text-critical signs. This resulted in readings from the Masoretic Text entering into the textual transmission of the Septuagint. This textual family was common chiefly in the areas where Origen's Hexapla was common, such as Palestine and the adjacent areas. Thus, the term Hexaplaric readings is still used in text-critical circles when discussing variants found in some Septuagint manuscripts containing readings in alignment with the Masoretic Text yet diverting from the majority of the Septuagint manuscripts. This was the text type of the Septuagint that was favored by Jerome, though he still viewed it as inferior to the veritas hebraica. Jerome concluded this because he mistakenly thought this was the least corrupted version, insofar as it was the one which approached the wording of the Masoretic Hebrew Text the most closely. This was the text which, he assumed, had been the source text used by the Seventy-Two translators originally.

Jerome also mentions a text associated with Hesychius, whose exact identity is somewhat of a mystery, which circulated in Egypt. However, the very existence of such a textual family has been brought into serious question,[234, 235] and its existence is now commonly rejected.[236] Some, though, grant its existence and associate it with a tendency toward a shorter text type, which is found in a small minority of manuscripts mostly in Egypt which fit Jerome's description. Ancient Alexandria was famous for its textual scholarship, which had developed in the three centuries before Christ and originated with text-critical work on the Homeric Epics. Here, certain principles were formed and the text-critical signs, later employed by Origen, were invented by these early Greek literary scholars. One of these principles, sometimes called the *Alexandrine principle*, was a methodology employed by some of the ancient scribes and also used in modern textual criticism, and it preferred the shorter of two variant readings.[237] On average,

---

[234] Graves, *Jerome, Epistle 106 (on the Psalms)*, 32.
[235] Fernández Marcos, *The Septuagint in Context*, 241.
[236] Jellicoe, *The Septuagint and Modern Study*, 151-53.
[237] Jellicoe, *The Septuagint and Modern Study*, 155.

PART IV: THE SEPTUAGINT IN THE THIRD MILLENNIUM CHURCH

this would naturally result in a shorter text. Thus, today the Homeric works are also found in different textual families—a shorter Alexandrine text, a longer common text, and a mixed type.[238]

Curiously, this actually matches up with the New Testament as well because the *Alexandrine* textual family of the New Testament, common in Egypt, is shorter than the more widespread majority text/Byzantine textual family. Without dealing too much with textual issues of the New Testament, this latter text type is not witnessed to early. One should remember that it was the same Christian scribes who copied the New Testament as well as the Old Testament. Indeed, the four great uncials are so large because they included both the Septuagint Old Testament and the New Testament and are major testaments to the literary product of the early church.

The last textual family mentioned by Jerome is the one already discussed above, namely the common or universal type which had recently, in Jerome's time that is, become known as the Lucianic. The Lucianic was named after the textual scholar and martyr Lucian, who died in A.D. 312, though this text type demonstrably did not originate with him but is much older. Indeed, Jerome himself says that it is was only recently that people had begun to associate this text type with Lucian. In the scholarship, this text is denoted as either Lucian, Antiochian, common/koine, or majority. Indeed, given its commonality, wide geographic spread, and its ancient readings, one can justly argue that it should be equated with simply being the original text of the Septuagint. Many variants, denoted as *Lucian*, are shared also by the very early *Vetus Latina* translation of the Septuagint,[239] thus long predating the very birth of Lucian the Martyr. Indeed, what is commonly classified as "Lucianic" readings have not only been found in the Old Latin translation, but also in Josephus' quotations of the Septuagint written down in the first century and even in manuscripts dating from the Maccabean period centuries before.[240, 241, 242]

Such considerations should give pause to those who wish to put too strong of a divide between the Lucianic, or common Septuagint, and the original autographs of the Septuagint's books. Indeed, talks of a *Lucianic*

---

[238] Mark Billington and Peter Streitenberger, eds., *Digging for the Truth: Collected Essays Regarding the Byzantine Text of the Greek New Testament; a Festschrift in Honor of Maurice A. Robinson* (Norden, Germany: FocusYourMission KG, 2014), 15, 61.

[239] Jellicoe, *The Septuagint and Modern Study*, 163-64.

[240] Jellicoe, *The Septuagint and Modern Study*, 290.

[241] Jellicoe, *The Septuagint and Modern Study*, 346-347.

[242] Fernández Marcos, *The Septuagint in Context*, 233.

revision, a term often used in this debate, seems like much too strong of a term, as noted by Siegfried Kreuzer, professor of Old Testament Studies and one of the foremost expects in textual criticism of the Septuagint. He writes, "These facts lead to the conclusion that the Antiochene or so-called Lucianic text is basically old and close to Old Greek",[243] which is putting it mildly. Indeed, Kreuzer mentions, though not denying that some variants crept into the Old Greek Septuagint text through the centuries, that talks of a *Lucianic recension* is overblown, and scholars are increasingly recognizing this.[244] He concludes, "To put it in general terms: The Antiochene text is a very good, or even the best, witness to the Old Greek, and there was a subsequent kaige recension, maybe not as strict everywhere as in the historical books and in the book of the twelve [Minor Prophets], but it was very widespread. Thus, there is no reason to assume a Lucianic redaction".[245]

It should also be noted that the features most often associated with the *revision* of Lucian, if one can even reasonably call it that, most often denotes stylistic features and minor grammatical improvements, many of which are wholly untranslatable into English and simply have to do with improving the Greek style of the text. The *T & T Clark Handbook on Septuagint Research* provides one short, though quite representative, example of this:

> Such grammatical and stylistic changes are not systematic and are affected by the context of each passage. For example, while the reviser often adds articles to nouns in line with a better Greek style, in some passages where one would expect such additions they do not occur. A good example of a passage where such additions do occur is 2 Sam. 15:2, where the desirable answer to Absalom's call is Ἐκ μιᾶς φυλῶν Ἰσραήλ ὁ δοῦλός σου ("your servant is from one of the tribes of Israel"), which the Lucianic reviser complemented with the requisite definite articles: Ἐκ μιᾶς τῶν φυλῶν τοῦ Ἰσραήλ ὁ δοῦλός σου.[246]

---

[243] Siegfried Kreuzer, "Old Greek, Kaige and the Trifaria Varietas – a New Perspective on Jerome's Statement," *Journal of Septuagint and Cognate Studies* 46 (2013): 74–85, https://ccat.sas.upenn.edu/ioscs/journal/volumes/jscs46.pdf, 80.
[244] Kreuzer, "Old Greek, Kaige and the Trifaria Varietas", 82.
[245] Kreuzer, "Old Greek, Kaige and the Trifaria Varietas", 82.
[246] Ross and Glenny, *T&T Clark Handbook of Septuagint Research*, 207.

PART IV: THE SEPTUAGINT IN THE THIRD MILLENNIUM CHURCH

It must also be strongly emphasized that, when discussing these features characteristic of the *Lucianic recension*, the vast majority of them have no bearing at all on the meaning of the text. They primarily deal with word order which, on account of Greek syntax, is very flexible. Indeed, Professor Kauhanen of Old Testament Studies, in a chapter dealing with the issue of the Lucianic text, cites a dissertation on the particularities of the Lucianic text and summarizes it in this way: "the most striking recensional features is as follows: "correcting" the gender of some nouns, interchange of first and second aorist endings and of aorist middle and passive, adding the definite article, using a participle to avoid parataxis, and removal of the historic present".[247] Grammatical alterations have zero impact on the meaning of the text.

If these are the most striking recensional features, then one can simultaneously grant that, first, the common/Lucianic text did indeed undergo some alterations, yet these pertained primarily to style and grammar with the content remaining unchanged. Second, the common/Lucianic text is simply a good, faithful, and ancient witness to the autographic texts of the Septuagint translation: "Barthélemy's theory, that the Antiochian text is essentially the Old Greek text [i.e. the autographic Septuagint], is still endorsed by some scholars, notably Kreuzer".[248] That the text underwent certain grammatical improvements could be in some ways compared to how modern Bibles also add many features to the text to aid in understanding. Punctuation, quotations for speech, question marks, and capitalization of letters are all aids which greatly help toward reading comprehension. It is in the same vein that these alterations can be viewed, the addition of definite articles, the smoothing out of noun genders, and more were likewise changes to help even out the text.

It is clear regardless of where one draws the exact lines that the framing employed by some scholars is vastly overblown. As Professor Boyd-Taylor of Trinity Western University concludes, the Lucian text type is *"loyal and conservative"*.[249] One should use equal weights and measures when dealing with these text-critical issues. For though one should not dismiss or ignore the textual issues of the Septuagint, one must also not blow them out of proportion. The vast majority of these variants have no bearing on the meaning of the text, and those few that do should be seriously considered

---

[247] Salvesen and Law, eds. *The Oxford Handbook of the Septuagint*, 539.
[248] Salvesen and Law, eds. *The Oxford Handbook of the Septuagint*, "septuagint", 543.
[249] Salvesen and Law, eds. *The Oxford Handbook of the Septuagint*, 24.

and dealt with, just as the text critic of the New Testament would do. The question of the ending of the Gospel of Mark, the pericope of the woman taken in adultery in John 7:53–8:11, the Comma Johanneum, and others present difficult and important questions for the reader of the New Testament, but it would be folly to talk about a plurality of New Testaments on account of this.

The New Testament is witnessed to by three or so different textual families, the Western, the Alexandrine (which closely align with most modern editions of the New Testament and the critical text employed by most scholars today) and the Byzantine majority text used historically from Jerome forward, and found today in some Bibles like the King James Version and the New King James Version. The Byzantine majority text is also used by a minority of scholars. One can rightly debate and discuss the benefits and reasons for preferring one or the other text, but only the most extreme would deny that all of these texts, though having important differences, are good and trustworthy editions of the Greek New Testament. Applying the same equal measurement to the Septuagint leaves the same conclusion. Though there are still some textual issues which must be dealt with, this does in no way undermine the fact that the Septuagint that is available today is an excellent and reliable text.

THE KAIGE

The last of the textual issues that deserve discussion is that of the kaige recension, its related matters, and the question of the book of Daniel. The term *kaige* describes a tendency found within some manuscripts to move the Septuagint into closer alignment with the particular Hebrew text available to the copyist, somewhat akin to the early Jerome. This recension and its influence should not be exaggerated though. It is limited to some manuscripts and is, for reasons not yet perfectly understood, "also limited to parts of the Septuagint and not all of it".[250] It is chiefly found within the text of Judges, 2 Samuel chapter 10 and onward, a few chapters in 1 Kings, and a few chapters in 2 Kings.[251] Though it must also be added that the Hebraizing tendency is, for a few manuscripts, also found in other books. The most famous example of this is the ancient fragments of a copy of the

---

[250] Salvesen and Law, eds. *The Oxford Handbook of the Septuagint*, 452.
[251] Salvesen and Law, eds. *The Oxford Handbook of the Septuagint*, 452.

PART IV: THE SEPTUAGINT IN THE THIRD MILLENNIUM CHURCH

Minor Prophets, dating from before the first century, that were found at Nahal Hever.

Again, talking about these differences abstractly can be misleading and cause one to overestimate the actual differences, which are in reality rather minute. The word kaige itself is one of the phenomena exhibited by the namesake text type, since the Hebrew phrase גַּם (and also) was translated more literally into the Greek καὶ γε (and also). Other features commonly associated with kaige is a more literal translation of the Hebrew term אִישׁ (man) but which can also be used as an indefinite pronoun (one, someone). The Septuagint translators translated this word depending on the text, either using the Greek word for man, ἀνήρ, or the indefinite pronoun, ἕκαστος, while the kaige recension changed this and consistently translated it as man regardless of the contextual meaning. Thus, in Judges 2:6 the common Septuagint reads, ἕκαστος εἰς τὸν οἶκον αὐτοῦ (each went to his house) while the kaige replaces the word each with man to bring it into closer conformity with the Hebrew, though it makes the Greek read less evenly.

Other features included etymological translations and more literal and less idiomatical translations, such as τὸ ἀρεστὸν ἐνώπιόν σου (what is pleasing before you), as found in the common Septuagint, to τὸ ἀγαθὸν ἐν ὀφθαλμοῖς σου (what is good in your eyes).[252] One can easily misunderstand and overvalue the influence and magnitude of these so-called recensions when they are discussed in isolation from concrete examples.

THEODOTIAN AND DANIEL

Finally, the issue of the book of Daniel should be touched upon. Here, a peculiar development took place. The original translation of the book of Daniel by the Seventy-Two was at some point, most likely in the third and fourth centuries onward, substituted by the translation of Theodotian in the use of most, though not all, of the church fathers.[253] At the time of Origen, this development was not yet accomplished, though some, like Hippolytus of Rome, quoted Theodotian's Daniel. Yet Origen explicitly distinguishes the two versions and compares their text of Daniel to each other, clearly juxtaposing them as two different editions (Letter to Africanus chapters 2 and 3). However, sometime following Origen, the original book of Daniel,

---

[252] Salvesen and Law, eds. *The Oxford Handbook of the Septuagint*, 453.
[253] Salvesen and Law, eds. *The Oxford Handbook of the Septuagint*, 292.

curiously, fell out of favor and was replaced by Theodotian's translation by most Christian authors.

Theodotian's translation is closer to the Masoretic Hebrew in some areas, but it is overall still closest to the Septuagint. Indeed, Theodotian's Daniel includes the passages of Susanna and of Bel and the Dragon—passages which Origen also underscored, *"is found in both"* that is, both the original Septuagint book of Daniel as well as Theodotian's translation. Rather than being a new translation made from the Greek, Theodotian's work is rather a revision and reworking of the original translation of the Seventy[254] into a more literal style closer to the Hebrew, yet a Hebrew text different from the Masoretic Text and related to the Hebrew Vorlage of the Septuagint, though not exactly the same.[255]

This is naturally a bit complicated, but on account of its wide circulation and use, many, if not most, of the English translations of the Septuagint have included the Theodotian version of Daniel as an alternative text in addition to the actual Septuagint book of Daniel, such as the Lexham, NETS. The difference between these two is not so much in actual content or passages being included, but rather the style, wording, and phrasing that is sufficiently different for it to be viewed as an actual recension of the original Septuagint's book of Daniel rather than being the result of textual variants.

This topic is further complicated by the fact that some scholars have concluded that the Theodotian book of Daniel is cited by the New Testament authors[256], which means that they had access to a text assumedly already in circulation around 150–200 years before it was translated by Theodotian. As an example, Mark 14:62 could be cited, where Christ says he will "come with the clouds of Heaven," that is, μετὰ τῶν νεφελῶν τοῦ οὐρανοῦ. This is, supposedly, a quotation from Theodotian's Daniel 7:13, which reads that the Son of Man will come μετὰ τῶν νεφελῶν τοῦ οὐρανοῦ *(with the clouds of Heaven)* just like the Gospel of Mark. This differs slightly from the Septuagint's book of Daniel, which reads, ἐπὶ τῶν νεφελῶν τοῦ οὐρανοῦ *(on the clouds of Heaven)* rather than μετὰ τῶν νεφελῶν with ἐπὶ τῶν νεφελῶν *(with the clouds of Heaven)*.

This problem with Theodotian's translation of Daniel is quite perplexing and needs further research, and it might very well be the Septuagint's equivalent of the Mark 16 question. However, it should also be noted that the difference is miniscule, and the sense is the same regardless

---

[254] Salvesen and Law, eds. *The Oxford Handbook of the Septuagint*, 294.
[255] Salvesen and Law, eds. *The Oxford Handbook of the Septuagint*, 295.
[256] Jellicoe, *The Septuagint and Modern Study*, 87.

of which rendition one takes. Indeed, many other probable causes for Mark's use of *with*/μετὰ could be given, such as a quotation from memory, rhetorical flair, intention to allude rather than quote verbatim, especially insofar as the connection hinges on a single word.

It should also be stated that the parallel passage citing the same passage of Daniel follows the wording of the original Septuagint's book of Daniel, ἐπὶ τῶν νεφελῶν τοῦ οὐρανοῦ, as found in the Gospel of Matthew 24:30 and 26:64. One should be careful about concluding too much from a single or a couple of quotations, which are sometimes not intended as verbatim renditions but as allusions or paraphrases, such as the Gospel of Luke which brings the reference to Daniel 7 as a much looser allusion, saying, ἐν νεφέλῃ μετὰ δυνάμεως (*in* [a] *cloud with power*).

This issue is complex and intriguing and would certainly be a fruitful field for further research. It should not be ignored, but neither should it be overblown. At the end of the day, the original text of the Septuagint's book of Daniel is rightly used and included. The Theodotian text should not be forgotten, though, and a good balance seems to have been struck by its inclusion as an alternative text, a kind of *deutero-Daniel*, which is, as Professor Olivier Munnich rightly notes, more correctly viewed as an actual recension of the original book of Daniel of the Septuagint.[257]

FROM THE MEDIEVALS TO THE MODERNS

A certain number of Septuagint manuscripts lay dormant in the European monasteries through much of the Medieval Era. But, as described earlier, the renaissance of Greek learning and the coinciding eclipse of the Byzantine Empire meant that many scholars and clergymen rediscovered old, native manuscripts as well as received, by purchase, gift, or through the belongings of refugees, many new Septuagint manuscripts from the beginning of the 400s A.D. and onward.

The earliest copy of the Septuagint to be made in Western Europe since the copyists stopped transcribing the Greek Septuagint by hand in late antiquity was Aldus Manutius' Aldine Septuagint published in 1518, which contained a copy of the Greek New Testament and the whole Old Testament Septuagint. It shared a good amount of text with the formerly mentioned Complutensian Polyglot described earlier. Sadly, none of these early editions provide adequate information about their manuscriptal basis, but

---

[257] Salvesen and Law, eds. *The Oxford Handbook of the Septuagint*, 294-95.

this edition has recently been re-appraised by scholars for bearing witness to some old readings of the Septuagint from now-lost documents.

The text was in part based on old European manuscripts, some lent by the Vatican Library and some bought in Venice, but also on a codex lent by Cardinal Bessarion himself, a native Greek born in the Byzantine empire who had fled to Italy, where he settled down and later died.[258] These editions, the Aldine and Complutensian texts, would later be supplanted by the official Roman Septuagint, an authoritative edition of the text promulgated and approved by Pope Sixtus V in 1587. This was, unlike the earlier text, almost wholly a diplomatic edition of the text of Codex Vaticanus, one of the four great ancient uncials.

Uncial is the term for a certain type of majuscule—capital letters only—manuscript which was common in antiquity. Of those surviving, four stand out and are known today as the four great uncials. These four codices are extent copies containing both Old and New Testaments bound into one large codex, a very costly and labor-intensive feat of work. One of these uncials is the so-called Codex Vaticanus, the other three being the Codex Alexandrinus, Codex Sinaiticus and Codex Ephraemi Rescriptus. The Roman Septuagint offers the text of the famous Codex Vaticanus,[259] most likely originating from Alexandria sometime around the 340s A.D. or so, during the episcopacy of Athanasius of Alexandria.[260]

Since that time, the textual quality and availability has only improved, and though the Roman Septuagint offered a good text, it was one marked by the shortcomings of relying on a single manuscript. It remained the standard edition until it was replaced by Rahlf's critical edition, published in 1935, which offered a corrected text recreating the original wording of the Septuagint by examining not only the great four uncials, but also patristic quotations and the thousands of other manuscripts of the Septuagint available. These available manuscripts were not just the later Byzantine and Medieval copies, but also the ancient papyri which, though fragmentary, go as far back as the third century B.C. Henry Barclay Swete's text-critical edition of the Septuagint, published at Cambridge University Press in 1909, must also be mentioned. This text, more or less based on the same approach as Rahlf's, offers a very similar text so, though useful, it provides a similar

---

[258] Salvesen and Law, eds. *The Oxford Handbook of the Septuagint*, 37.
[259] Jellicoe, *The Septuagint and Modern Study*, 155-156.
[260] Jellicoe, *The Septuagint and Modern Study*, 178.

PART IV: THE SEPTUAGINT IN THE THIRD MILLENNIUM CHURCH

final result as Rahlf's, which remains the standard Septuagint text in use today.[261]

These latter two editions are also equipped with a textual apparatus providing an overview of the textual variants and the manuscripts supporting those readings, much akin to the most common editions of the Greek New Testament available today, such as the Nestle Aland *Novum Testamentum Graece* and the UBS Revised Edition. The work on the Greek Septuagint continues still, with the Göttingen project that incorporates new findings and publishes a text with a much larger and much more thorough apparatus useful for researchers, scholars, and clergy.

Akin to the procedure of the textual enterprise of the New Testament, it is likewise the goal of the textual work of the Septuagint to the "recovery of the text as it left the hand of the translator".[262] Indeed, as mentioned above, the ongoing Göttingen Septuagint project works along the same lines with an aim toward *"recovering the proto-Septuagint"*.[263]

SEPTUAGINT TRANSLATIONS

As seen earlier, translations of the Septuagint were common throughout the ancient church as it served as the textual basis for the Old Testament for languages as diverse as Latin, Gothic, Coptic, and Armenian. This trend has been rejuvenated, and the Septuagint has also been translated into many modern languages. It has been available in English since 1808, and with Lancelot Brenton's excellent translation from 1854 it is now freely available online. Other English versions deserving mentioning are The Lexham English Septuagint 2012, which is a diplomatic translation based on the text of Codex Vaticanus, and the New English Translation of the Septuagint from 2007, also known as NETS, which is a translation of Rahlf's critical edition and the Göttingen edition when available.

The Septuagint is also available in many other languages, such as the French *La Bible d'Alexandrie*, though this is somewhat of a specialist's edition with a large amount of textual information, commentary, and more. In German, the newly-published *Septuaginta Deutsch* from 2009 offers an available translation based on Rahlf's critical edition. Other translations

---

[261] Salvesen and Law, eds. *The Oxford Handbook of the Septuagint*, 35.
[262] Jellicoe, *The Septuagint and Modern Study*, 1.
[263] Jellicoe, *The Septuagint and Modern Study*, 8.

include the Spanish *La Biblia griega* of 1992 and the Italian *La Biblia dei Settanta*.

CONCLUSION

"In turn, the LXX, now generally exonerated and shown to be basically a faithful translation of one ancient Hebrew text form of each book, sometimes earlier than or superior to the MT, may be used judiciously both to correct the MT and to reconstruct the text of scrolls when they are fragmentary." [264]

— Professor Eugene Ulrich

Though much more could be said—and for those who would like to look further into these issues the bibliography will be helpful—some lines must be drawn up. This chapter provides only a window into a complicated field which will likely benefit from further research in the future, yet, this does not change certain conclusions.

The Septuagint has never been more readily available for those interested in reading and studying it. With just a few clicks on a computer, one can access a freely available translation online in the world's most commonly spoken language—Brenton's English translation of the Septuagint. This and other translations into multiple common modern languages, as well as the many published critical editions of the original Greek text with detailed textual apparatuses, allows the reader a thorough overview of the textual issues and differences present in the Septuagint's transmission.

These modern editions, whether text-critical editions such as Rahlf's Greek Septuagint or the English NETS translation, or diplomatic editions like Lexham's translation, provide the public with very solid texts of the Septuagint. Indeed, too much noise and criticism has unjustly been thrown toward the Septuagint. Discussions of important questions regarding its transmissional history have sometimes been greatly exaggerated and often detached, at least at lay and popular levels, from its proper proportions, resulting occasionally in pure caricature.

The ancient witnesses are surprisingly clear in their acknowledgement of a single, common, and widespread text of the Septuagint, the common or *koine* Septuagint. Jerome and Augustine take this for granted and mention it as a matter of fact. Jerome even presents this view as not only that of the

---

[264] Salvesen and Law, eds. *The Oxford Handbook of the Septuagint*, 445.

PART IV: THE SEPTUAGINT IN THE THIRD MILLENNIUM CHURCH

Latin fathers but of the ancient authors, such as Eusebius and Origin, as well as the contemporary Greeks. This information, it should be noted, is postdated by generations the time from which the earliest complete Septuagint codices have survived.

This is not stated to deny the textual issues the Septuagint faces, as do all ancient texts, but it is said to provide context to the discussion of the problem. For different recensions, textual trends, and more have shaded the form in which the Septuagint has been handed down till this day. Some of these are innocent and stylistic, such as the grammatical improvements found in the common Septuagint, while others have a stronger impact. Yet neither of these should give cause doubt as to whether the Septuagint today is substantially the same. This is certainly the case, just as it is the case for the New Testament, even though it has some textual difficulties and tricky transmissions of some pericopes. When equal weights and measures are used, the conclusion is the same—this is a great witness to the skills and tenacity of the ancient Christian scribes.

LAST REMARKS
BETWEEN THE MASORETES AND THE SEVENTY-TWO

"*The Masoretic Text was not selected in antiquity because of its textual superiority. In fact, it was probably not selected at all. From a certain point onward it was simply used.*" [265]

— Professor Emanuel Tov, as cited by Timothy Law

he choice between the Masoretic Text and the Septuagint as the textual basis for the Old Testament is an important one, and these two are the prime candidates. As the conclusion above shows, the Septuagint was simply the Old Testament of the Christian church in the first half of the millennium, yet today it has almost been wholly replaced by the Masoretic Text, and of that by one single medieval manuscript from Rabbinic Judaism. The *Biblica Hebraica Stuttgardensia* (BHS) today serves almost exclusively as the textual basis for all modern translations of the Old Testament,[266] which rarely depart from its wording. The BHS is a so-called diplomatic edition of the Leningrad Codex, the oldest complete manuscript covering the whole Old Testament, excluding though the deuterocanonical books. The Leningrad Codex was written in the eleventh century and is the premier representative of the Masoretic tradition. The name stems from a group of learned Rabbinic Jewish scholars in the seventh and eighth centuries who edited a group of Hebrew manuscripts,[267] the so-called proto-Masoretic Text, which would result in the codification and stabilization of the Masoretic Text type from early medieval times onward.

This edition brought about certain changes to the Hebrew Text, such as the addition of a complete set of signs and marks denoting the vowel sounds to the otherwise purely consonantal Hebrew text. The Biblica Hebraica then, it must be noted, is *not* a copy of or a reconstruction of the original Old Testament, that is to say an approximation of the autographic texts thought to have been in circulation in ancient Israel, an approach akin to the text-

---

[265] Salvesen and Law, eds. *The Oxford Handbook of the Septuagint*, 75.
[266] Salvesen and Law, eds. *The Oxford Handbook of the Septuagint*, 21.
[267] German Bible Society, "BHS: The Biblia Hebraica Stuttgartensia," academic-bible.com, 2020, https://web.archive.org/web/20230325225541/https://www.academic-bible.com/en/bible-society-and-biblical-studies/scholarly-editions/hebrew-bible/bhs/#c5549.

PART IV: THE SEPTUAGINT IN THE THIRD MILLENNIUM CHURCH

critical editions of the New Testament such as the Novum Testamentum Graece. Rather, the Biblica Hebraica is a diplomatic edition of a single Rabbinic Jewish manuscript dating around 1,000 years after Christ and, in the words of the publishers, "Unlike the scholarly editions of the Greek New Testament, the Biblia Hebraica Stuttgartensia does not set out to reconstruct the original text of the Hebrew Bible".[268]

This does not mean, however, that the Masoretic Text type goes no further back than to the eleventh century. As discussed earlier, textual families related to the Masoretic Text are represented by multiple manuscripts found in the Dead Sea Scrolls, meaning that the parentage of the Masoretic Text goes back to very beginning of the first millennium. Likewise, it is important to note that, though the Masoretic Text is by far the most dominant text during the Medieval era, it is far from the only Hebrew textual tradition which survived antiquity and was passed down. Emmanuel Tov, in all likelihood the greatest living authority on Old Testament textual criticism, recognizes this as well and comments how medieval Hebrew manuscripts will at times depart from the wording of the Leningrad Codex and rather support the Septuagint's reading. He remarks how one must keep in mind how "the medieval [Hebrew] manuscripts cannot be taken as a single entity, as is often done in analyses of this issue".[269]

Much too often the debate is simplistically reduced to a discussion of the Septuagint against one singular and uniform Hebrew Text but, as demonstrated earlier, this simply was not the case at the time of Christ nor even in the Medieval era, given how much change the Masoretic Text underwent and how the Hebrew never offered one uniform text type. The Masoretic Text did indeed end up as the most common text, but it was far from the only one in circulation, both in antiquity and subsequently. Thus, even the textual plurality witnessed to by the Hebrew manuscripts of the Medieval is demonstrative of the textual variation found in documents of earlier ages from which the latter texts were copied. These differences are represented both in regard to the consonantal text as well as the interpretative tradition of the vowels, which often results in a different reading of the same consonantal text.

These different and mutually exclusive interpretative traditions can easily be seen when one compares the Medieval Hebrew manuscripts from Yemen and Cairo. Though both stem from the rabbinical tradition, many

---

[268] German Bible Society, "BHS: The Biblia Hebraica Stuttgartensia".
[269] German Bible Society, "BHS: The Biblia Hebraica Stuttgartensia".

variants are present. The original autographic Hebrew text was by nature purely consonantal, lacking not only vowels but also word divisions. Thus, the Hebrew text suffered from a large degree of intrinsic underdetermination. Emmanuel Tov examines many such examples where, depending on word division, vocalization, and interpretation, one can come up with multiple valid but mutually exclusive interpretations. One such example is Jeremiah 17:16, where the Masoretic Text reads *"and the horrible day"* while the Septuagint reads *"and the day of man"*. Both are fully compatible with the consonantal Hebrew text, the difference only being found in how the words are vocalized (וְיוֹם אָנוּשׁ vs וְיוֹם אֱנוֹשׁ).

The problematic nature of this feature is skillfully presented by Professor Law, who provides the follow illustration:

> One can imagine the difficulty of reading without vowels and the different interpretations that could arise from such a text, as in the following sentence of consonants. Note the increasingly ridiculous different possibilities that follow it:
>
> Jn rn t th str t by brd.
> Jon ran to the store to buy bread.
> Jon, run to the store to buy bread!
> Jon ran to the store to buy a board.
> Jan ran to the stair, at a bay beard.
> Jane, I run to thee, a star to obey, a bride!
>
> These are laughable examples, but they show that, even if one is competent in the language, various interpretations can arise—some plausible, some absurd.[270]

This inherent characteristic of the inspired autographical Hebrew text played an important role for the church's reception of the Septuagint in that the Septuagint, apart from being an inspired translation itself, also served in a derived sense as a divine illumination of a dim Hebrew text. This is not to say that the Hebrew text was not inspired, it was affirmably so, yet as part of God's ongoing revelation, the Septuagint acts as a further revelation illuminating the earlier one even more. The Pentateuch was followed by the

---

[270] Law, *When God Spoke Greek*, 22.

PART IV: THE SEPTUAGINT IN THE THIRD MILLENNIUM CHURCH

writings of the Prophets, and the hidden Hebrew was made clear by the Septuagint, just as the New Testament served as the final, not only fulfillment, but also illumination of the Old Testament.

This theme of the Septuagint as an expositor of the Hebrew is expressed by authors such as Justin Martyr, who makes comments about the translators not only being translators, but also being ἐξηγήσεων (*exegeters or interpreters*). Hilary of Poitiers also commented about the Seventy-Two having received the sacred teaching of Moses so that their translation would be a correct, determinative exposition of the underdetermined Hebrew text.

The question at hand then, cannot be reduced to a discussion of the merits of the Septuagint over and against that of the Hebrew text, the only valid representative of which is assumed to be the Masoretic Text. The "*Hebrew Text*" of our time, often quite simplistically understood to be ideally expressed in the Leningrad Codex, is a grave misunderstanding. Such a view fails to properly identify the inspired sacred text's nature as consonantal which much, much later received an additional interpretative and explanatory grid of vowels and word divisions by the rabbinical Masoretic scholars of the late first millennium. Therefore, the question is not just one of the Septuagint versus the Hebraica Veritas, but it is first a question of which Hebrew textual family? Then, when that is decided, it is a question secondly of which interpretation of that dim consonantal text is true?

The fact of the Hebrew text's intrinsic indeterminacy is too often overlooked, even when granting the additions and edits of the Masoretes. For, unlike that of the Septuagint with its developed vowel system and with access to the enormous corpus of Greek literature, the interpretation of the Hebrew text is by nature much more difficult on account of the much smaller amount of biblical Hebrew in existence—there are countless examples of rare vocabulary, uncommon consonant roots, and unclear semantic range of words in the biblical Hebrew that still exists. Professor Grinfield, commenting on this issue, notes how it is often the case that less frequent Hebrew words must be understood through comparisons with foreign languages such as Ugaritic, Moabitic, Arabic, and even much more distant Semitic languages such as Ethiopian and even Coptic.[271] This is the case not only with scores of words concerning especially names of plants, animals, and the like but also in regard to important terms and titles. Many

---

[271] Grinfield, *An Apology for the Septuagint*, 57.

such examples could be made, but in the interest of brevity one case will help to exemplify this issue.

One such case is the important title of God as *El Shaddai* (אֵל שַׁדַּי) which in the Septuagint is translated into *God almighty*, which is a very common appellative of God. But the meaning of the Hebrew term *Shaddai* is very controversial. This puzzle is amply illustrated by the biblical scholar Margaret Barker who, in her analysis of the term's meaning, affirms the murky and difficult nature of the problem at hand. She writes, *"etymology, however, offers some interesting possibilities"*.[272] Latching on to this approach, she discusses whether the title might not justifiably be translated as *God with breasts* if not *The God of breasts*, that is, as a certain epitaph underscoring the divine feminine's blessing of the patriarch with fertility. As support for these *"interesting possibilities"*, she cites the scholarly article *"The God with Breasts"* by the biblical scholar Biale, who, with a foundation in comparative linguistics, compares the Akkadian term *shadu* and the Coptic root *shdi*, denoting the act of suckling,[273] and interprets *El Shaddai* as *The God with Breasts*, or *The Suckling El*.[274]

Though etymologies can often be relevant, such an approach as presented above must be strongly criticized as languages, even closely related ones, can differ very greatly in meaning even for closely related etymological terms. One such example could be the King James Version's translation of Jeremiah 32:27 as *The God of all flesh* which in the German Textbibel is translated as *der Gott alles Fleisches* (*the God of all flesh*). The English term *flesh* is equivalent etymologically with the German term *Fleisch*, which also happens to share the same meaning in both languages. This is not that surprising, considering that these two languages are closely related Germanic languages. But the highly problematic nature of this sort of etymological equivocation can be seen when trying to interpret the Danish sentence *al flæsks Gud* which, though being cognates and etymologically closely related, means something wholly different. For the God of all *flæsk* would not mean the God of all flesh, but rather the God of all pigmeat, a meaning one would not at all arrive at unless one had a concrete knowledge of Danish, no matter how well one had studied the German and English

---

[272] Margaret Barker, "Wisdom: The Queen of Heaven," *Scottish Journal of Theology* 55, no. 2 (April 17, 2002): 154, https://doi.org/10.1017/S0036930602000224.

[273] David Biale, "The God with Breasts: El Shaddai in the Bible," *History of Religions* 21, no. 3 (1982): 248-9, https://doi.org/10.2307/1062160.

[274] Biale, "The God with Breasts: El Shaddai in the Bible," 249.

cognates of the word. Therefore, though one should not necessarily exclude this etymological method, their results are tied to subjective taste and conjecture to such a degree that they are practically bereft of certitude.

Such an example illuminates the uncertainties in trying to decipher semantic range by comparing cognates, even for three closely related Germanic languages. This is a problem which is only exacerbated when done not just with less closely related languages like Hebrew, Ugaritic, and Moabitic, but much more so when done through the lens of distantly related languages such as Coptic, Arabic, or Akkadian. At best, one can only arrive at an uncertain approximation of the probable meaning of the term at some certain time. The issue is that this method, though ridden with uncertainties, very often is absolutely necessary in deciphering difficult Hebrew terms and roots whose rare appearance or use make it impossible to pin down their meaning by appeal to the Biblical Hebrew literature alone, the amount of which is rather limited. This stands in very stark contrast to Koine Greek, the dominant socio-dialect used by the New Testament's authors as well as the Septuagint, the amount of literature truly is an embarrassment of riches. This begs the question of why such desperate measures should be employed when the clarity of the Greek Septuagint is comfortably within reach?

THE INSUFFICIENCY OF THE MASORETIC TEXT

"As in Jeremiah, scholars knew that there were radical divergences between the Septuagint and Hebrew Bible, but Samuel is special because all scholars will admit that the Hebrew Bible contains a highly corrupted text. Modern English Bibles even give evidence in their footnotes where often the editor has been forced to resort to another ancient version to determine what the text says. The NRSV, for example, has at the end of 1 Samuel 10 the paragraph about King Nahash, which is absent from the Hebrew Bible and also from most other English translations. Some scholars propose that this paragraph was original to the text (as seen in the Qumran fragment) and was only later accidentally lost by a scribal error." [275]

— Professor Timothy Law

As pointed out in the introduction to this book, the Masoretic Text is not a bad text. It has served many Christians well for centuries, but this does not mean that the text is adequate or sufficient. The Masoretic Text suffers from

---

[275] Law, *When God Spoke Greek*, 80.

multiple deficiencies resulting in the fact that no translation is able to rely wholly on it. Christian translations never do so consistently, but incorporate elements from the Septuagint sometimes greater and sometimes in smaller degrees. This can range from things as minor as the ordering of the canonical books as well as the naming and divisional conventions. For example, modern translations present Genesis rather than *Bereshit*. They use a Septaugintal ordering of books: five books of Moses, the historical books, Joshua–Esther, the wisdom literature, and lastly the prophetic books. This ordering is in contrast to the Masoretic ordering of *Torah*, *Nevi'im* (*the prophets*, though Joshua and Kings are also included her), followed by the loose category of *Ketuvim* (*writings*, encompassing books like the Psalms, Job, and Daniel, who the Masoretes apparently did not reckon among the prophetical writings, and others).

Normally, however, the reliance on the Septuagint is greater than on the Masoretic Text. As will be seen in the following chapter, messianic passages are curiously missing at times from the Masoretic Text, and the majority of Christian translations follow the inspired authors of the New Testament in their quotations of the Old Testament, even going so far as to insert the wording of the Septuagint in what is otherwise a translation of the Masoretic Text. Thus, almost all translations of the prophecy of the Virgin Birth in Isaiah follow the Septuagint, apart from a few exceptions, such as the New American Bible, NET Bible, and the New Revised Standard Version—an odd choice which can at least be praised on account of the consistency it expresses.

Putting the question of tendencies and editions aside for a moment, one of the more daunting deficiencies of the Masoretic Text is the explicit corruption and simply erroneous text which it at times transmits, being of a particularly bad quality in some of the historic books such as Kings and Samuel. Concerning this issue, Professor Jellicoe writes, "The Hebrew text of these books [Samuel and Kings] has reached us in a state of considerable disorder, and the main value of the LXX has not unnaturally been measured in terms of an aid to restoration. In brief, it may be stated at the outset that the study of the LXX of the four Books of the Kingdoms points strongly to an underlying Hebrew text superior to that which has come down to us." [276]

This should not be read as a general indictment of the Masoretic Text which, in general, is a fairly good transmission of a version of the Hebrew

---

[276] Jellicoe, *The Septuagint and Modern Study*, 282.

PART IV: THE SEPTUAGINT IN THE THIRD MILLENNIUM CHURCH

text that was in circulation around 100 B.C., but it should be read as a note on the deficiencies found in the Masoretic Text.

Other times, the Septuagint preserves readings and passages which have not suffered corruption, as they have simply been dropped out or lost in the Masoretic Text due to the errors or carelessness of the Jewish scribes. One such example is found in 1 Samuel 14:41. Below, the top quotation is according to the Masoretic Text, v. 40-41, and beneath this quotation is according to the Septuagint with the text omitted by the Masoretic Text in bold:

> Then he said to all Israel, "You be on one side, and my son Jonathan and I will be on the other side." And the people said to Saul, "Do what seems good to you." Therefore Saul said to the Lord God of Israel, "Give Thummin." And Saul and Jonathan were taken, but the people escaped.
>
> — 1 Samuel 14:40–41 [Masoretic Text]

> Then he said to all Israel, "You shall be on one side, and I and Jonathan my son will be on the other side." And the people said to Saul, "Do what seems good to you." Therefore Saul said, "O LORD God of Israel, **why hast thou not answered thy servant this day? If this guilt is in me or in Jonathan my son, O LORD, God of Israel, give Urim; but if this guilt is in thy people Israel, give Thummim.**" And Jonathan and Saul were taken, but the people escaped.
>
> — 1 Samuel 14:40–41 [Septuagint]

Here, the Masoretic Text has omitted a rather large piece of text which makes the narrative quite incomprehensible. The mistaken was likely not purposeful but rather is due to the inattention of the scribe whose eyes jumped from the first *Israel* to the second *Israel*, thus skipping the text in between.[277] This passage simply slipped out of the entire textual tradition of the Masoretes and is today found only in the Septuagint. Professor Tov, the leading authority on Old Testament Hebrew textual criticism, concurs and writes:

---

[277] Law, *When God Spoke Greek*, 50.

SEVENTY-TWO SERVANTS OF THE WORD

Of special interest are some sections which were omitted from the Hebrew text by way of parablepsis and which therefore are now pluses [i.e. additional text omitted by the Masoretic Text] in the LXX (cf. p. 56). If the analysis of a presumed case of parablepsis in MT (*homoioteleuton* or *homoioarcton*) is correct, it is legitimate to retrovert the original Hebrew text from the LXX. There are often favorable conditions for such retroversions if the words occurring in the Greek plus are paralleled by Greek-Hebrew equivalents in the context (...) There seems to be no way of explaining the text except with the aid of the section which has been transmitted solely by the LXX (and V) and which, incidentally, provides the only description of the functioning of the oracle of the Urim and Thummim. This section must have been omitted accidentally.[278]

These kind of deficient omissions in the Masoretic Text are not confined to 1 Samuel alone, but Professor Tov also provides examples from 2 Chronicles 23:18. Additionally, one must not forget the quite infamous example of Psalm 145, which is an acrostic psalm except for a single verse.

An acrostic psalm is a genre of tight composition in which the verses follow the Hebrew alphabet: the first verse begins with *aleph*, the next with *beth*, and so on. Yet curiously, the Masoretic Text omits a whole verse, ruining the acrostic nature of the psalm because it skips the verse which was supposed to begin with *nun*. Interestingly, this verse is found within the Septuagint and also survives in other textual traditions, such as Syriac translation as well as in a few manuscripts from the Dead Sea Scrolls. This is quite intriguing insofar as, when translated out of the Hebrew and into the Greek, the psalm no longer contains the acrostic structure, making it highly unlikely that the verse is an addition, but when retranslated from Greek into Hebrew the verse is found to begin with the letter *nun* in the position where the composition of the psalm would demand it. Indeed, a single late Hebrew manuscript has been found that includes the verse that is missing in all the manuscripts of the Masoretic Text. The verse reads in the Septuagint, "Faithful is the Lord in all his words, and holy in all his works." The Greek word for *faithful*, δίκαιος, is in Hebrew נאמן (he is faithful, *niphal*, from the root *aleph-mem-nun*, where the famous word *amen* is also taken from, meaning *truthful, trustful, faithful*).

---

[278] Emanuel Tov, *The Greek and Hebrew Bible: Collected Essays on the Septuagint* (Leiden ; Boston: Brill, 1999), 177.

PART IV: THE SEPTUAGINT IN THE THIRD MILLENNIUM CHURCH

One last example of missing text in the Masoretic Text is the famous story of David and King Saul. The episode that introduces the meeting of these historic characters is actually quite shorter in the Septuagint compared to the amount of text provided by the Masoretic Text. Yet this additional text bears signs of being later additions, both insofar as they are lacking from the earlier Septuagint and because the narrative itself makes much better sense without the interpolation.

In 1 Samuel 16:15f, both the Masoretic Text and the Septuagint agree and introduce David the son of Jesse the Bethlehemite as a solution to the torments suffered by King Saul. The text is the same in both textual traditions for the rest of the chapter and both describe that Saul loved David, that David found favor with Saul, became his armourbearer, and played the harp for him. The agreement continues in the first 11 verses of chapter 17 as well, but after that the Masoretic Text adds 20 or so verses before both texts realign again. That is to say, the passage found in the Masoretic Text's 1 Samuel 17:11–31 is not found in the Septuagint. The passage provides further details about David's background and how he brought supplies for the Israelite army, yet this passage is not the only addition, for at the end of chapter 17, in verse 54, where the chapter ends in the Septuagint the Masoretic Text adds a few further verses describing what happened after David's defeat of Goliath:

> When Saul saw David going out against the Philistine, he said to Abner, the commander of the army, "Abner, whose son is this youth?" And Abner said, "As your soul lives, O king, I do not know." So the king said, "Inquire whose son this young man is." Then, as David returned from the slaughter of the Philistine, Abner took him and brought him before Saul with the head of the Philistine in his hand. And Saul said to him, "Whose son are you, young man?" So David answered, "I am the son of your servant Jesse the Bethlehemite."
>
> — 1 Samuel 17:55–58 [Masoretic Text]

This passage is undeniably very awkward, along with the addition between verses 12–32, and it makes the narrative quite odd. According to both the Septuagint and the Masoretic Text, David is taken to the royal court of King Saul to become a court musician and armourbearer, King Saul comes to love him and give him favor. Then the Masoretic Text adds a passage describing how David occasionally went home to feed the sheep of the family flock, a chore which the favorite member of the royal court supposedly had time and need of tending to. Then David, in verse 17, is told by his father to go to the army of King Saul and carry with him cheese and other food stuffs, meaning that David, the king's armourbearer, apparently was not present with the army. Making the situation even more odd, David's brother Eliab, who was present with Saul's army according to verse 28, is surprised to see David there and inquires who he left to guard the sheep. That King Saul's armourbearer is found on the battlefield rather than tending sheep, being a favored member of the royal court, should only be expected by those familiar with the text preceding this addition.

Worse yet is the last addition quoted above, where Saul is described as not knowing who David is and, apparently, meets him for the first time in verse 58, this only hours after their last conversation in verses 32–33, which comes after an extended period of service in Saul's court where David finds his love and favor. The text is, to put it mildly, very confused and clearly edited in some haphazard manner, while the same story reads smoothly and evenly in the Septuagint, which doubtless represents the original unedited version in contrast to the altered edition of the Masoretic Text.

THE LOST MESSIANIC TENDENCY OF THE MASORETIC TEXT

"In a similar vein, the passages that came to be understood in a messianic sense during the Roman period in the Second Temple and following periods (e.g. Aquila) seem to have been de-messianized and depoliticized as well" [279]

— Professor Michaël N. van der Meer, discussing the post-Christian rabbinical translation of the Old Testament of Aquila

In a certain regard, the Septuagint was itself a messianic project, as was noticed by many of the early Christian authors. By virtue of its translation into the lingua franca of the time, the story of God's dealing in human history and the promises and prophecies made by the prophets concerning the coming Savior were revealed to all in the common tongue of the Mediterranean. What had before been hidden in Hebrew and available to only a few quickly spread to all the major port cities and urban centers and beyond—first to the Hellenic empires and later to the Roman Empire as

---

[279] Salvesen and Law, eds. *The Oxford Handbook of the Septuagint*, 447.

PART IV: THE SEPTUAGINT IN THE THIRD MILLENNIUM CHURCH

well. This important aspect of the Old Testament's translation cannot be understated.

In fact, this revolutionary development plays a large part in the New Testament as well where its results are seen again and again. Here, the so-called *God fearers* (φοβούμενοι τὸν Θεόν or θεοσεβεῖ) play a large role, especially in the Acts of the Apostles. For the wide circulation of the Septuagint, in a period of fundamental shifts in Greco-Roman religious praxis, the flourishing mystery cults, the rise of the religio-philosophical schools such as Epicureans, Stoics, and more meant that forms of Old Testament monotheism were able to spread to many gentiles. In that period of general religious disruption, a new religious class of *God fearers*, that is, gentile believers in the one God of the Old Testament, began arising in the Roman Empire, mediated through the Greek Old Testament.

Proselytes, itself a Greek term originating from the Septuagint, were in large part a phenomenon resulting from the Septuagint and the preaching and religious missionizing it facilitated. Professor Marcos also notes how it was also only after the translation of the Septuagint that Greco-Roman authors began interacting with Jewish religion.[280]

---

[280] Fernández Marcos, *The Septuagint in Context*, 306.

SEVENTY-TWO SERVANTS OF THE WORD

Luke 7:5	
"For he loves our nation, and has built us a synagogue."	ἀγαπᾷ γὰρ τὸ ἔθνος ἡμῶν, καὶ τὴν συναγωγὴν αὐτὸς ᾠκοδόμησεν ἡμῖν.
Acts 10:2	
Cornelius (...) a devout man and one who feared God with all his household, who gave alms generously to the people, and prayed to God always.	εὐσεβὴς καὶ φοβούμενος τὸν θεὸν σὺν παντὶ τῷ οἴκῳ αὐτοῦ, ποιῶν τε ἐλεημοσύνας πολλὰς τῷ λαῷ, καὶ δεόμενος τοῦ θεοῦ διὰ παντός.
Acts 13:16	
Then Paul stood up, and motioning with his hand said, "Men of Israel, and you who fear God, listen!	Ἀναστὰς δὲ Παῦλος, καὶ κατασείσας τῇ χειρί, εἶπεν, Ἄνδρες Ἰσραηλῖται, καὶ οἱ φοβούμενοι τὸν θεόν, ἀκούσατε!
Acts 13:26	
"Men and brethren, sons of the family of Abraham, and those among you who fear God, to you the word of this salvation has been sent.	Ἄνδρες ἀδελφοί, υἱοὶ γένους Ἀβραάμ, καὶ οἱ ἐν ὑμῖν φοβούμενοι τὸν θεόν, ὑμῖν ὁ λόγος τῆς σωτηρίας ταύτης ἀπεστάλη.
Acts 16:14	
Now a certain woman named Lydia heard us. She was a seller of purple from the city of Thyatira, who worshiped God. The Lord opened her heart to heed the things spoken by Paul.	Καί τις γυνὴ ὀνόματι Λυδία, πορφυρόπωλις πόλεως Θυατείρων, σεβομένη τὸν θεόν, ἤκουεν· ἧς ὁ κύριος διήνοιξεν τὴν καρδίαν, προσέχειν τοῖς λαλουμένοις ὑπὸ τοῦ Παύλου.
Acts 17:4	
This Jesus whom I preach to you is the Christ." ⁴And some of them were persuaded; and a great multitude of the devout Greeks, and not a few of the leading women, joined Paul and Silas.	Καί τινες ἐξ αὐτῶν ἐπείσθησαν, καὶ προσεκληρώθησαν τῷ Παύλῳ καὶ τῷ Σίλᾳ, τῶν τε σεβομένων Ἑλλήνων πολὺ πλῆθος, γυναικῶν τε τῶν πρώτων οὐκ ὀλίγαι.
Acts 17:17	
Therefore he reasoned in the synagogue with the Jews and with the Gentile worshipers, and in the marketplace daily with those who happened to be there.	Διελέγετο μὲν οὖν ἐν τῇ συναγωγῇ τοῖς Ἰουδαίοις καὶ τοῖς σεβομένοις, καὶ ἐν τῇ ἀγορᾷ κατὰ πᾶσαν ἡμέραν πρὸς τοὺς παρατυγχάνοντας.
Acts 18:7	
entered the house of a certain man named Justus, one who worshiped God, whose house was next door to the synagogue.	ἦλθεν εἰς οἰκίαν τινὸς ὀνόματι Ἰούστου, σεβομένου τὸν θεόν, οὗ ἡ οἰκία ἦν συνομοροῦσα τῇ συναγωγῇ.

Table 8 – God-Fearers and Gentile Inclusion in Luke-Acts

In the New Testament, many of these *God fearers* are described, such as Cornelius, who was described in Acts 10:2 as one who *"was pious and feared the one God*" (εὐσεβὴς καὶ φοβούμενος τὸν θεόν). In other places, these *God fearers* are described as constituting whole groups, which indicates their not-so-inconsiderable number. As shown in the table below, these *God fearers* represented not only gentiles who had settled in Roman Palestine, such as Cornelius, but quite often also gentiles far removed from the Jewish lands, such as Lydia, or the many Greek speaking *God fearers* found in the Synagogue in, for example, Thessaloniki. Timothy is also described in 2 Timothy 3:15 as having known the *"Sacred Scriptures from childhood"*, though he was only half-Jewish himself—his mother being a Jew while his father was most likely a Greek because Timothy himself was uncircumcised.

Needless to say, these *God fearers* knew Scripture and had heard proclamations of the God of Israel through the Septuagint. The church fathers also, as described at length by Eusebius in his *Praeparatio evangelica*, acknowledge this as an intrinsic feature of the Septuagint, which itself was messianic, in that it helped prepare the road for Christ in its proclamation of the one true God of all the world, and in its disclosure of the prophecies which enabled many gentiles to convert and await the arrival of the promised *Messiah*, which in the Greek Septuagint simply was *Christ*, the Greek term for Messiah. This accessibility to the Holy Scriptures enabled many gentiles to leave their former religious persuasions behind and to convert, so much so that these proselytes and *God fearers* were common all over the Roman Empire, even to such an extent that at the time of Paul, some uncircumcised gentiles had grown up with a thorough knowledge of Scripture, such as Timothy.

According the fathers, it was not just in this formative way that the Septuagint served in a messianic and salvific manner. Also in regard to the content of the pages themselves did they notice significant differences, actually to such an extent that one can justly speak about a missing messianic tendency in the Masoretic Text as compared to the Septuagint. In the centuries leading up to the time of Christ, Judaism had entered a period of religious upheaval with many strains of Jewish thought moving in a very universalist direction, foreshadowing the Christian message in some ways. Yet in the decades following Christ's death, and with the final break between what would become Rabbinic Judaism and Christianity, a much more defensive and closeknit posture would be taken.

Following the destruction of the Second Temple in Jerusalem, Judaism especially became much more in-group oriented and began defining itself more strongly over and against Christianity. This movement in religious thought is also clearly expressed in the changing attitude of Judaism toward the Septuagint. Professor Marcos, noting this development, describes how the clear rejecting of the Septuagint and the embrace of the Masoretic Text is closely connected to this shift. Increasingly, the Septuagint began to be seen as so closely connected with Christianity and a more messianic and universal expression of Judaism, that it proved incompatible with the attitude of Rabbinic Judaism[281]. Professor Jellicoe also concurs and calls this Christian takeover of the Septuagint, and later Judaism's abandonment of it, as "one of the most remarkable take-over bids in history".[282] As remarked on in the chapters about the patristic reception, this departure from the Septuagint resulted in many heated debates between the early Christians and the Jews concerning the multiple biblical passages, which the Jews were accused of having altered or edited, since the copying and transcription of the Hebrew manuscripts had been an exclusive activity of the Synagogal Jews who had firmly rejected Christianity. Thus, it became in the Synagogue alone that the Hebrew text would survive, and it would survive almost exclusively in one single text form, namely the Masoretic Text.

Though it would be easy, and for many people tempting, to write off the patristic comments as biased Christian polemics against the Jews, that would be much too simplistic. For there truly is a tendency of the Masoretic Text, especially in passages with a messianic or universalistic touch, to have a different reading than that which is found in the Septuagint. One must also note that, because of the very polycentric distribution of the Septuagint being transmitted and copied by both Jews and Christians in the first couple of centuries A.D., it is very difficult to imagine some sort of organized Christian conspiracy to remove or alter certain passages, especially those cited by the New Testament, as they by their very nature must predate Christianity. The Masoretic Text, however, actually did experience such a confined transmissional bottleneck, in that it was copied, edited, and modified with an extensive system of vowel points and accentuations by a small and definite group, the Masoretes, in a relatively defined geographical area in northern Israel near Lake Tiberias.[283]

This final text which left the hands of the Masoretes cannot at all be assumed to be a better reflection of the original Hebrew manuscripts of the Old Testament books, as Professor Law also writes, "*one thing is clear, it should*

---

[281] Fernández Marcos, *The Septuagint in Context*, 109.
[282] Jellicoe, *The Septuagint and Modern Study*, 75.
[283] Law, *When God Spoke Greek*, 22-23.

PART IV: THE SEPTUAGINT IN THE THIRD MILLENNIUM CHURCH

not be postulated that the Masoretic Text better or more frequently reflects the original text of the biblical books than any other text"[284]. Thus, neither should one give a priority judgement of reliability in view of the Masoretic Text when comparing its readings to the Septuagint, and markedly not when, unlike the Septuagint, the Masoretic Text was much less immune to centrally organized alterations and editing on account of its transmissional history.

These vulnerabilities, however, prove nothing by themselves but should be kept in mind when discussing demonstrative examples and apparent examples. One such demonstrative example of a Jewish alteration of a very important messianic passage, at least in the eyes of the church, is found in Psalm 22, a psalm cited by Jesus himself at the crucifixion. Verse 16 has special significance, as it reads, *"they have pierced my hands and my feet"*. The Masoretic Text, quite curiously, reads something quite different, namely *"like a lion* [they are] *at my hands and my feet"*. In the Masoretic Text, כָּאֲרִי יָדַי וְרַגְלָי is a nominal sentence, which is quite common, meaning that the verb is implied and specified by the context. The translation *like a lion they are at my hand and my feet* is the plain meaning of the Hebrew text and is also the translation given by NET Bible, Tanakh (1985), Jewish Bible (1998), and others. Only by changing the very consonantal text itself can the reading of the Septuagint be arrived at. The Hebrew word כָּאֲרִי (*like a lion*) must first have its *yod*, the final letter, changed into a *vaw*. But even if this change is made, and it is an easy error to make, as the two Hebrew letters *yod* and *vaw* look like each other, then one would still end up with a less than satisfying result. For even if the *yod* is changed into a *vaw*, one would end up with the word כָּאֲרוּ, which is somewhat odd. The Hebrew root כרה does indeed mean *to dig*, and it would fit fine in the sense of *they have pierced*. However, the issue is that the normal third person plural form of כרה/*to dig* is כָּרוּ and not כָּאֲרוּ as is found in Psalm 22:16, even when changing the final *yod* into a *vaw*. This is peculiar, for the verb כרה is quite common in the Old Testament, occurring approximately 17 times. Yet not once does it appear with an *aleph* regardless of the form, and when it does appear in the third person plural form, as it does twice, then in both cases it is written כָּרוּ.

---

[284] Fernández Marcos, *The Septuagint in Context*, 23.

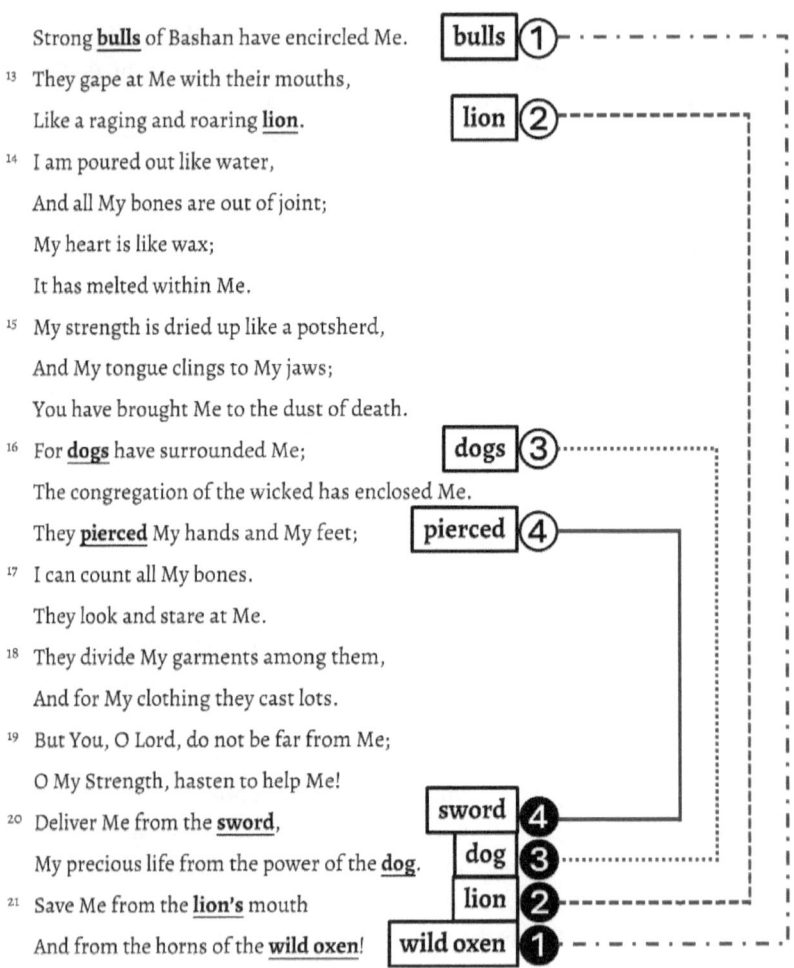

Figure 7 – Chiastic structure of Psalm 22:12-21

The attempt by some of salvaging the Hebrew text at best results in a rather *ad hoc* solution which, regardless, still has to alter the consonantal text, and even when this is done, the result is far from convincing.

The important question that must be asked, nevertheless, is if the writing as found in the Hebrew Masoretic Text of *"like a lion they are at my hands and my feet"* is the correct and original reading, or if the reading reflected by the Septuagint, *"they have pierced my hand and my feet"* is correct and original instead? If the Septuagint's reading is correct, then how does this reflect on the Christian accusation of anti-Christian changes to the text by the Jews?

PART IV: THE SEPTUAGINT IN THE THIRD MILLENNIUM CHURCH

The example here has been chosen because this textual difference is one example where it can be demonstrably shown that the difference is a result of active Jewish editing. This can be shown by intertextual reasons when examining Psalm 22:13-22, which follows a strict poetic structure as shown in the figure above. This passage is an example of an exquisite chiasm, a sort of poetic device where a tight parallel structure is employed to emphasize a dramatic core, often following a pattern such as 3 2 1 0 1 2 3 with more or fewer couplets. The complex chiastic structure of Psalm 22 is shown in the figure above, where the three couplets encompass a dramatic climax in the central couplet, namely the piercing which stands in parallel to the sword, which becomes even clearer when considering the type of sword common in antiquity. Unlike the much larger broadswords and longswords of Medieval Europe, the swords employed then were much shorter, around 50-60 cm/20-24 inches, like the Egyptian *khopesh*, the Greek ξίφος, or the famous Roman *gladius*—swords which were often used as short swords for thrusts, hence the piercing.

The Masoretic Text's reading, on the other hand, must be firmly rejected, as it reads *"like a lion"* rather than *"they have pierced"* in verse 17, on account of the intertextual arguments. First, this would break the parallelism with the sword, which *"lion"* is not a parallel word to. Secondly, and much more significantly, the word *"lion"* already explicitly serves as a couplet in verses 14 and 22. Thus, the carefully constructed poetic architecture of the psalm itself disproves the Masoretic reading and affirms that of the Septuagint.

This example's usefulness is shown because the alteration of the text itself is easily demonstrated from the text itself. This is rarely possible, but it lends further support to the overall tendency of the Masoretic Text to lack messianic prophecies, a tendency which must be viewed in conjunction with the particular textual transmission of that text type. Keeping this in mind, the following examples can serve as probabilistic support, though neither of them on their own could be used as any sort of conclusive evidence. However, viewed together the result seems to be a compelling vindication of the patristic claims as being much more than unfounded anti-Jewish polemic.

These following examples are in no way exhaustive, but they should be viewed only as illustrative of the bias of the Masoretic Text:

SEVENTY-TWO SERVANTS OF THE WORD

Deuteronomy 32:43, LXX	Deuteronomy 32:43, Qumran, 4QDeut_q	Deuteronomy 32:43, MT
εὐφράνθητε, οὐρανοί, ἅμα αὐτῷ, καὶ προσκυνησάτωσαν αὐτῷ πάντες υἱοὶ θεοῦ, εὐφράνθητε, ἔθνη, μετὰ τοῦ λαοῦ αὐτοῦ, καὶ ἐνισχυσάτωσαν αὐτῷ πάντες ἄγγελοι θεοῦ	ה רנינו שמים עמו והשתחוו לו כל אלהים	הַרְנִינוּ גוֹיִם עַמּוֹ כִּי דַם־עֲבָדָיו יִקּוֹם
Rejoice, O Heavens! With Him, and worship him, all ye Sons of God Rejoice, O ye peoples! With His people, and strengthen Him, all ye Angels of God!	Rejoice, O Heavens with Him! And worship Him, all ye Gods	Rejoice, ye peoples, *with* his people! For he will revenge his servants' blood

Table 9 –*Deuteronomy 32:43 in the Septuagint, Dead Sea Scrolls, and Masoretic Text*

This example is found in the Song of Moses in Deuteronomy 32. Multiple church fathers comment on this passage and see in it a prophecy of Christ by Moses, as he foretells the arrival of a coming Messiah who will be worshiped by the heavenly host. This verse plays an important part in the New Testament as well, as Christ explicitly states that Moses foretold his arrival; in Hebrews 1:6 it is also quoted, though with a minor variance, *"let the angels of God worship him"* rather than *"let the sons of God worship him"*. The Masoretic Text, on the other hand, mentions nothing about worship nor angels which is peculiar, as Hebrews mentions this passage as a quotation. Lastly, and interestingly enough, one Hebrew fragment, 4QDeut_q, has been found supporting the wording of the Septuagint over and against that of the Masoretic Text.

PART IV: THE SEPTUAGINT IN THE THIRD MILLENNIUM CHURCH

Amos 4:13, LXX	Amos 4:13, MT
διότι ἰδοὺ ἐγὼ στερεῶν βροντὴν καὶ κτίζων πνεῦμα καὶ ἀπαγγέλλων εἰς ἀνθρώπους τὸν χριστὸν αὐτοῦ	כִּי הִנֵּה יוֹצֵר הָרִים וּבֹרֵא רוּחַ וּמַגִּיד לְאָדָם מַה־שֵּׂחוֹ
Therefore, see! I am He making strong thunder and creating wind, and am proclaiming His Christ to mankind	Therefore, see! I am creating mountains and wind, and I proclaim to mankind, what his thought is.

Table 10 –Amos 4:13 in the Septuagint and the Masoretic Text

This verse from Amos was used by many church fathers as a reference to the revelation of the future Messiah, which is a poignant term in the Septuagint because it simply speaks about the revelation of *the* χριστὸς *(of Christ)*. The Masoretic Text, however, contains no reference to either a Messiah or Christ, but a reference to the revelation of God's plan, שֵׂחוֹ *(communication or thought)*.

SEVENTY-TWO SERVANTS OF THE WORD

Acts 15:15-18	Amos 9:11-12, LXX	Amos 9:11-12, MT
καὶ τούτῳ συμφωνοῦσιν οἱ λόγοι τῶν προφητῶν καθὼς γέγραπται Μετὰ ταῦτα ἀναστρέψω, καὶ ἀνοικοδομήσω τὴν σκηνὴν Δαυὶδ τὴν πεπτωκυῖαν· καὶ τὰ κατεσκαμμένα αὐτῆς ἀνοικοδομήσω, καὶ ἀνορθώσω αὐτήν· ὅπως ἂν ἐκζητήσωσιν οἱ κατάλοιποι τῶν ἀνθρώπων τὸν κύριον, καὶ πάντα τὰ ἔθνη, ἐφ' οὓς ἐπικέκληται τὸ ὄνομά μου ἐπ' αὐτούς, λέγει κύριος ὁ ποιῶν ταῦτα πάντα.	ἐν τῇ ἡμέρᾳ ἐκείνῃ ἀναστήσω τὴν σκηνὴν Δαυιδ τὴν πεπτωκυῖαν καὶ ἀνοικοδομήσω τὰ πεπτωκότα αὐτῆς καὶ τὰ κατεσκαμμένα αὐτῆς ἀναστήσω καὶ ἀνοικοδομήσω αὐτὴν καθὼς αἱ ἡμέραι τοῦ αἰῶνος ὅπως ἐκζητήσωσιν οἱ κατάλοιποι τῶν ἀνθρώπων καὶ πάντα τὰ ἔθνη, ἐφ' οὓς ἐπικέκληται τὸ ὄνομά μου ἐπ' αὐτούς, λέγει κύριος ὁ θεὸς ὁ ποιῶν ταῦτα	בַּיּוֹם הַהוּא אָקִים אֶת־סֻכַּת דָּוִיד הַנֹּפֶלֶת וְגָדַרְתִּי אֶת־פִּרְצֵיהֶן וַהֲרִסֹתָיו אָקִים וּבְנִיתִיהָ כִּימֵי עוֹלָם: ¹² לְמַעַן יִירְשׁוּ אֶת־שְׁאֵרִית אֱדוֹם וְכָל־הַגּוֹיִם אֲשֶׁר־נִקְרָא שְׁמִי עֲלֵיהֶם נְאֻם־יְהוָה עֹשֶׂה
And with this the words of the prophets agree, just as it is written After this I will return and will rebuild the tabernacle of David, which has fallen down; I will rebuild its ruins, and I will set it up So that the rest of mankind may seek the Lord, even all the Gentiles who are called by My name, says the Lord who does all these things.	On this day I will raise up the tabernacle of David, which has fallen down; I will rebuild its ruins, and I will set it up as it was in days of old. So that the rest of mankind may seek the Lord, even all the Gentiles who are called by My name, says the Lord God, who does all these things.	On that day I will raise up the tabernacle of David, which has fallen down, and I will mend its broken [walls] and its ruins. I will rise up and rebuild it as in the days of old. That they may posses the remnant of Edom, and all the Gentiles who are called by my name, against them is the declaration of the Lord who does this.

Table 11 – Acts 15:15-18 vs. Amos 9:11-12 in the Septuagint and Masoretic Text

PART IV: THE SEPTUAGINT IN THE THIRD MILLENNIUM CHURCH

Amos chapter 9 is also interesting, as it is directly cited in the New Testament. Herein its use by the Apostle James is clearly contingent on the universalist tendency in verse 12, as found in the Septuagint, describing how all people and nations are able to seek the Lord. Though this passage is witnessed to by both the New Testament and the Septuagint, it is lacking the Masoretic Text, which rather discusses national Israel's takeover of the remnant of Edom

Luke 3:6	Isaiah 40:5 LXX	Isaiah 40:5 MT
καὶ ὄψεται πᾶσα σὰρξ τὸ σωτήριον τοῦ θεοῦ	καὶ ὄψεται πᾶσα σὰρξ τὸ σωτήριον τοῦ θεοῦ	וְרָאוּ כָל־בָּשָׂר יַחְדָּו כִּי פִּי יְהוָה דִּבֵּר
And all flesh will see the salvation of God	And all flesh will see the salvation of God	And all flesh, together, will see, for Lord's mouth has spoken.

Table 12 – Luke 3:6 vs. Isaiah 40:5 in the Septuagint and Masoretic Text

This bias is also seen in Luke chapter 3 and its quotation of Isaiah chapter 40. Again, it is seen how the universalist tendency of the Septuagint is expressed in Isaiah, who ties together the notion of the universality of salvation being witnessed by all living, while the Masoretic Text restricts the implication to be concerning God's proclamation only. The verse here, though being quite a short passage, is noticeable as it is quoted in the Gospel of Luke as *"what is written in the Book of the words of Isaiah the Prophet"* (Luke 3:4):

Romans 15:12	Isaiah 11:10 LXX	Isaiah 11:10 MT
καὶ ὁ ἀνιστάμενος ἄρχειν ἐθνῶν, ἐπ' αὐτῷ ἔθνη ἐλπιοῦσιν	καὶ ὁ ἀνιστάμενος ἄρχειν ἐθνῶν, ἐπ' αὐτῷ ἔθνη ἐλπιοῦσιν	עֹמֵד לְנֵס עַמִּים אֵלָיו גּוֹיִם יִדְרֹשׁוּ וְהָיְתָה
And He who shall rise to reign over the Gentiles, in Him shall the Gentiles hope.	And He who shall rise to reign over the Gentiles, in Him shall the Gentiles hope.	He who shall stand as a sign to the people, him shall they ask *about*

Table 13 – Romans 15:12 vs. Isaiah 11:10 in the Septuagint and Masoretic Text

The trend continues and is also seen in Paul's use of Isaiah 11:10 in Romans 15:12. Here, Paul quotes verbatim from the Septuagint, this *"root of Jesse"* who will rise up and rule the nations applies to Christ, and that the nations in turn will trust/believe in him further underscores the Messianic witness and usefulness of the Septuagint. Interestingly enough, though, this part is again absent from the Masoretic Text.

A text that also deserves to be mentioned is Psalm 40:7, which was seen as a clear prophetic reference to the Incarnation by many of the church fathers. This text says, *"a body have you prepared for me"*.[285] It is likewise used in Hebrews 10:5. This text, yet again, differs strongly from the Masoretic Text, which says, *"you have opened my ears"*.

Another very popular reference to the incarnate Christ in the Old Testament among the church fathers was Zephaniah 3:8.

Zephaniah 3:8	
Septuagint	Masoretic Text
Διὰ τοῦτο ὑπόμεινόν με, λέγει κύριος, εἰς ἡμέραν ἀναστάσεώς μου εἰς μαρτύριον, διότι τὸ κρίμα μου εἰς συναγωγὰς ἐθνῶν τοῦ εἰσδέξασθαι βασιλεῖς τοῦ ἐκχέαι ἐπ' αὐτοὺς πᾶσαν ὀργὴν θυμοῦ μου, διότι ἐν πυρὶ ζήλους μου καταναλωθήσεται πᾶσα ἡ γῆ	לָכֵן חַכּוּ־לִי נְאֻם־יְהוָה לְיוֹם קוּמִי לְעַד כִּי מִשְׁפָּטִי לֶאֱסֹף גּוֹיִם לְקָבְצִי מַמְלָכוֹת לִשְׁפֹּךְ עֲלֵיהֶם זַעְמִי כֹּל חֲרוֹן אַפִּי כִּי בְּאֵשׁ קִנְאָתִי תֵּאָכֵל כָּל־הָאָרֶץ
Because of this, wait for me, says the Lord, **for the day of my resurrection, for a witness.** On account of my judgement, to gather the peoples, to welcome in kings, to pour upon them all my fierce wrath, for with fire will my zeal consume the whole world.	Therefore wait for me, says the Lord, for the day when I raise up to *catch* the pray, for my determination is to gather the nations, to my assembly of kingdoms, to pour on them my wrath, all my fierce anger, all the earth will be consumed with the fire of my jealousy.

Table 14 – Zephaniah 3:8 in the LXX and MT

Here, God himself explicitly mentions the "day of my resurrection as a witness," while the Hebrew text, albeit a bit murky (compare the translation above with the countless others available) has a very different wording and lacks the reference to the Lord's Resurrection.

Many other verses deserve mentioning, many of which were seen as prophetic references to the Messiah by the fathers, such as Ezekiel 17:22–23, Numbers 24:7, 17, and many others. But in the interest of length, these two

---

[285] Rahlf's Septuagint writes *ear* here, which is witnessed to by only a single manuscript while codex Vaticanus, Sinaticus and Alexandrinus all write *body*, σωμα.

PART IV: THE SEPTUAGINT IN THE THIRD MILLENNIUM CHURCH

examples must suffice. In Ezekiel 17, the prophet mentions how the Lord will *"plant him on a high hill, hang him on the hill [or mountain] of Israel high in the air"*. Hereafter, the text goes on to state how he will produce much fruit and how the birds of the air will find rest with him. In this passage, they saw a prophetic foreshadowing of Christ's Crucifixion on the hill of Calvary, in close proximity to Mount Zion, around 700 meters north of it, where Christ was planted on the tree and hung high on the hill of Israel. In this Crucifixion, he won eternal rest for all those who would flee to him and make their nest beside him.[286]

In Numbers 24, the heathen prophet Balaam prophecies concerning a future ruler over the nations, a star of Jacob, a man from Israel. Here, the fathers saw Christ foretold, who would destroy the powers of wickedness, symbolized by Moab's princes, and rule all the tribes and peoples. The Masoretic Text fails to mention this coming Messiah here, but narrates how water will be poured out from buckets in Numbers 24:7.

The overall tendency of the Masoretic Text is curious, in that it time and time again either lacks or differs in regard to the more universalist language inclusive of the gentiles and messianic tone found in the Septuagint. Though this by itself does not prove mischief or purposeful alteration, the example of Psalm 22 ought, in conjunction with this prevalent bias, to make the statements by the church fathers concerning rabbinical editions of the Old Testament texts with a strong anti-Christian bent seem much more likely. At minimum, one cannot seriously reject them as mere anti-Jewish polemic.

---

[286] Origen, Homilies 1-14 on Ezekiel, etc.

FINAL CONCLUSION
THE SEVENTY-TWO SERVANTS OF THE WORD OF GOD

he end of this journey spanning millennia is reached, and has been summed up in under 200 pages. From God's written word's inception in Egypt during the time of Moses, its sojourning to Israel, the prophets and kings, its precarious state, its rediscovery, and then, curiously, its return back to Egypt. Here, the prophet Jeremiah ministered, and his scribe Baruch wrote. But as time went on confusion arose, forgetfulness and inattention crept in, and though God's Word never perished, it lay dormant for periods as Israel slipped into idolatry, wars, sieges, and internal strife. Textual confusion resulted, and different textual recensions and families of the different Old Testament books evolved. Yet God was active, and 282 years prior to the birth of Christ he began turning the soil in preparation for the sowing of his Son. At the request of the gentile Greeks, the High Priest of Jerusalem sent the copies from the very Temple of Jerusalem itself to serve as the authoritative basis for what would become the Septuagint, the divine Scriptures translated into the Greek.

For this task, providence chose out of the twelve tribes of Israel Seventy-Two godly and learned men, as Christ himself would do again during his earthly ministry, so that during these short 300 years the world would be prepared for the Lord's coming through the preaching and reading of all that was foretold in these divine books. As the Hebrew prophets once had spoken with increasing clarity concerning the Messiah, the immortality of the soul, the bodily resurrection, things only dimly stated in the Pentateuch, in like manner God's divine light brought forth still greater clarity by these Seventy-Two servants of the Word of God. By the authority of the divinely instituted High Priest of Jerusalem, one text was chosen and sent from the temple down to Egypt. Egypt is where Scripture itself had once been born and where it would now be born again in Greek form, so that nations in the fullness of time might recognize the Christ which they and their fathers had read about. The Jews received the translation with joy and the gentiles with great interest, and soon men and women began to join the Jews in their worship of the one true God preached to them by the Seventy-Two, prefiguring the church's ingrafting of Jew and gentile into one body.

PART IV: THE SEPTUAGINT IN THE THIRD MILLENNIUM CHURCH

For this reason, Jesus again spoke out the words of Isaiah, once spoken by God himself through the prophet, then again by the Seventy-Two whose very words now rung out in the Synagogue of Nazareth from the mouth of Christ, as he read the Septuagint he himself had authored. Christ is the lamp for our feet and the shepherd of the flock. who points us toward the written Word of God which in turn bears witness to him. His deliverance of the Septuagint into the hands of the apostles was confirmed by the apostolic preaching and witnessed to by the ancient church, whose fathers and councils passed on what they themselves had been faithfully entrusted, a witness and gift now being handed on to current generation, as well.

THE DEPARTURE

It was in many ways a surprising development which Jerome, perhaps unintentionally, set in motion. Ultimately, the many loud protests against Jerome's break with the Septuagint and the church's use of it in the last 400 years were futile. Despite this, the Septuagint remained the Old Testament of the West some centuries still, and Isidore of Saville, who died 236 years after the translation of the Jerome, still used the Septuagint and described how the reception of the Vulgate was caused rather by its beauty of style and prose, compared to the rough and ancient Vetus Latina[287] than its content. It was in this regard that something of a historical coincidence, rather than a conscious choice, displaced the Septuagint in the West. In the Eastern Orthodox Church, as well as in the Eastern Oriental Churches, as well as a few other places, the Septuagint never lost its place of pride. It should therefore be asked, was departing from this path wise?

This book has sought to shed light on the origin of the Septuagint by looking at earliest sources describing its translation, its reception by Judaism prior to the advent of Christ, and its reception by the authors of the New Testament. On the opposite side, it has sought to show how the major reason for the shift away from the Septuagint and over to the Masoretic Text was based on the assumption of a correlation between the Masoretic Text and the autographical Hebraic texts, an assumption which is simply untenable and contrary to the data. The Masoretic Text cannot be presumed to reflect the original Hebrew text, as Professor Law says,

---

[287] Edmon L. Gallagher, "The Septuagint in Patristic Sources," in *T&T Clark Handbook of Septuagint Research*, ed. William A. Ross and W. Edward Glenny (New York: Bloomsbury Publishing Plc, 2021), 309.

SEVENTY-TWO SERVANTS OF THE WORD

We must recognize that the Hebrew Bible editions in our hands today, those based on the medieval Masoretic Text, do not represent the "original text" of the Bible. The greatest modern authority on the Hebrew textual tradition puts it bluntly: "One thing is clear, it should not be postulated that the Masoretic Text better or more frequently reflects the original text of the biblical books than any other text.[288]

On the contrary, it has been laid out how the Masoretic Text reflects the religious biases and views of Rabbinic Judaism, which rejected the Messiah, and whose Masoretes also edited and transmitted the Hebrew text in the centuries following Christ independently of the church. That these texts became the foundation of the Old Testament of the Christian Church, on account of a flawed assumption of their fidelity, is an intolerable situation.

Viewed through the lens of a Christian approach to Scripture, with due theological considerations, this outcome must be rejected. It is not only an unjustified novelty, principally brought about by a single individual who tore asunder the link between the Bible of the church and that of Christ himself and his apostles. It must therefore be asked, can the church be served by another testament than that which Christ, the foundation and chief cornerstone of the church, handed on and entrusted to his flock? This is a question which this book has confidently answered *no*.

The answer is relevant for everyone, whether Roman Catholic or Reformed, whether clergyman or layman. In our pursuit of Christ and the Word of God we should eagerly welcome him and sit down at his feet to hear the words that he spoke and handed on to our church in the pages of the Septuagint, for therein is found full fidelity to the words as they were written, and nothing less than that should satisfy us.

---

[288] Law, *When God Spoke Greek*, 23.

APPENDIX: TIMELINE

All dates are approximate (circa)

c. 721 B.C.	The Fall of the Northern Kingdom Israel and the dispersion of the Ten Tribes of Israel.
c. 586 B.C.	The Fall of Jerusalem and the Southern Kingdom of Judah. The Babylonian Exile begins.
c. 600–500 B.C.	The Hebrew alphabet falls out of use and is replaced by the Aramaic used by the Babylonians.
c. 539 B.C.	King Cyrus of Persia permits the Jews to return to Jerusalem and rebuilt the Temple.
c. 600–500 B.C.	Jewish settlements are established in Egypt and grow. The Prophet Jeremiah flees to Egypt.
c. 500s B.C.	First Greek loan words enter the Old Testament and Aramaic begins to become vernacular among the Jews.
c. 400–300s B.C.	Spoken Hebrew begins to die out as the vernacular among the Jews as Aramaic supplants it.
c. 331 B.C.	Alexander the Great, King of Macedon and Hegemon of Greece, defeats the Persians at Gaugamela and ushers in the fall of the Persian Empire.
c. 323 B.C.	Alexander the Great dies and leaves Hellenistic successor kingdoms stretch from Greece in the West to the Indus River in the East and Greek language and culture and colonization rapidly expands throughout the Mediterranean and the Near and Far East.
c. 281–246 B.C.	Rule of King Ptolemy II of Egypt under whose auspices the translation of the Septuagint began.
c. 280s B.C.	The translation of the Septuagint begins.
c. 221–205 B.C.	Demetrios the Chronographer is active and shows a high textual dependency on the Septuagint.
c. 200–100s B.C.	The Ryland 488 papyrus was written providing the earliest archeological find of the Septuagint.
c. 150–50 B.C.	Spoken Greek becomes common throughout the Levant and Israel.

SEVENTY-TWO SERVANTS OF THE WORD

c. 160 B.C.	Judas Maccabeus begins a revolt against the Greek Seleucid Empire and succeeds in establishing first independent Judaic state since the Fall of Jerusalem in 586 B.C.
c. 132 B.C.	Jeshua ben Sirach notes how the Law, the Prophets and the rest of Scripture is translated in the Septuagint.
c. 30 B.C.	The last Hellenic ruler of Ptolemaic Egypt, Queen Cleopatra, is deposed by the Romans.
c. A.D. 130	Jewish convert Aquila publishes the first new translation of the Old Testament into Greek since the Septuagint.
c. A.D. 132	The Bar Kokhba revolt begins and is crushed by the Romans leading to the major decimation of the Jewish population of Israel and North Africa.
c. A.D. 300s	Codex Vaticanus and Codex Alexandrinus, the earliest fully extend copies of the Septuagint, were written.
c. A.D. 380s	Damasus, the bishop of Rome, commissions Jerome to make a new translation of the Old Testament into Latin.
c. A.D. 381	The Council of Nicaea takes place.
c. A.D. 393	The Synod of Carthage canonizes the Septuagintal books of First and Second Esdras.
c. A.D. 600s–700s	The Hebrew Masoretes compile and edit the Hebrew Masoretic Text.
c. A.D. 1000s	The earliest fully extend copy of the Hebrew Old Testament, the Leningrad Codex, was written.
c. 1488	The printed version of the Hebrew Old Testament is published.
c. 1514	The Greek New Testament is printed and published for the first time.
c. 1518	The Aldine Septuagint, the first printed copy of the Septuagint, is published.

BIBLIOGRAPHY

Barkay, Gabriel, Marilyn J. Lundberg, Andrew G. Vaughn, and Bruce Zuckerman. "The Amulets from Ketef Hinnom: A New Edition and Evaluation." *Bulletin of the American Schools of Oriental Research* 334 (May 2004): 41–71. https://doi.org/10.2307/4150106.

Barker, Margaret. "Wisdom: The Queen of Heaven." *Scottish Journal of Theology* 55, no. 2 (April 17, 2002): 141–59. https://doi.org/10.1017/s0036930602000224.

Bellarmine, Robert. *Controversies of the Christian Faith*. Translated by Kenneth Baker. Saddle River, New Jersey: Keep The Faith, Inc, 2016.

Biale, David. "The God with Breasts: El Shaddai in the Bible." *History of Religions* 21, no. 3 (1982): 240–56. https://doi.org/10.2307/1062160.

Billington, Mark, and Peter Streitenberger, eds. *Digging for the Truth: Collected Essays Regarding the Byzantine Text of the Greek New Testament; a Festschrift in Honor of Maurice A. Robinson*. Norden, Germany: FocusYourMission KG, 2014.

Calvin, John. *Institutes of the Christian Religion*. Translated by Henry Beveridge. Grand Rapids, MI: Christian Classics Ethereal Library, 1845.

Chemnitz, Martin. *Examination of the Council of Trent*. Translated by Fred Kramer. Concordia Publishing House, 1971.

Filastrius Brixiensis. *Diversarum hereseon liber*. Edited by Friedrich Marx. Vol. 38 of *Corpus Scriptorum Ecclesiasticorum Latinorum*. Vienna: F. Tempsky, 1898.

———. *Loci Theologici, Part I, II and III*. Concordia Publishing House, 1989.

Closer To Truth. "N.T. Wright - Philosophy of the Bible." YouTube, June 28, 2018. https://www.youtube.com/watch?v=ZQU83Lfdi8w.

Dean, James Elmer, ed. *Epiphanius' Treatise on Weights and Measures: The Syriac Version*. Chicago, Illinois: University of Chicago Press, 1935.

Fassberg, Steven E. "Which Semitic Language Did Jesus and Other Contemporary Jews Speak?" *The Catholic Biblical Quarterly* 74, no. 2 (April 2012): 263–80. https://doi.org/10.2307/43727847.

Fernández Marcos, Natalio. *The Septuagint in Context: Introduction to the Greek Version of the Bible*. BRILL, 2000.

Flavius Josephus. *Jewish Antiquities, Volume I: Jewish Wars*. Translated by H. St. J. Thackeray. Books 1–3. Cambridge, Ma ; London: Harvard University Press, 1998.

fleetwd1. "On the Invention and Problem of the Term Septuagint - Peter Williams - ETS 2016." YouTube, December 12, 2016. https://www.youtube.com/watch?v=xhmMKwl3KeE.

Forestell, James T. "Old Testament Background of the Magnificat." *Marian Studies* 12, no. 12 (2016): 205–44. https://ecommons.udayton.edu/marian_studies/vol12/iss1/12.

Gallagher, Edmon L. "The Septuagint in Patristic Sources." In *T&T Clark Handbook of Septuagint Research*, edited by William A. Ross and W. Edward Glenny. New York: Bloomsbury Publishing Plc, 2021.

Gallagher, Edmon L., and John Daniel Meade. *The Biblical Canon Lists from Early Christianity : Texts and Analysis*. Oxford: Oxford University Press, 2017.

Gerhard, Johann. *On Interpreting Sacred Scripture and Method of Theological Study*. Edited by Benjamin T. G. Mayes. Translated by Joshua J. Hayes. St. Louis, Missouri: Concordia Publishing House, 2017.

———. *On Justification through Faith*. Translated by Richard J. Dinda. St. Louis, Missouri: Concordia Publishing House, 2018.

BIBLIOGRAPHY

German Bible Society. "BHS: The Biblia Hebraica Stuttgartensia." academic-bible.com, 2020. https://web.archive.org/web/20230325225541/https://www.academic-bible.com/en/bible-society-and-biblical-studies/scholarly-editions/hebrew-bible/bhs/#c5549.

Gleaves, G. Scott, and Rodney Eugene Cloud. *Did Jesus Speak Greek? : The Emerging Evidence of Greek Dominance in First-Century Palestine.* Eugene: Pickwick Publications, 2015.

Graves, Michael. *Jerome, Epistle 106 (on the Psalms).* The Society of Biblical Literature, 2022.

Grinfield, Edward William. *An Apology for the Septuagint.* London: William Pickering, 1850.

Hill, Robert C. *Fathers of the Church: Saint John Chrysostom: Homilies on Genesis 1-17.* Washington, D.C.: Catholic University of America Press, 1986.

Jellicoe, Sidney. *The Septuagint and Modern Study.* Eisenbrauns, 2013.

Jerome. *Epistulae.* Edited by Isidor Hilberg. Corpus Scriptorum Ecclesiasticorum Latinorum. Vol. 55. Leipzig: G. Freytag, 1922.

Jewish Publication Society. *Tanakh: The Holy Scriptures.* Philadelphia: Jewish Publication Society, 1985.

Jones, R. Grant. "Notes on the Septuagint," 2006. https://www.scriptureanalysis.com/wp-content/uploads/2016/09/Grant-Jones-LXXNotesFeb06.pdf.

Jorink, Eric, and Dirk van Miert. *Isaac Vossius (1618-1689) between Science and Scholarship.* BRILL, 2012.

Kittel, Rudolf, and Wilhelm Rudolph, eds. *Biblia Hebraica Stuttgartensia.* Stuttgart: Deutsche Bibelgesellschaft, 1997.

Kreuzer, Siegfried. "Old Greek, Kaige and the Trifaria Varietas – a New Perspective on Jerome's Statement." *Journal of Septuagint and Cognate Studies* 46 (2013): 74–85. https://ccat.sas.upenn.edu/ioscs/journal/volumes/jscs46.pdf.

Lange, Armin, Emanuel Tov, and Matthias Weigold. *The Dead Sea Scrolls in Context: Integrating the Dead Sea Scrolls in the Study of Ancient Texts, Languages, and Cultures.* 2 Vols. BRILL, 2011.

Lauer, Edward Henry. "Luther's Translation of the Psalms in 1523-24." *The Journal of English and Germanic Philology* 14, no. 1 (1915): 1–34. https://doi.org/10.2307/27700635.

Law, Timothy Michael. *When God Spoke Greek: The Septuagint and the Making of Western Civilization.* New York: Oxford University Press, 2013.

Leuchter, Mark. "The Aramaic Transition and the Redaction of the Pentateuch." *Journal of Biblical Literature* 136, no. 2 (January 1, 2017): 249–68. https://doi.org/10.1353/jbl.2017.0018.

Lundeen, Erik T. "Luther's Messianic Translations of the Hebrew Bible." *Lutheran Quarterly* 34, no. 1 (January 1, 2020): 24–41. https://doi.org/10.1353/lut.2020.0004.

Metzger, Bruce M. *The Bible in Translation: Ancient and English Versions.* Grand Rapids, Michigan: Baker Academic, 2001.

Meyers, Eric M. "Jesus and His Galilean Context." In *Sepphoris in Galilee: Crosscurrents of Culture,* edited by Rebecca Martin Nagy. North Carolina Museum of Art, 1996.

Müller, Møgens. "Septuaginta Som Udfordring Til Den Bibelske Kanon." *Religionsvidenskabeligt Tidsskrift* 73, no. 73 (June 22, 2022): 84–114. https://doi.org/10.7146/rt.vi73.132568.

———. *The First Bible of the Church: A Plea for the Septuagint.* Journal for the Study of the Old Testament Supplement Series. Vol. 206. 1996. Reprint, Sheffield Academic Press, 2009.

BIBLIOGRAPHY

Nodet, É. "Josephus and the Pentateuch." *Journal for the Study of Judaism* 28, no. 2 (January 1, 1997): 154–94. https://doi.org/10.1163/157006397x00138.

Norlin, Goerge, trans. "Panegyricus." In *Isocrates, Volume I*, 49–50. Cambridge, Massachusetts: Harvard University Press, 1980.

Pearce, N. D. F. "Grinfield, Edward William (1785–1864), Biblical Scholar." In *Oxford Dictionary of National Biography*, edited by Sinéad Agnew. Oxford University Press, September 23, 2004. https://www.oxforddnb.com/.

Philo. *On the Confusion of Tongues*. Translated by F. H. Colson and G. H. Whitaker. Loeb Classical Library. Vol. IV. 1932. Reprint, Cambridge, Massachusetts: Harvard University Press, 1985. 10.4159/DLCL.philo_judaeus-confusion_tongues.1932.

Porter, Stanley E. "The Septuagint: A Greek-Text-Oriented Approach." In *T&T Clark Handbook of Septuagint Research*, edited by William A. Ross and W. Edward Genny, 363–80. Bloomsbury Publishing, 2021.

Rajak, Tessa. "Josephus and the Septuagint." *Oxford University Press EBooks*, February 10, 2021, 420–33. https://doi.org/10.1093/oxfordhb/9780199665716.013.55.

Rex, Richard. "St John Fisher's Treatise on the Authority of the Septuagint." *The Journal of Theological Studies* 43, no. 1 (1992): 55–116. https://doi.org/10.2307/23965451.

Rivera, Letizia. "Multilingualism and Rebellion in 2nd-Century Judaea ." Edited by Pedro Jesús Molina Muñoz. *Researchers in Progress II: Languages in Contact: Languages with History*, 2017, 117–24.

Roberts, Alexander. *Fathers of the Second Century: Hermas, Tatian, Athenagoras, Theophilus, and Clement of Alexandria (Entire)*. Edited by James Donaldson and A. Cleveland Coxe. The Ante-Nicene Fathers. Vol. 2. Buffalo, New York: Christian Literature Company, 1885.

Ross, William A., and W. Edward Glenny. *T&T Clark Handbook of Septuagint Research*. Bloomsbury Publishing, 2021.

Run2Christ. "Why I Don't Believe in the Septuagint - Dr. Peter Williams, PhD." YouTube, September 8, 2015. https://www.youtube.com/watch?v=RmpnJ1cgh58.

Sæbø, Magne, Christianus Brekelmans, Menahem Haran, Michael A Fishbane, Jean Louis Ska, and Peter Machinist. *Hebrew Bible / Old Testament: The History of Its Interpretation*. Vandenhoeck & Ruprecht, 2008.

Salvesen, Alison G., and Timothy Michael Law, eds. *The Oxford Handbook of the Septuagint*. Oxford University Press, 2021.

Schaff, Philip. *A Select Library of the Nicene and Post-Nicene Fathers of the Christian Church*. Translated by J. G. Cunningham. Vol. 1. Buffalo, NY: Christian Literature Company, 1886.

———. *A Select Library of the Nicene and Post-Nicene Fathers of the Christian Church*. Translated by Marcus Dods. Vol. 2. Buffalo, NY: Christian Literature Company, 1887.

———. *A Select Library of the Nicene and Post-Nicene Fathers of the Christian Church*. Translated by Richard Stothert. Vol. 4. Buffalo, NY: Christian Literature Company, 1887.

———, ed. *Nicene and Post-Nicene Fathers, First Series*. Translated by Rev. John Gibb. Vol. 7. Buffalo, NY: Christian Literature Publishing Co., 1888.

Scheck, Thomas P., trans. *Origen: Commentary on the Epistle to the Romans. Books 6-10*. Washington, D.C.: Catholic University Of America Press, 2002.

Scott, S. P. *The Civil Law*. Vol. 17. Cincinnati: Central Trust Company, 1932.

Seleznev, Mikhail G. "The Septuagint in the Eastern Orthodox Tradition." In *T&T Clark Handbook of Septuagint Research*, edited by William A.

BIBLIOGRAPHY

Ross and W. Edward Glenny, 283-98. Bloomsbury Publishing, 2021.

Smith, Jr., Henry B. "Methuselah's Begetting Age in Genesis 5:25 and the Primeval Chronology of the Septuagint: A Closer Look at the Textual and Historical Evidence." *Answers Research Journal* 10 (2017): 169-79.

Stern, David H. *The Complete Jewish Bible: An English Version of the Tanakh (Old Testament) and B'rit Hadashah (New Testament).* Clarksville Jewish New Testament Publications, 1998.

Tov, Emanuel. *The Greek and Hebrew Bible: Collected Essays on the Septuagint.* Leiden ; Boston: Brill, 1999.

———. *The Text-Critical Use of the Septuagint in Biblical Research.* Winona Lake, Indiana: Eisenbrauns, 2015.

Twining, T. "Richard Simon and the Remaking of Seventeenth-Century Biblical Criticism." *Erudition and the Republic of Letters* 3, no. 4 (October 24, 2018): 421-87. https://doi.org/10.1163/24055069-00304003.

Wavers, John William. *Notes on the Greek Text of Exodus*, April 9, 2019. https://doi.org/10.2307/j.ctv1xsm8mk.

Wearne, Gareth. "Cave of Horror: Fresh Fragments of the Dead Sea Scrolls Echo Dramatic Human Stories." The Conversation, March 18, 2021. https://theconversation.com/cave-of-horror-fresh-fragments-of-the-dead-sea-scrolls-echo-dramatic-human-stories-157423.

Wevers, John William. *Notes on the Greek Text of Exodus.* Septuagint and Cognate Studies Series 30. Atlanta, GA: Scholars Press, 1990.

William, John, and Udo Quast. *Septuaginta II.1: Exodus.* Göttingen Septuagint. Göttingen: Vandenhoeck & Ruprecht, 1991.

SEVENTY-TWO SERVANTS OF THE WORD

Wright III, Benjamin G. "The Septuagint and Second Temple Judaism." In *T&T Clark Handbook of Septuagint Research*, edited by William A. Ross and W. Edward Glenny. New York: Bloomsbury Publishing Plc, 2021.